NANCY WILSON ROSS

THREE WAYS OF ASIAN WISDOM

HINDUISM

BUDDHISM

ZEN

AND THEIR SIGNIFICANCE FOR THE WEST

A TOUCHSTONE BOOK
PUBLISHED BY SIMON AND SCHUSTER

PRE

CONTENTS

FOREWORD

My reason for undertaking the writing of a book on Eastern religions, designed for the general reader, was essentially a simple one. There has never been a time in world history when East-West relationships have been of such intense, immediate concern to all mankind. For hundreds of millions of Asians their religion—no matter what form it takes—is the most vital concern of their daily lives, very far indeed from a mere one-day-a-week observance. Yet it is undeniable that the average Westerner knows very little, if anything at all, about the powerful spiritual motivations, religious convictions and ways of worship of the people who live on the other side of the globe.

In the past, many sincere and dedicated Westerners have gone out to Asia to face with admirable courage the severest hardships and dangers in order to spread the word of Christian beliefs and customs. Since these missionaries were, on the whole, judging from the record, received politely, listened to and patiently tolerated, it does seem now no more than the smallest return courtesy to make increasing attempts to understand certain beliefs about God, man and the universe that have been the basis of brilliant cultures and superb art in the long, rich and complex history of Asia. A quickened Western understanding of the mysteries that rise from the deepest level of mankind's common life seems acutely important today when East-West confrontation on more obvious levels grows hourly of greater concern to everyone alive.

Although my reason for undertaking a layman's explanation of three Asian religious philosophies, and the arts that grow from them, was simple and direct, I think it fair to add this does not imply that writing such a book was equally simple. Of Hinduism, for example, it has been often and truly said that nothing can be asserted about it that cannot also be denied. What is more, the Christian vocabulary and the vocabularies of Eastern faiths by no means dovetail with neat exactitude. A Westerner cannot write about religion without making use of such basic terms as God and the soul. The word God, signifying the creator of man's universe and the supporter of strict moral law, though relevant in writing of Christianity—as it would be of Mohammedanism or Judaism—does not, however, quite fit the concepts of a Supreme Being or First Cause in either Hinduism or Buddhism. Where Hinduism appears able to manage, with dazzling adroitness, to combine the worship of innumerable gods and goddesses with a seemingly paradoxical monotheism, Buddhism considers the concept of a Creator of the Universe so far beyond the scope of man's limited powers of comprehension, and so essentially irrelevant to following the Buddha's ethical Middle Way and training in "mindfulness," that it prefers to keep silent on the subject. As for the soul—Hinduism holds that there does reside in every man a spark of the divine, known as the *atman,* and that this spark can, by methods both mystical and specific, rejoin its Divine Source—infinite, immutable Brahman—while still on earth. Buddhism, in general, holds that there is no such thing as an individual ego, personal self, or soul—in our sense of the word—but only an ever-changing, forever-in-flux "aggregate of energies."

Both religions, however, with varying degrees of personalism or abstraction believe in the Law of Karma or "As ye sow so shall ye reap," and this Law extends itself through more lives than one, as expressed in the theory of reincarnation, basic to both faiths as it is to almost the whole Eastern world. Yet with all the innumerable differences in viewpoint or emphasis—not only between East and West but between Eastern religions themselves and even among their various sects—it is evident that all seekers of salvation, deliverance, Nirvana, Heaven, *moksha, samadhi, satori,* truth, or even merely "meaning," are obviously working with the same materials: unknown man and his unknown universe.

During the writing of this book, my own search for personal understanding of Eastern religious thought and its related art forms has been considerably expanded. I have come to see with increased clarity, and without forcing all possible parallels, that there does exist a larger number of paths of connection between Eastern and Western points of view than I had seen before. The range of interests that have become so much a part of Western thought in the present century—physics, astronomy, astrophysics, psychology, psychoanalysis, psychotherapy, even the new so-called "science" of mythology—are offering us fresh clues every day to clearer comprehension of ancient beliefs and concepts born long ago in the profound depths of Asian consciousness. It is wise, however, not to press too hard for similarities; it is better to allow one's mind, rather, to be stimulated by the significant differences. Perhaps, indeed, the reader might bear in mind the remark once made by the great Vedantist Swami Vivekananda, who during his first trip to the West late in the last century made such a profound and lasting impression on all who met him and heard him speak. Vivekananda said: "I accept all the religions of the past and I worship God with every one of them. Can God's book be finished? Must it not be a continuing revelation? Difference is the first sign of thought. I pray that the sects may multiply until at last there will be as many sects as human beings." If this seems an exaggerated and even alarming point of view, perhaps the advice given by Edmond Taylor in his useful book *Richer by Asia* could prove helpful. Taylor remarked that after an interest in Eastern religion had overtaken him during war years in India, Ceylon and Japan, he determined in his study of simple Buddhist and Hindu religious experiences to try as best he could "to *feel* rather than *think* them."

Carl Jung, whose psychological insight and wide scholarship have done so much to create more viable relationships between Eastern and Western ways of thought, once expressed some of the feeling with which I have ended this work of the past few years: "The wisdom and mysticism of the East have, indeed, very much to give us even though they speak their own language which is impossible to imitate. They should remind us of that which is familiar in our own culture and which we have already forgotten, and we should direct our attention to that which we have pushed aside as insignificant, namely the fate of our own inner man."

Perhaps some word of explanation is needed on why there were omitted from this volume the two classic philosophies of China: Confucianism and Taoism. Their omission was based entirely on the fact that they are not, insofar as one can judge at this distance from China's present state, playing a living part in the life of the country that gave them birth. I must admit that I was sad to bypass Lao-tzu, the father of Taoism (though I was able to touch on him briefly in the Zen chapter). Lao-tzu's viewpoint, born of a time of troubles not unlike the present, seems unusually attractive and appealing just now, for he advocated *wu wei* or "yielding to win," stressed *being* rather than *doing,* and emphasized the good sense, even the unarguable logic, of returning good for evil. What is more, as far back as the sixth century B.C., he was decrying the growing infringement on the rights of individual man by an amorphous entity called the State. It is impossible to forego at least one quotation from this legendary sage, who is said to have given expression to one side of the basic Chinese character—the intuitive—as Confucius laid form on the other—the behavioristic and formal:

> He who stands on tiptoe does not stand firm;
> He who takes the longest strides does not walk
> the fastest.

One final note on the absence of diacritical marks in the following pages. In works of original scholarship, words from Pali or Sanskrit are given diacritical marks to distinguish between vowels and consonants represented by the same English letter. Since this book is, however, aimed at a general readership, there seemed little reason to add unfamiliar marks to already unfamiliar words, as for instance, in the names of the Indian gods, which are spelled approximately as pronounced—that is, Shiva and Vishnu instead of Śiva and Visnu. Also where, as in the two main schools of Buddhism, there exist two words describing the same thing, one in Sanskrit, one in Pali, I have used what seemed to me to be the more familiar of the two: thus the Sanskrit *Nirvana* instead of the Pali *Nibbana*; the Sanskrit *karma* and *dharma* instead of the Pali *kamma* and *dhamma*; but the Pali *anatta* (no self) instead of the Sanskrit *an-atman*, and the Pali *tanha* (craving or thirst) instead of the Sanskrit *trishna*. In this procedure I have followed the example of such authoritative writers on Buddhism as Professors E. A. Burtt and Floyd Ross, Christmas Humphreys, head of the English Buddhist Society, and a number of others who have written books in this field designed for general readership.

—N.W.R.

HINDUISM

He who tries to give an idea of God by mere book learning is like the man who tries to give an idea of the city of Benares by means of a map or a picture.

—Shri Ramakrishna

When Svetaketu, at his father's bidding, had brought a ripe fruit from the banyan tree, his father said to him,

"Split the fruit in two, dear son."

"Here you are. I have split it in two."

"What do you find there?"

"Innumerable tiny seeds."

"Then take one of the seeds and split it."

"I have split the seed."

"And what do you find there?"

"Why, nothing, nothing at all."

"Ah, dear son, but this great tree cannot possibly come from nothing. Even if you cannot see with your eyes that subtle something in the seed which produces this mighty form, it is present nonetheless. That is the power, that

is the spirit unseen, which pervades everywhere and is
all things. Have faith! That is the spirit which lies at the
root of all existence, and that also art thou, O Svetaketu.
                                        —*Chandogya Upanishad*

> *Who sees his Lord*
> *Within every creature*
> *Deathlessly dwelling*
> *Amidst the mortal:*
> *That man sees truly. . . .*
>
> *Who sees the separate*
> *Lives of all creatures*
> *United in Brahman*
> *Brought forth from Brahman,*
> *Himself finds Brahman.*
>   —*Bhagavad-Gita*
>   (Translated by Swami Prabhavananda
>   and Christopher Isherwood)

H INDUISM, generally considered to be the oldest of the world's existing faiths, is the broad term used to designate a large, conglomerate, socio-religious organism to which belong today well over three hundred million Hindus in India proper and some fifteen to twenty million inhabitants of other Asian countries, the West Indies region, and South Africa. An example of active Hinduism outside the geographic boundaries of India was the world-famous nonviolent resistance movement (*Satyagraha*), first set in motion by Mohandas K. Gandhi when a South African resident from 1893 to 1914. As a discriminated-against, though highly successful, emigrant lawyer, Gandhi began in South Africa to develop a classic Indian tenet of *ahimsa* (the doctrine of refraining from the harming of others or the taking of life) into an invincible political instrument. After his return home, application of this ancient religious law not only helped free his countrymen from British rule but led them to worship him as a mahatma or Great Soul.

Not all Indians are followers of Hinduism. There are hundreds of thousands of Muslims, Sikhs and Jains, as well as a fair number of Parsis, Buddhists and Jews, scattered over the vast subcontinent, which includes, of course, the new Muslim state of Pakistan created from India proper in 1947. There are even very old, still vital communities of Indian Christians. The Syrian Church of Kerala, on the Malabar coast, claims to be the oldest Christian community extant. It traces its perhaps apocryphal origins back to the arrival in India, in the first century A.D., of the missionary apostle St. Thomas himself. Indian Christians are today the third-largest religious group; Muslims the second. Hinduism, however, in its many social and religious forms represents the faith of eighty-five per cent of the population of the Republic of India and is unquestionably the cultural foundation of national life. In the face of centuries of major, as well as countless minor, invasions from a wide variety of non-Hindu settlers, traders, and warriors, it has managed to retain its powerful influence on India's manners, morals, rituals, customs, economics, science, medicine and art, including literature, music, dance, painting and sculpture. Such all-pervasive, unbroken cultural-religious continuity is rare, if not unique, in the history of nations.

Travelers to north India who have been educated only in Western history (unfortunately, still the vast majority) are often surprised to find on their itinerary so many magnificent mosques and palaces plainly Islamic (Muslim) in design. These elegant, domed and high-arched buildings, of which the Taj Mahal at Agra is the most famous, are the architectural legacy of the lordly and opulent Moguls, the most powerful and civilized of the various aggressive, restless peoples of Mohammedan faith who, as early as the eighth century A.D., began invading the land of the Hindus through the Himalayan passes. Decades of intermittent infiltration and many regional conquests culminated around the thirteenth century in virtual Muslim rulership of India for some five hundred years. No matter what their geographic origins, early followers of the prophet Mohammed were fanatic believers in their one God, Allah, and ready forcibly to convert all "infidels" in his name. The warrior Muslims, with their cohesive, regimented religion, their grim opposition to idol worship, and a firm belief in the realities of the material world, could hardly have differed more sharply from the native Hindu with his views of the world as *maya* (a relative reality), his hundreds of thousands of divine images, and his subtle delineations between good and evil. Despite, however, ruthless destruction of Indian temples and art by the early Muslim hordes and in later years—at the other extreme—the fabled marvels and glories of the Mogul courts, Islam's total effect on Hinduism's ancient traditions was singularly negligible. While there were, of course, certain inevitable adaptations, exchanges and influences at the upper sociological level, the Hindu masses in the main continued to follow the religious customs of their remote ancestors. Even the world-conquering British, who succeeded Muslims in the seats of power and confronted the Indian mind with modern Western science and technology, did not too drastically disturb the mysterious depths of India's ancient faith. Nor have the violent events of postwar years revolutionized the religious behavior of Hindu villagers, who —representing as they do the overwhelming proportion of the Indian people—still sustain popular Hinduism, as they have done for centuries, by their strict daily adherence to private sacerdotal duties, obligations and pleasures.

Although large gatherings of devout Hindus watch priestly performances in Hindu temples, they do not constitute a congregation in the Western sense of the term; they might more accurately be called an audience. Temples are open at all times with special services held during festivals when large numbers of pilgrims and devotees gather for prayer and to make votive offerings. Daily worship in Hinduism, however, takes place in the home, where devotional procedures are each individual's personal responsibility; no priest, regardless of his hierarchical rank, can serve as another man's spiritual proxy. Of paramount importance, therefore, is an orthodox Hindu's own prescribed observance of the ritual minutiae whereby he maintains an intimate, often complicated, relationship between himself and whatever expression of Divinity he has chosen to worship from a crowded pantheon of male and female deities. Like the temple priests—and only to a slightly less demanding degree—every orthodox householder learns and practices devotional skills that might almost be classified as technical, for the complex rituals of Hindu *puja* (worship of a god by way of his image or an abstract symbol) requires expert use of fire, water, lights, scents, sounds, flowers, grasses and leaves. Priests, householders and *sadhus* (holy men) also employ in their worship a variety of meaningful postures, gestures and utterances, and it is this intense personalism and ritual intimacy that have unquestionably helped Hinduism maintain, for so many centuries, its immemorial usages.

It has been often remarked that almost all thought in India is, in a sense, "religious thought" and that the national consciousness has, for millennia, found its real fulfillment in religious activity of one sort or another. It is quite true that even in modern India conversations on spiritual matters, or religious beliefs, are considered eminently suitable, and certainly enjoyable, forms of social exchange. Yet it must be kept in mind, as stated in the Foreword to this volume, that nothing can be asserted about Hinduism that cannot also be denied. It is essential to approach even the most cursory study with extreme care in order to avoid leaping to the wrong conclusions. There is encountered in Hinduism not one single religion but a variety of popular, metaphysical and symbolic expressions spread over an immense area of humanity. On the one hand one sees the country people still living in intimate communion with some personal god chosen from among the many thousands, even millions, of deities that enliven this ancient land's rich mythology. The Hindu masses' meticulous observance of immemorial ritual, often childish and superstitious in the modern view, is balanced by the presence in Hinduism of many great teachers and disciples of a purified faith rooted in humanism and universalism. Dr. Amiya Chakravarty has pointed out an interesting fact: Down the centuries India's greatest religious leaders have all been "iconoclasts" in one way or another, and scarcely one of its many gifted scholars, philosophers, poets, saints or periodic reformers has been a "professional Brahmin" abiding by the strict behavior patterns of the hereditary sacerdotal caste.

Perhaps it is the wide range of accepted practice and credo in this long-enduring socio-religious organism that helps to account for Hinduism's absence of aggressive proselytizing force. Whatever the reason, Hinduism's history has, in general, been marked by a live-and-let-live tolerance extended to other world faiths, founded on very different interpretations of God's function in the universe, as well as to the widely divergent approaches to Divinity included within its own boundaries. The charge of heresy by which Christians, Jews and Muslims have rejected unfamiliar theological concepts has relatively little place in Hinduism, which holds that there are innumerable valid ways to serve and worship the transcendent all-pervasive One who rules the world. There have been, of course, minor persecutions among sects in the long history of Hinduism and, with the rise of the modern spirit of nationalism, the inevitable bristly antagonisms and assumptions of spiritual and cultural superiority natural to a repressed colonial people rediscovering their inherent worth. Hinduism has, however, never fostered a church militant or organized all-out crusades against infidels and unbelievers in the name of a One True Faith—nor does it seem likely that it ever will. Even the modern conflict between the post-partition Muslim state of Pakistan and the new Indian Republic appears to be, on India's side at least, more political and territorial than ideological in any religious sense, and certainly Mahatma Gandhi's remarkable pattern of behavior in the midst of the tragic internecine strife of the postwar period was considered by the vast majority of Hindus to represent an exemplary expression of true Indian ideals of tolerance and harmlessness.

Although it is not altogether easy to account for Hinduism's record of permissiveness and its lack of organized missionary zeal, it seems fair to speculate that some of this tolerance has its source in the ancient Indian theory of *karma*. Karma—about which more will be said later—is in simplest terms the belief in predestination or "what is to be will be." Such a belief is bound to modify or exclude any fanatical proselytizing as it also encourages, to some degree, an attitude of passivity and acceptance that remains basic to Hinduism even though some teachings about karma suggest how man's individual destiny can be altered by the development of higher faculties. The Hindu view of the nature of time may also have played its part in minimizing conversion pressures. Time, for Hindus, does not move, as in Western thought, from past through present to future. Instead it swings eternally, like the seasons, in immense cycles, forever recurring, waxing and waning. In such a scheme of endless periodicity final goals are bound to be more abstract than the type of destination basic to belief in such relatively static, not so remote futures as the Heavens and Hells of the Christians, Jews and Muslims.

Unlike Christianity, Islam, or that other great India-born religion, Buddhism, Hinduism had no single founder. Its main spiritual source is traced back to a body of very ancient and anonymous "revealed scriptures," the Vedas, which in turn had their origin in even older hymns of worship sung for centuries by light-skinned Aryan nomads (common ancestors of Northern Europeans) who came into India through the Himalayan passes at about the time Moses was leading the people of Israel out of Egypt.

The great migration of these pastoral tribes from their homelands on the high central Asian plateau is believed to have begun around the middle of the third millennium B.C. Some part of this migratory flow (which also reached Greece and ancient Persia) entered northern India between 1500 and 1000 B.C. These earliest known invaders of the Indian subcontinent—whose name for themselves was Aryas, "nobles"—brought with them to the Gangetic plains, and to far-northern areas now a part of Afghanistan, their own bardic priests who already possessed oral teachings said to have been born of "the very breath of God."

The most ancient Vedic teachings are designated in Hinduism as *shruti* or "that which was heard." Less archaic, though also sacred, Hindu literature is described as *smriti* or "that which was remembered." The "eternal revealed" Vedas, Hinduism's primary scriptures, are four in number. Of these four the Rig Veda is generally accepted as the oldest text among the world's living religions. It is written in antique Sanskrit (which, it should be remembered, is a remote relative of most of the languages of Europe) and contains among many hymns and prayers an ancient song of worship with which countless Indians to this day greet the morning sun:

Let us meditate upon the adorable
Glory of the Divine Life-Giver
And may He direct our thoughts.

The earth and higher celestial atmospheres are also mentioned in this very
old hymn from mankind's infancy, along with a central spiritual source of
man's intellect and divine consciousness.

Our knowledge of the early Aryans in India is dim, but we do know the
Vedic religion soon felt the deep impact of the still earlier cultures that
flourished in the subcontinent before the Aryans arrived. India's complicated
ethnic web is well reflected in the complexity of its religious forms. The vast,
many-layered structure of Hindu cosmology, though traditionally based on
the Aryan scriptures just mentioned, owes many of its richest elements to
India's pre-Aryan inhabitants who were contemporaneous with the most
ancient Sumerian and other Near Eastern cultures. These proto-Indians—
dark-skinned, mysterious and gifted—have been loosely termed Dravidians.

It has become increasingly plain to modern scholars that the population of
India's remote unrecorded past was by no means composed of simple
primitives. As far back as 2500 B.C.—well over a thousand years or more
before the first Aryan invasions—these early Indians were already living in
large, well-planned communities. Three of their ancient cities in the Indus
River region, Mohenjo-Daro, Harappa and Chanhu-Daro, have been extensively excavated, and the diggings have yielded proof of an advanced state of
civilization and a keen aesthetic sensibility revealed in sculptured human
figures, animal models, children's toys and, in particular, many brilliantly
engraved seals.

When the agricultural and town-dwelling inhabitants of northwestern
India were invaded by the horse-owning wanderers from the Asian steppes,
the vigorous newcomers soon acquired the dominant position. They were
able to repress, or push southward and eastward, many of the indigenous
people. Quite naturally the Aryans also substituted their own gods and ways
of worship for those they found on the spot. Yet even so, the religion of
India's early inhabitants was never entirely lost. It disappeared underground
and stayed alive among the people, emerging in due course to make its own
special contribution to the manifold subtleties and facets of Hinduism. Some
of the recognizable elements of pre-Aryan Indian beliefs are the ritual use of
water, veneration for the holy *lingam* (phallus) as the symbol of divine
creativity, the worship of trees, serpents, bulls and other animals. The

powerful idea of God as Mother, the age-old Mother Goddess in her many aspects, also dates back to Dravidian cults. So too, it is generally believed, does the great god Shiva, whose flame-circled bronze figure in the role of Cosmic Dancer (an icon created in southern India) gives magnificent expression to Hindu belief in the eternal dualistic creation-destruction rhythm of the universe. (A third element in the usual Indian trinity is that embodied in Vishnu, the Sustainer, or Divine Power seen as the Preserver of Creation, a symbolic expression which will be developed in more detail further on.)

The multiple and often seemingly contradictory aspects of Hinduism lend it a peculiar power and fascination, deepened rather than diminished by study. An initial open-mindedness is essential, and it is necessary, as Heinrich Zimmer once remarked, to relinquish the idea that a high school education and four years of college have automatically established access to the *sanctum sanctorum* of "utter truth"—and that that truth belongs to the West. It cannot be denied, however, that even the most open-minded Westerner's first response to Hinduism's metaphysical labyrinth is apt to be one of bewildered recoil, largely because there appears to be no single guiding thread through the maze of subtly interwoven theologies, conflicting modes of worship of fantastic gods and goddesses, diverse rituals, ceremonial observances and spiritual disciplines, as well as the innumerable sects, cults and philosophic systems that constitute this complex, flexible and persistent religious organism.

Nevertheless, and contrary to all appearances, Hinduism's seeming chaos does contain a basic universal concept: the underlying belief in one immutable, ultimate, indescribable Reality known as Brahman.

A somewhat confusing inconsistency prevails in the English spelling of three very common Hindu words: Brahman, Brahma (with either a capital or a lower-case "b") and Brahmin. In these pages, Brahman will be used to indicate the indescribable Supreme Principle of Life—an abstract *metaphysical* concept; Brahma to indicate the third member of the powerful Vishnu-Shiva-Brahma *mythological* triad of gods; Brahmin for a member of the first of the four major Indian castes.

Brahman, the nonpersonal Supreme One, pervades all things and transcends all things. Of this great Principle, the Rig Veda states, "Though men call it by many names, it is really One." An essential part of the teaching regarding Brahman is the belief that a man can, by personal effort, and use of inner knowledge, attain union with this Divine One while still on earth.

Such blissful union is made possible because the Ultimate Reality and the individual soul (*atman*), though seemingly apart, are, in actuality, one and the same substance. This identity of soul and God in Hinduism is given terse expression in an often-quoted Sanskrit formula: *Tat tvam asi*, or "That art Thou." It has been pointed out that this particular Hindu formula presents a good example of the relationship existing between the English tongue and its Indo-European root language, Sanskrit. Tat is related to our word "that," tvam to "thou" (in Latin "tuam"); asi is the copula "is" or "are." So the English translation of this ancient Sanskrit formula expressing the fundamental identity of the individual soul and God is "That art Thou."

The attainment of individual mystic union with the Divine Reality which exists eternally behind the world's ever-changing maya is Hinduism's highest aim, and it cannot be too often repeated that this belief in one supreme Divinity serves to place Hinduism among monotheistic world faiths, in spite of its bewildering acceptance, on certain levels, of devotional practices polytheistic or animistic in nature.

Hinduism's basic tolerance for bizarre or unfamiliar types of human behavior in acts of worship is curiously offset in the social realm by many strict tabus having their source in the time-honored organization of Indian society into a rigid system of castes. These contradictory traits of easy acceptance and rigid exclusiveness, so characteristic of the Hindu attitude toward life, are also outgrowths of that universal law of moral compensation already referred to as karma. The doctrine of karma is inseparably tied to the theory of reincarnation, and reincarnation in its most rudimentary interpretation is the belief that each man existed before and will exist again and again until at last he has effected his final escape from the eternal round of "becoming."

In the Hindu view, as a consequence of the operation throughout the entire universe of the inescapable karmic law of periodic return, men are to be found living at many different stages of development along a many-lived path or "process." It would therefore be sheer folly to expect everybody to approach the Divine in the same manner. An intellectual would naturally strive toward God-consciousness by way of abstract metaphysical speculation, meditation, or some of the many forms of specific spiritual disciplines known as yoga. A simple villager, on the other hand, might find it necessary to satisfy his personal religious needs with colorful childish ceremonies and the worship of images whose exaggerated number of heads and arms are simply the popular Hindu way of expressing a deity's various powers and attributes.

It is perhaps worth mentioning here (by way of keeping values in balance) that while many Hindu images are horrifying to Western tastes, there are Indians who, in the face of outspoken Western revulsion, find it genuinely puzzling that these critical Christians are not repelled by the Cross of Calvary with the crucified and bleeding figure of a man impaled upon it, or the ritual eating of the body and drinking of the blood of Christ in the sacrament of the Eucharist. Not that a Hindu would condemn such iconography as the Crucifix or the ritualism of the Mass or Holy Communion. He would take it for granted that there will always be wide differences in modes of worship. This permissive viewpoint makes it possible for many worldly, even intellectual Hindus to look on with detached equanimity at their less-evolved brothers, including many temple priests, playing sacred games like so many children with dolls: bathing and feeding images of gods, taking them on outings, swinging them in swings, putting them to bed at night, dressing them in different costumes for various ceremonial occasions. Quite obviously all this is more to the participants than merely playing games with toys of stone and wood. After certain rites of sanctification have taken place, it is believed that a particular god has, in some sense, come to dwell in his image. He, or she, must, therefore, be treated like an honored guest: wakened ceremoniously, diverted during the day, like a king of ancient times, with outings, swingings, performances of dance and song and generous banquets of which the deity will eat only the "subtle" part, leaving the "gross" portion for consumption by his worshipers or as an offering to the poor.

In India, where the collective imagination has always been peculiarly fertile, the status of the myth has never declined or disappeared into the unconscious as it has in the West. One might say that mythology to the Hindu is merely one expression of Reality, or, with equal validity, that it is an expression of Unreality, for if Brahman alone exists and the world, as it appears to us, is essentially an illusion—a "projection," to use a popular Western term—then the gods are as real, or as unreal, as anything else. Hindu myths can therefore be described as true in the sense that poetry and art are true. It has been remarked that even learned Indian philosophers tend to react toward the entire cosmic and human spectacle more like critics analyzing a piece of art than like engineers explaining how something works. The Indian regards the world less as a battlefield of principles than as a "theater for the display of natural forces." This latter concept is given specific expression in the idea of all nature seen as *lila*, the creative activity of the Divine in playful or sportive mood. A line in the scripture known as the Bhagavata Purana tellingly makes this point: "Let us meditate on the Lord who is omniscient and self-luminous, who through his heart extended *to the prime poet* [Brahma] the knowledge in the form of the Veda."

Such ideas are not wholly unfamiliar to Western thinkers and poets, some of whom have suggested that it is just as possible to conceive of Nature mythologically as an artist working in metaphors, images and rhythms, as to think in terms of an engineer, architect or large-scale planner abiding by a fixed (though invisible) blueprint, trying to do the job efficiently, save material, make things "come out right" and so on.

In Hinduism divinity pervades all things. Mountains, rivers, water of any kind (even in a jar in the household shrine), trees, flowers, stones, plants, insects, animals may therefore be found worthy of veneration. Best known to the West among India's sacred animals is the cow. Originally, perhaps, honored as a life-giving necessity for a nomadic people living by their herds, the cow, a multipurpose animal, has become down the centuries a creature of special privilege and of such inviolate sanctity that it may be seen in modern cities wandering unmolested through the busiest traffic or entering temple precincts where priests are the only persons admitted. Even a man of Gandhi's intellectual stature defended reverence for the cow as a "practical application of the belief in the oneness, and therefore the sacredness, of all life." To Gandhi, as to many other educated Hindus, it was possible for the cow to symbolize "the whole dumb creation of God" and thus to deserve its distinctive place in Hinduism. (Gandhi was, however, in most respects an unflinching realist, and he once remarked that the pathetic Indian cows, often half starved for lack of proper pasturing, were a "disgrace" and that, in general, cattle in India were "treated worse than anywhere else in the world" in spite of their holy status. It is also a matter of record that he sanctioned, on one occasion, the killing of a suffering calf.)

Monkeys too, in India, are deemed worthy of special veneration and privilege, though less exalted than the cow in the hierarchy of worship. These mischievous pampered creatures—against whose sly kleptomania unwitting temple visitors must be warned—acquired their present place in the complex Hindu pantheon in part because of the heroic role played in prehistoric days by Hanuman, an astute and valiant member of the species.

As told in the Ramayana, one of India's ancient epic sagas, Hanuman was instrumental in rescuing from a royal demon-kidnaper the flawless Hindu queen, Sita.

Presumably, too, early man's observation of the often humanlike behavior of this particular animal species could account for a special regard and tenderness for his monkey brother. Although nowadays large numbers of monkeys are sold by Hindus for export and medical uses abroad, still such instances of a universal breakdown in the Hindu's sense of life's organic unity only serves to point up the rare feeling for all existence from plant to animal that animated the sculptors and cave muralists of India's past. This rare sensibility can be readily observed even in photographic reproductions of such national monuments as the great carved gates guarding the *stupa* (Buddhist relic mound) at Sanchi in central India, the superb frescoes and sculptures in once holy caves like Ajanta and Ellora in Hyderabad and Elephanta near Bombay and on the immense seashore monoliths at Mahabalipuram near Madras. The artists of the past were plainly and deeply conscious of an indestructible eternal principle, a "transmigrating life-monad" infusing all forms of existence, subtly uniting them one to another in the unending flow of phenomena known as *samsara*. This mystical perception of unity expressed itself in aesthetic relationships linking humans, animals, birds, trees, flowers, demons, nymphs and other divinities in a sustained rhythmic rapport. With the sculptured image of an animal, for instance, more appears involved than a merely brilliant observation and representation of anatomical aspects; there is also suggested some secret common bond shared by the animal with his fellow creature, man. In this context one thinks, in particular, of the kindly protective serpents of Indian folklore and sculpture portrayed guarding World Teachers like the iconoclastic, Indian-born Buddha, or the Saviors of the ascetic Jain sect, or serving as a bed for the powerful Hindu god Vishnu while he sleeps on the cosmic sea. As human-faced reptilian creatures known as Nagas, they are given dreamy and tender miens and the status of royalty. It is even said that some ancient families boast Naga ancestry as part of their proud lineage, and serpent worship still persists in some parts of rural India.

It is Hinduism's basic conception of the subtle interfusion and interconnection of life that also makes it possible for simple Hindus to worship in their home shrines such a powerful god as Vishnu by way of small river-worn stones called *salagramas*. These stones, believed to be Vishnu's response to an extremely devout river goddess who prayed that he might, in one of his incarnations, be reborn in her womb, are lovingly gathered from certain streams to serve as the god's living presence in the household. While some Indians honor riverbed stones sacred to Vishnu, others worship those of different shape sacred to Shiva, or circular ones representing Shakti, the Divine Mother of the Universe. This prehistoric Mother Goddess—whose worship was dominant in pre-Aryan India as in so many ancient cultures— has again assumed a powerful place in Hinduism. She appears under many different names and guises ranging from the archaic stone symbols just mentioned, through the blissful repose of the divine bride, Parvati, to the dark and tribal Kali for whom animal sacrifices are still offered even in such a great industrial metropolis as Calcutta.

Ritualistic greeting of the rising sun and the ceremonial morning and evening ablutions are universally observed among all devout Hindus. Although his personal appearance, because of dust, heat, and the frequent scarcity of water, may often make him appear otherwise, the orthodox Hindu is strict about personal cleanliness to the point of fanaticism. Thus, for instance, although he may be seen with a green leaf as his plate, eating food with his fingers, the rules about the uses to which the right and left hand may be put, and the washing of hands before and after meals are prescribed with a strictness quite unknown to the "sanitary" West. More than this, the daily care of mouth, teeth and tongue, usually only with the help of a twig of the medicinal neem tree, goes on so long and with such assiduity that it might well shame any television toothpaste commercial.

Orthodox Hindus begin their private devotions well before sunrise, repeat them at noontime and again just before sunset. To strengthen or more successfully to focus this worship, they employ specified means: bodily postures (*asanas*), gestures (*mudras*, also used in the classic art of Indian dance) and the utterance of given sacred sounds called *mantra*. All of these prescribed techniques are designed to aid the individual in identifying himself with the Divine—the aim of his worship. Among the most potent of many sacred Hindu words is the one-syllable mantra "*Aum*"—or "*Om*," as it is sometimes spelled. The sounding of Aum is used as a help in achieving concentration, or in quieting the mind preparatory to deep meditation. This single syllable is said to contain the same creative and sustaining energy present at the origin of the universe when the utterance of certain sounds helped bring forth the world—a teaching that calls to mind the cryptic line in St. John, in the Christian Bible: "In the beginning was the Word . . . and the Word was God."

As mentioned earlier, various forms and degrees of mental and physical discipline aimed at spiritual advancement belong to a large and influential branch of Hinduism known as yoga. The word yoga comes from the Sanskrit and means to yoke: specifically, in spiritual exercises, it signifies the joining, or yoking, of the individual soul to Brahman. Those who set out to practice yoga in its higher forms must receive, from an adept, exact guidance in the prescribed steps by which eventual *moksha*, or "release" from earthly bonds, can be achieved. (For all of Hinduism's seeming permissiveness, it does not hold that really high spiritual attainment can come about by accident but only by the employment of a precise methodology and definite disciplines.) Common to all schools of yoga is careful instruction in the use and control of breath as the very source of life itself. Bodily postures designed to achieve proper concentration of physical energies are also taught; of these the most familiar is the cross-legged "lotus posture" seen in many contemplative figures of saints, gods and teachers in Asian art.

There are five important yoga "paths," characteristically designed to reach people at different stages of mental and spiritual development. The five paths, or methods, are: bhakti-yoga, the way of devotion or selfless love; jnana-yoga, the way of the intellect or knowledge; karma-yoga, the way of action, deeds and service; raja-(or contemplative) yoga, "king among yogic practices," intended only for those already well advanced in meditation procedures; hatha- (or physical) yoga, the way of bodily development or strength. Of the various yoga systems, it is hatha-yoga that has aroused the most interest outside India, in large measure due to a number of reputable observers who have written about spectacular feats they have witnessed: sustained control of "involuntary" bodily processes such as pulse and heartbeat; prolonged deliberate trances in which sadhus (holy men) have been buried alive and recovered after hours or even days—still breathing—and similar superhuman feats.

The exotic terminology employed in some rather extreme yoga practices (many of them dating back to a form of medieval mysticism called Tantrism) has aroused a degree of curiosity among Westerners that could be potentially dangerous since almost no yoga, except the most simple physical exercise, is designed for novices. In particular, one might mention the esoteric teaching about the *kundalini*, "serpent power" (sometimes called "thermal power"), said to lie in quiescent state at the base of the spine behind the sexual organs. Some yogis, it is asserted, learn to awaken this sleeping kundalini and raise it up the spinal column, or central nervous system, by way of five *chakras* (centers or "wheels" of psychic energy) lying at definite bodily points.* The uniting of the kundalini with the potent "lotus center" at the crown of the head, by way of this chakra chain, is claimed to give a yogi extraordinary powers not only over himself but over other life forces and phenomena.

Putting to one side the inevitable fanaticism that accrues to all body cults, it is undeniable that objective study has revealed the attainment by highly trained yogis of amazing powers difficult to account for in Western scientific terms; but these powers are referred to by adepts merely as "efficiencies" which "only appear supernatural" to the uninitiated. From the medical and scientific point of view, unprejudiced observers have come to the conclusion that Hinduism's ancient and mystical physiology could yield valuable findings if opened to serious study by modern biologists, physiologists and psychologists. The purest forms of yoga practice have been described by the French scholar, Louis Renou, as essentially a "discipline of the unconscious."

Since for centuries in India life's most meaningful pursuit has been the attainment of liberation from samsara (the endless round of existence) to a higher state of consciousness, holy men of all descriptions have always been, and still are, a part of the Indian social scene. The most exaggerated types are those who believe that the path to what the West would term "salvation" must come by way of triumph over the body's weaknesses and limitations. With this form of escape as their aim, they may be seen gazing unblinkingly into the fierce noonday sun, or, half naked, with grotesquely painted bodies, assuming physical poses of extreme contortion. Some, relinquishing all possessions, wander the cities and countryside as ragged, homeless mendicants. Still others, more sophisticated *swamis* (initiated members of a holy order) choose to live more ordinary lives and may even put in appearances, in their flowing white and yellow robes, on social occasions.

Although many Indian holy men (and women too, for the life of the voluntary ascetic is not confined to the male sex) have given up their lives to seek for union with Brahman, they are not necessarily priests or even members of the highborn priestly caste of Brahmins. They are merely individual seekers who have abandoned conventional existence to pursue moksha for its own sake, a decision that anyone may make with impunity at any time in India, where the "retreat to the forest"—particularly in the later

* *There are seven* chakras *in all.*

stages of life—is an ancient and honored prerogative open to all. This tradition, which has so marvelously survived to the present, in theory at least, goes back as far as the remarkable "forest thinkers" of the sixth to fourth centuries B.C. Even then, in voluntary exile, these sages were turning their considerable analytical and intellectual powers to speculation on the origin of the cosmos, the nature of God and the soul, the relationship of mind to matter and other profound subjects subsequently developed in the various schools of Indian philosophy.

There is also among Hindus the old and honored tradition of the *guru*, or spiritual instructor, to whom earnest pilgrims may come for guidance on how best to attain divine knowledge or to live a more meaningful life. Seekers and disciples often gather in large numbers around a particular guru and set up an *ashram*, a community of like-minded people who have relinquished their personal and private lives for group endeavor. Others may join such groups for briefer periods of instruction, rest, or spiritual renewal.

One of the most influential and relatively recent mystics and teachers, who serves as a prototype of many Indian gurus, was Shri Ramakrishna (1836–1886). The life and teaching of this unlettered, deeply human and spiritually endowed Bengali saint were brought to the attention of the West early in the present century by his highborn disciple and "St. Paul," Swami Vivekananda (1863–1902), organizer and founder of the Vedanta Societies of Europe and America. Shri Ramakrishna, who was regarded by his followers as an incarnation of divinity, approached religious experience with both fervid passion and an almost scientific spirit of inquiry. He set out deliberately to experiment with various paths to "God-consciousness" as taught in other great world religions such as Islam, Buddhism and Christianity. He finally professed to have attained the state of highest *samadhi*, or blissful union with God, by way of each of these seemingly alien methods. Therefore, though remaining a Hindu, he emphasized to his followers that all men who truly worship are in truth worshiping one and the same Great Principle or Almighty God. Here Ramakrishna was merely stressing once again an often-quoted tenet from an ancient Indian scripture: "In whatever way men approach Me, even so do I reward them, for it is My path that men follow in all things."

Hindus of both high and low degree do not believe that God, or the Supreme Source of Life, has made only one appearance among men. It is therefore held possible for Hindu deities—all reflections of Brahman in one way or another—to assume different names and forms to meet various challenges and crises in the world of men and gods. Since the Hindus in the main, as already indicated, do not believe that they have exclusive hold on religious truth, it follows that they can also readily honor the Buddha and Jesus Christ as special appearances on earth of Divine Reality in human form. Authority for this belief in *avatars* is found specifically in the Bhagavad-Gita, the most widely read and influential scripture among modern literate Indians. In the Gita—as it is generally called—the god Krishna (one of the several incarnations of the often-incarnated great god Vishnu) makes this statement:

> In every age I come back
> To deliver the holy,
> To destroy the sins of the sinner,
> To establish righteousness.

The hypothesis of the appearance of Divinity on earth at periodic intervals is a related part of that underlying belief in karma, common not only to India, as stated before, but to most of the Asian world. In fact, this theory is so fundamental to the life attitude of the majority of Eastern peoples that its validity does not lend itself to argument. The idea of a succession of lives for each human creature would be no more debatable to the average Hindu than a Westerner's fixed belief that continuity from childhood to adulthood exists in a single life, even though the past may be largely forgotten. (It might be pertinent to mention here that many educated Indians sincerely believe there are people capable of recalling their former existences in some detail.)

Quite apart, however, from any proofs of a former life, the concept of karma seems to the Hindu the only sensible way to account for the manifest inequities of human existence. How else, he asks, can one explain the ease, beauty and happiness of one man's lot as compared to another's seemingly undeserved misery, deformity, poverty, unless each is reaping the results of action in some former existence? Karma would thus seem to represent in essence the familiar teaching "As ye sow, so shall ye reap," but a rather more adequate phrasing would describe it as a self-operating law of Action-Energy —in speech, deed and thought—functioning through a series of lives, producing, by the inescapable rhythm of cause and effect, certain inevitable results; results however—and this is of vital significance—that do not involve the participation of a bookkeeping deity, meting out personal rewards and punishments. Someone has put it in these words: "Karma is the Master Law of the Universe but there is no Law Giver." To the Hindu mind, this law works as naturally, one might almost say as automatically, as any other law of the universe, such as gravity.

Inasmuch as a man's personal inherited karma dictates his present place in life, and his present attitude toward human existence, it has inevitably given support to the caste system, already referred to as the framework on which Hindu society has been built for centuries. Since the original Sanskrit word for caste was *varna*, "color," it has been suggested that the light-skinned invading Aryans used color distinctions as an aid in keeping the darker-skinned indigenous peoples subjugated. The castes—once only four in number—have down the years proliferated into a vast structure with a multitude of offshoots, resulting in utmost confusion and complication as each subcaste developed its own special customs and tabus. Color is no longer a specific factor (if, indeed, it ever was), although it is undeniable that light-skinned Indians—the pale Kashmiri Brahmins, for example—pride themselves on their pigmentation, and dark-skinned girls have often been required to furnish larger dowries in the marriage market.

The original four castes—mainly vocational—were headed by the Brahmins, learned interpreters and hereditary custodians of the sacred Vedas, and, as such, the wielders of special spiritual influence. The Brahmins' power—born originally of exceptional knowledge and fabulous memories—inevitably moved on into the social sphere, bringing the sacrosanct members of this leading caste, in addition to many strict duties and obligations, many valued privileges.

Next to the Brahmins came the Kshatriyas, equally aristocratic, representing the worldly rulers, the regional rajahs and nobles and, in early days, the warriors. Third in line were the Vaisyas, who ranged from merchants to artisans. At the end came the Shudras, to whom fell the menial tasks of Hindu society. Though they are at the bottom of the original caste ladder, the Shudras have produced a number of remarkable leaders as well as many wealthy citizens and are considered by some social historians to be the real bulwark of Hinduism.

Outside the four main caste divisions, and the multiple branches and extensions of this ancient social system, there has also existed from the earliest times a group familiarly known as the Untouchables. They were called Panchamas, literally "the fifths"; that is to say, all those people outside the four castes forming the single largest miscellaneous group; in other words the "outsiders" or outcasts. To these unfortunates without any caste distinctions, whose very shadow was considered polluting and who might not even use the common village well, Gandhi gave the name Harijans or Children of God. He and many other modern Indian statesmen, including Nehru, have vigorously championed the cause of these hapless people, and today Harijans have able leaders on a national level and enjoy full constitutional rights—though the actual behavior patterns, particularly at the village level, are only very gradually altering. (Some sociologists even assert that caste lines are temporarily hardening under the threat of forced change, a familiar social phenomenon in many other parts of the globe.)

If discriminations, hierarchies and "establishments" seem to resist change with particular stubbornness in most of India, it is not for want of effort on the part of many renowned Indians who have earnestly sought to alter the ancient patterns. In the Middle Ages such great preachers as Kabir and Ramanand taught the brotherhood of all men before God and attempted to draw Hindus and Muslims more closely together; yet ironically enough they found their followers organizing into sects that took on the characteristics of new castes. Nanak (1469–1538), the gentle and enlightened founder of the Sikh community, following in the footsteps of Kabir, also sought to incorporate the best of Hinduism and Islam into one faith; yet neither he nor the leaders and teachers who succeeded him ever brought about a total eradication of a sense of caste among the Sikhs. Buddhism, which from its pre-Christian beginnings opposed caste distinctions and offered its teachings openly and freely to all who desired to learn, was destined to die out in India though it conquered most of the rest of Asia. Even the invader Muslims, according to A. L. Basham, in spite of the alleged equalitarian basis of their doctrine, tended to form caste groups in India, and the Malabar Syrian Christians divided, in time, into sections that assumed a castelike character. Perhaps, however, in spite of this long, disheartening record, since Gandhi set the example of encouraging intercaste marriages and even deliberately and publicly performed such Untouchables' tasks as cleaning out latrines and doing other menial work of a supposedly degrading nature, India may dare hope for the eventual disappearance of an ancient social order which—no matter what its original justification—can hardly be considered tenable in the context of modern sociological attitudes and beliefs. This position is firmly taken by virtually all men in public life in India today and by the vast majority of educated Indians.

THE ART OF HINDUISM

Examples of the art of Hinduism shown in these pages have been selected with the simple aim of opening the eyes of an average reader to an unfamiliar aesthetic without at the same time burdening him with too many details of chronology and nomenclature. Nothing more has been attempted with these all too few examples and necessarily brief text than to give a general sense of some of the ways in which the artists of Hinduism—that vast, socio-religious organism with its manifold ethnic and geographic variations—have expressed the paradoxical attributes of leading deities or sought to represent in sculpture and painting the richly creative myths, theories and life attitudes that lend Hinduism its rewarding diversity, depth and color. The many magnificent sculptured caves and carvings from living rock to be found in different parts of the Indian subcontinent comprise this country's greatest contribution to world art. The Indian artist of the past was challenged to bring forth from "dead" stone the myriad forms of natural life and the ever-shifting panorama of his people's living myths. A few examples from Hindu-influenced cultures such as those of Cambodia and Nepal have been included. No exact chronological sequence has been followed in the choice of illustrations, and there has been no consistent attempt to characterize the precise historical periods to which various examples belong. Although Hinduism's temple architecture is particularly rich and varied in symbolic meanings, the vastness and profundity of the subject made it seem expedient to omit specific examples in this necessarily brief space.

The bibliography includes books in which the interested reader can, if he wishes, pursue at greater length the engrossing subject of the art of Hinduism.

Shiva as King of the Dancers, an embodiment of eternal cosmic energy. A familiar icon from South India, 12th century A.D.

The god carries in his upper right hand a drum representing sound as the first element in the unfolding of the universe, while the upper left bears a tongue of flame, the element of the world's final destruction. The gestures of his other hands suggest the eternal rhythmic balance of life and death. One foot, resting on the demon of "Forgetfulness" (who holds a cobra), the other raised in dancing pose, denote, says Heinrich Zimmer, "the continuous circulation of consciousness into and out of the condition of ignorance."

"The essential significance of Shiva's dance is threefold. First it is the image of his rhythmic play as the source of all movement within the cosmos, which is represented by the arch. Secondly, the purpose of his dance is to release the countless souls of men from the snare of illusion. Thirdly, the place of the dance, Chidambaram, *the Center of the Universe, is within the heart.*

"In the night of Brahma,* Nature is inert and cannot dance till Shiva wills it. He rises from his rapture and dancing sends through inert matter pulsing waves of awakening sound, and lo! matter also dances, appearing as a glory round about him. Dancing, he sustains its manifold phenomena. In the fullness of time, still dancing, he destroys all forms and names by fire and gives new rest. This is poetry; but none the less, science."

Ananda Coomaraswamy

The theory of the periodic cosmic dissolution and recreation of all life—occurrences that would be catastrophic in the Western view—are accepted with equanimity by Hindus. It has been said that the destruction of a whole universe is to the Hindu "as certain as the death of a mouse and to a philosopher no more important." (See text, page 17.)

* In the present text the term *Brahman* has been used for this essentially metaphysical, *not* mythological, concept. (See text, page 19.)

1

2

3

4

5

The dramatic archaeological discovery in the present century of ancient pre-Aryan cities in Northern India drastically changed the history of Indian art, pushing it back at least to the third century B.C. The Indus Valley civilization, *circa* 3000–1500 B.C. (see text, page 18) had attained a notable degree of civilization, revealed in the ruins of its towns, in its pottery, toys, animal sculptures and, above all, in its many remarkable seals. Certain themes and subject matter of these pre-Aryan artists foreshadow later developments in Indian art and worship. (2) Statuette of a man in an ornamented robe, probably a priest's portrait. (3) Seal showing three-faced deity in yoga posture, seated among animals. Perhaps an early form of the god Shiva. (4) Glazed ceramic monkey. All from Mohenjo-Daro. (5) Sacred animal standing before an altar or incense burner. Still undeciphered script. Found near Ahmedabad.

6

7

A fine observation of their animal brothers and a subtle recognition of kinship with them pervades the best of Indian sculpture, a characteristic whose source may in part lie in the Hindu belief that each life monad passes through many different forms of transmigration on its way to final union with the Supreme One. (6) Reclining deer, a detail of the massive rock carving long known as the Descent of the Ganges, from the deserted seashore site at Mahabalipuram, southern India, early 7th century. (See also illustrations 28 and 29.) (7) A monkey family from the same site. (8) Nandi, the white bull sacred to Shiva, reposing in the hall of one of the many sculptured caves at Ellora, *circa* 700–750 A.D.

8

(9) A Naga or Serpent King, a favorite subject in Indian sculpture. Nagas are superhuman creatures who may assume the forms of men or half-men, although when asleep they take on wholly their serpent nature. They are often shown guarding various "Saviors" with the protection of their canopied hoods. In early Hindu myths birds and beasts associated freely with men and communicated easily with them. In Hindu iconography animals appear as the inseparable companions, in a sense almost as alternate forms, of the leading deities. Each god has his special *vahana* (vehicle), often represented as a mount; thus the Mother Goddess, as Durga, rides a lion, Brahma a swan, Shiva a white bull and Vishnu the sunbird, Garuda, here portrayed (10) by a Khmer artist (Cambodia, *circa* 13th century A.D.) as a forceful, almost arrogant creature, half man, half bird; a diminutive bronze figure, only 9¾

9

inches in height, yet full of tremendous power. (11) Ganesh, the zoomorphic son of Shiva, a genial potbellied god of luck and powerful "overcomer of obstacles," often depicted with his companion, the rat, an equally useful "finder of the way" after his own sly fashion. (12) Hanuman, the monkey god. (See text, page 54.)

10   11   12

13

14

(14) The supermundane bliss of the sleeping Vishnu expressed in a Cambodian (Khmer) head. Early 12th century A.D.

15

When the god Vishnu rides through the air he uses the sunbird, Garuda (illustration 10). When he sleeps he reclines on the cosmic serpent Ananta ("Endless") also known as Sesha ("the Remainder"—that which abides even after the periodic dissolutions of the universe). (13) Here reposing on the watery abyss from which all creation periodically emerges, Vishnu represents the transcendent Lord of Life. (The perplexing interchange of cosmic roles among leading Hindu deities (see illustrations 17 and 23) is explained by the theory that in substance all divinities are identical. Any major Hindu deity might be described as a manifestation through which the Supreme Brahman—superpersonal, immanent, abstract—makes himself approachable. Each individual worshiper is free to choose the divine manifestation most appealing to his own needs and tastes:—Vishnu, Shiva, Kali, or a lesser divinity. (15) Vishnu's serene composure shines forth in this standing figure from Western India, 12th or 13th century A.D. His left hand holds his weapon, the discus, a familiar circular form often seen in Indian iconography, suggesting originally the sun's wheel and ancient solar myths.

16

(16) Shiva Ardhanari, Shiva in hermaphroditic form, half male, half female, a figure which has magnificently triumphed over physiological incongruities. One can sense the artist's perception of a single unceasing current of strong yet gentle life underlying the rhythmic swaying movement of the god's androgynous body, shining forth also in a countenance whose serene compassionate detachment is indescribably moving to the beholder. Elephanta, 8th century A.D. (17) One of the most famous of the many great sculptures of Shiva, who has many different forms and titles, represents him as Shiva Mahesvara, or Mahadeva, the Great God in his three aspects. An immense image some 23 feet high by 19½ across, the three faces represent: on the god's right the male force of the universe; at his left, the female; while the center visage expresses the sublime transcendent union of the two polarities or "the undifferentiated essence of the creative void." Caves of Elephanta, near Bombay, 8th century A.D. (18) The simple form of Shiva's lingam (phallus), often found in quiet and holy sanctuaries, symbolizes the life force of the universe, its generative, creative essence (see text, page 60). Ellora, 750–850 A.D.

17

18

19   20

(19) Shiva with his wife the Great Goddess in her most charming form as Parvati, his beloved bride, sit together at home on Mount Kailasa under which there resides Ravana, the demon who was chained eternally in the nether world for his crime in abducting Sita, the theme of the epic Ramayana. (See text, page 54.) The firm placement of Shiva's right foot here and in many of these familiar sculptures indicates that the god can feel, but is repressing with godlike imperturbability the earthshaking threat of the hidden demon chained below. (20) Shiva and his consort seated in state on the sacred white bull, Nandi, in a happy scene of court life, 10th century A.D. The gods' embrace may be taken as another representation of the eternal procreative activity of the universe, a profound theme, which the Hindus variously express as a trinity, a duad, one god in two forms, or by a single symbol like the lingam. (See illustrations 16, 17 and 18.) (21) Here Shiva with divine imperturbability makes himself a dancing platform for his consort in her fearful Kali form; a theme of Time and Eternity. (See text, page 61, and illustration 25.)

21

22   One of the Great Goddess's most marvelous exploits, the subduing of a mythological cosmic monster, embodied in the form of a demon buffalo. (22) With youthful insouciance and assurance the Goddess as Durga (one of her several names and forms) rides her lion mount against the god-defying tyrannical foe, still on his feet and dangerous but obviously soon to be conquered. From Mahabalipuram, early 7th century A.D. (23) Here, with her foot on the creature's back, she prepares the death-blow with an almost dreamlike detachment from the mighty deed to which the gods have assigned her in the role of primary life force expressed in the being of the

23   Divine Mother of the Universe. From one of the caves at Ellora, 7th century A.D.

24

Two paintings that also express dynamic aspects of the Mother Goddess. (24) A
painting from the Punjab Hills, *circa* 1700. The relevant text, translated by A. K.
Coomaraswamy, reads: "Thus it is said: She destroyed the *asura* (demon) Smoke-eye.
Making the sound *Hum*, forsooth, Ambika (the Mother) burnt him to ashes then
and there." (25) *Durga (Kali) Stirs by Her Movement Shiva, the Corpse, to Life.*
The scene is a Hindu burning-ground with the goddess Kali shown placing her foot
on a mysterious double figure (Shiva-Shava) laid out in seeming death. The god
Shiva, one of the two recumbent figures, is seen awakening and beginning to shake
a small drum producing the vibration of sound by which creation comes about. (The

25

lower figure has been identified by
Dr. Stella Kramrisch as possibly, in
this instance, representing a devotee
identifying himself with an aspect of
the god.) The symbolism underlying
this powerful, enigmatic painting implies that Shiva, in the role of supreme Deity, exists beyond creation
and without any attributes until the
living touch of Kali brings him alive
to create and animate the world. The
burning-ground here symbolizes, says
Dr. Kramrisch, "the heart of man
freed from all the fetters which tie
men to life. Only when freed is it
possible to realize Kali in her dance
on Shiva." (Kangra, 18th century.)

26

(26) The Khmer civilization in Cambodia made magnificent use of many themes of transplanted Hinduism. This is brilliantly exemplified in the façades of Angkor Wat, where, in their own inimitable fashion, the Khmers set out to tell in incised stone relief the Hindu legend of the Churning of the Milk Ocean, a contest between gods and titans for the attainment of immortality. The illustration here shows the hosts of the gods pulling manfully on their half of the Cosmic Serpent which they are using as a churning rope to twirl Mount Mandara on its axis and bring up various priceless treasures from the ocean's depths, including the elixir of eternal life. (27) Among the many treasures of Hindu medieval art and architecture from Mahabalipuram, the deserted stone pilgrimage site of southern India not far from Madras, is a prodigious rock wall depicting in detailed, finely executed sculptured forms the theme of the Descent of the Ganges,* 7th century. The river, according to legend, descended to earth high in the Himalayas through Shiva's matted hair—the god's way of breaking the destructive force of the immense Heaven-born body of water. A large vertical cleft, natural to the rock itself, represents the descent of the river, and at certain seasons water from a pool at the top falls across the face of the twenty-foot-high carving.

* This title is currently debated among scholars, some of whom incline to a re-naming of the sculpture, the Penance of Arjuna. I have, however, preferred to use the original and more familiar name.

27

28

29

Details from the Descent of the Ganges.
(28) In the cleft representing the river, a
Serpent (Naga) King and his consort dis-
port themselves, and to either side a vast
assemblage of animals, birds, demons, an-
gelic couples and human beings celebrate
in their special ways the miraculous event.
A bearded man on one leg stands in a classic yoga posture not far from a figure of
a four-armed Shiva; an old man seated in
meditation beside a little temple has been
taken to represent the sage who by his
fearsome austerities brought to earth the
boon of the sacred river. Below him may
be seen the deer from illustration 6. (29)
Heavenly couples seldom move by wings
in Hindu art but rather by airy flowing
movements of their own limbs.

30

One of the epic deeds of Krishna (that popular, beloved incarnation of the often incarnated god Vishnu) was the subjugation of an annoying river serpent named Kaliya. (30) A Rajput painting from the Punjab Hills shows Krishna in almost a dancer's pose, holding the mighty serpent over his head while the Naga's wives, risen from the river, beg him to spare their now repentant spouse, and Krishna's companions extol his deed from the river's bank. *Circa* 1700. (31) As Tamer of the Serpent in a southern Indian bronze, Krishna is seen here as a boy who conquers the poisonous reptile simply by dancing blithely on his head, an action which the Naga himself seems to find not too unpleasant. *Circa* 900 A.D. (32) A Nepalese sculpture presents Krishna as a sturdy, self-assured child easily overcoming the same fearsome creature. *Circa* 7th century A.D.

31

32

33

34

Sculptured themes of lovers from medieval Indian temples gave expression to the Tantric view that the path to realization or "release" might lie not alone through world negation and asceticism but also through the profound experiences of human love and sensual bliss. In these often ineffably beautiful Hindu sculptures one clearly senses the unknown artists' awareness of the interior energy of all life flowing outward to express itself in the forms and movements of passionate human bodies. (34) Sculptured stone lovers from a temple at Khajuraho, *circa* 1000 A.D. Many centuries later this subtle and meaningful, one could even say spiritual, voluptuousness appeared on a less monumental scale in charming and romantic paintings from northern India. In this relatively recent art the amorous protagonists were often the god Krishna and his *gopi* love, Radha. (33) Krishna and his adored Radha in an intense though deliberately restrained, almost mannered, pose, from Rajasthan, late 18th century.

The allegorical story—with devotional and erotic overtones—of the god Krishna (a Vishnu incarnation), who led part of his life in a pastoral environment, a simple cowherd among other cowherds and cowgirls (*gopis*), became the subject matter of innumerable sensuous and delicate, rapturous and vivid paintings from northern India during the 17th to the 19th centuries. (35) Here Krishna, in a Matisse-like setting of brilliant stylized trees and a pond full of lotus flowers, flutes his irresistible song. (36) Krishna and his chief love, Radha, are seen in a rainstorm sheltered under a lotus-leaved umbrella while frolicsome cows sport alongside. (37) A painting in two sections; above, Radha and Krishna with a maid churning butter; below, Radha watching Krishna milk a cow.

35

36   37

(38) The mighty subject of the Churning of the Milk Ocean, which the Cambodian Khmers depicted so magnificently on the immense façade at Angkor Wat in the early 12th century (see illustration 26), is here expressed 600 years later in an amusing painting from northern India. It shows Vishnu seated atop Mount Mandara while the gods and demons twirl their respective ends of the cosmic serpent, which has already brought up from the Milk Ocean various gifts and wonders, including a snow-white bull and elephant, a seven-headed horse and the goddess Padma Lakshmi. (39) A Himalayan idyll: The god Shiva as a simple mountain dweller, trident in hand, walks ahead of his wife Parvati who is mounted on the white bull, Nandi. In her lap she holds their elephant-headed son, Ganesh, while on his right shoulder Shiva carries their other son, the six-headed god of war, Karttikeya. 17th century.

38

39

40

(40) The soft late afternoon—known in an Indian village as "the Hour of Cowdust," when the venerated cows return from pasture—is also the classical hour associated with the wandering storytellers who have kept alive, down the centuries, the countless timeless legends of Hinduism. Rajput, 18th century. (41) Two sages in a landscape. Although painted as late as the 18th century, this painting is descriptive of the very earliest practices of Vedic India when sages, holy men, or those who were merely world-weary retired to the forest to think their own thoughts or to receive and give instruction on life's meaning and man's proper conduct. Punjab Hills, Garhwal.

41

In general Hinduism, as practiced among the people, has never lacked for drama in terms of its social distinctions or its religious observances. Hardly a day passes without lively goings-on around one of the major or countless minor deities: feasts, fast days and festivals, large and small; pilgrimages to holy cities like Puri or Benares, where every pious Hindu hopes to attain his final rest, to the shores of the Bay of Bengal, to the sources of the Ganges high in the Himalayas, or to this sacred river's junction with the Jumna. As recently as February, 1954, a congregation of four million people, most of whom came on foot, assembled at this last spot with the intention of immersing themselves in the two rivers' joined waters on the most auspicious day for the performance of such holy rites in one hundred and forty-four years of reckoning. (Dr. Amiya Chakravarty has made the point that such immemorial customs are unconnected with genuine Hinduism but are a part of ancient folkways that still exist, though in steadily lessening measure, along with modern India's growing hunger for technology and science. The immense adjustive power manifesting itself in India's cities today contrasts vividly with many old patterns of behavior, giving this land its paradoxical fascination for outsiders and leading to the hope on the part of friends of India that it may, in due course, in spite of all its current problems, come to serve as a truly significant link between East and West.)

There are four "great abodes of the Lord" in India, one north, one south, one east, one west, and seven special "holy sites" also strategically scattered over the Indian land. To these pilgrimage spots Hindus travel—often for hundreds of miles on foot—to make or renew vows, to offer penance for misdeeds, to ask for altered fortunes, or simply to make an act of devotion to some aspect of the One whom they may be worshiping under the form of Rama, Krishna, Shiva, the Divine Mother or any other of the various guises of Divinity. There are fifty-one "footrests" sacred to the Great Goddess in the form of Sati (an early incarnation of Shiva's wife—she of so many different names and forms). As told in one arresting myth, these particular pilgrimage sites represent the spots where segments of Sati's corpse fell to earth, deliberately fragmented and scattered over the land by Vishnu. This seemingly unfeeling and violent deed on Vishnu's part has been symbolically interpreted as the god's way of impressing on his fellow divinity, Shiva, the idea of death "as a human phenomenon necessary to accept." By his drastic action Vishnu was able to return Sati's grieving consort to his senses and his godlike duties and prevent him from continuing his further aimless and blind wandering, dazed with grief, carrying his earthborn wife's lifeless body on his back.

A number of once-sacred Indian sites—asterisked as historic and aesthetic landmarks in all official guides to India's monuments—inexplicably ceased to be pilgrimage centers well before the days of tourism. One of these mysteriously abandoned sites is the Sun Temple of Konarak in Orissa where remarkable sculptures that take as their subject matter the whole gamut of life from birth to death have—by certain startlingly frank erotic details— often proved as disturbing to modern Hindus as to unprepared Western travelers. Sometimes pilgrimage sites, neglected for centuries, will for no apparent reason again become pilgrim goals.

One of the most famous holy occasions of Hinduism is the annual Car Festival at Puri when Jagannath (another Krishna manifestation) is attired in his most splendid raiment and drawn through the streets in a wooden cart so immense it takes hundreds of devotees to move it. (This, incidentally, is the origin of the English word "Juggernaut"—a dark word having its source in the reputed accidents and deaths caused by the rolling wheels in the frenzied throngs of worshipers.) Other Hindu festivals range from the rather rowdy, though joyous, springtime Holi, when colored water and powders are thrown on all passersby, to the lovely Diwali, or Festival of Lights, when at twilight of the October–November full moon, flickering oil lamps appear in every home, shrine and temple, floating, too, on the shore of the sea, on streams, rivers and sacred tanks.

Until very recent times hardly any art or literature in India could have been said to be secular in the strictest sense of the word. Dance and theater were—and still are—largely given over to the fanciful activities of various deities in their manifold manifestations. Even the majority of modern films deal with the proliferating stories of these same gods and goddesses. The magnificent sculptured façades and interiors of the hundreds of ancient temples and caves scattered across the face of the Indian land, and in Hindu-influenced countries like Bali and Cambodia, also provide a vast pictorial encyclopedia of Hindu mythology. Each little shrine in house or village further reflects some aspect of this enormous storehouse of continuing legend.

India's ancient classic literature has been one of the strongest cohesive forces holding together a people of so many creeds and practices. Such early scriptures as the Upanishads, together with the subsequent learned commentaries on them, have always belonged, by the very nature and range of their sublime inquiry, to people of exceptional quality of mind. The Upanishads—"Upanishad" literally means a "session" in the sense of sitting at the feet of a master who imparts wisdom—can surely be numbered among humanity's most ambitious attempts to express the inexpressible. Of these primary testaments to man's burning desire to solve the mysteries of his own being, a modern Indian scholar, D. S. Sarma, has said, "They are the Himalayan springs from which have flowed the rivers of the Spirit which have watered the Indian peninsula for the last twenty-five centuries." During these twenty-five centuries philosophers and scholars have systematized the Hinduism based on the Upanishads into various schools called *darsanas,* or "views of life." Of these several views of life one of the most important and influential is known as Vedanta.

Vedanta, literally "end [from the Sanskrit *anta*] of the Vedas," has been designated "the loftiest peak of Vedic knowledge." Its teachings are based on the mystical and philosophical elaboration of the ancient *shruti* or "revealed" truth. Vedantists are often termed nonsectarian since they belong to no body of worshipers of any particular deity; they dwell entirely on Hinduism's highest philosophic and intellectual plane. Many of India's scholars and distinguished men at the forefront of public life—like the Nobel Prize poet, Rabindranath Tagore, and Dr. Sarvepalli Radhakrishnan, India's learned President who once taught Comparative Religion at Oxford—have expressed deep reverence for Vedantist thought. As the accepted philosophy of intellectual Hinduism, Vedanta has also attracted to it in recent times a number of Western thinkers and artists.

Vedantists, who place little emphasis on the performance of orthodox rites or duties, approach "liberation" by means comparable in many ways to certain types of Buddhist training. (In fact they are sometimes accused of being crypto-Buddhists because of the stress they lay on active individual search for enlightenment.)

Vedantist teachings stem from the thirteen principal Upanishads. In these Upanishads, whose dates range from 1000 to 100 B.C., there are, ever more strongly developed, certain themes of unity and comprehensiveness already apparent amid the diffuse and frequently confused material of the Vedas proper. Vedanta emphasizes Brahman, the Ultimate Reality, the "One-Without-a-Second," infinite, eternal, omniscient, omnipresent and incomprehensible, from whom the universe eternally evolves, appears and disappears. (The nonpersonal, noncorporeal concept of Divinity—intensely spiritual and metaphysical and in no way mythological—did not, it must be noted, succeed in doing away with those other polytheistic tendencies so deeply rooted in the Indian consciousness: one more illustration of Hinduism's singular elasticity, its acceptance of a wide variety of religious needs related to people at different stages of intellectual and spiritual evolution.)

Vedanta, although conceived far back in the early Upanishadic schools of philosophy, is today the result of a continuous process of development. The ideas embodied in the rather general term "Vedantism" have never been combined in one fixed system. They are, as Dr. Radhakrishnan has said, "simply the thoughts of the wise, not always agreeing in detail, and presented as independent utterances, each with its own values." An example of this deliberate absence of theological systematization can be cited in a volume of general essays, *Vedanta for the Western World,* published in the United States in 1946. Distinguished Western contributors included Aldous Huxley, Gerald Heard, John van Druten and Christopher Isherwood, along with many eminent Hindu swamis and *sannyasins* (wise men). The subject matter was wide in range: essays on "The Sermon on the Mount," "The Lord's Prayer," "The Teachings of Shri Ramakrishna," "The Practice of Yoga" and "Proper Methods for Meditation," including "The Meaning and Use in Contemplative Exercises of the Sacred Syllable Aum (or Om)."

Among the many approaches to God possible in different Vedantist schools there might be briefly mentioned two means designated as "the method of the monkey" and "the method of the cat." In the latter concept man is "saved" by God without participation or effort on his part, just as a kitten is carried to safety by the scruff of the neck. In the former a man wishing salvation must turn and cling to God as a baby monkey clings to its mother.

The higher types of Vedantist training are concerned with shifting the center of attention from the exterior to the interior world. In a sense it might be claimed that Vedanta offers its followers a map and guidebook to the unknown inner world from which alone, in its view, the mysteries of the so-called objective world may be understood and put in proper perspective. Dr. Radhakrishnan has written: "From the outward physical fact, attention shifts to the inner immortal self situated at the back of the mind, as it were. We need not look to the sky for the bright light; the glorious fire is within the soul."

Specific exercises are considered essential to bring about this direct apprehension of Spirit in its pure form. Training comprises the study of certain religious texts, sessions with an approved teacher, listening to him and also, significantly, exchanging discussion with him in an analytical manner. These first stages are to be followed by ever more profound reflection and a deepening of meditation until the student has arrived at a certain one-pointed inner concentration "beyond the sphere of argument or reasoned thought." At this point he has reached the state described in classic Upani-shad lines: "Just as when salt has been dissolved into water the salt is no longer perceived separately and the water alone remains, so likewise the mental state that has taken the form of Brahman, the One-Without-a-Second, is no longer perceived, only the Self remains."

The daily meditation which forms so essential a part of a Vedantist's discipline finds ultimate realization in the phrase already quoted in these pages: *Tat tvam asi*, "That art Thou"; in other words, a man's hidden self or soul is identical with the World Soul, Brahman. One might, therefore, briefly describe Vedanta as a method of instruction and practice leading to a personal experiencing of the living Reality which lies behind the world of appearances. This Absolute Reality is Brahman or *sat-chit-ananda*, pure Existence-Consciousness-Bliss. Of this basic concept a modern Vedantist, Swami Nikhilananda, who has lived and taught in the West, has written:

> Brahman does not exist as an empirical object—for instance, like a pot or a tree—but as Absolute Existence, without which material objects would not be perceived to exist. Just as a mirage cannot be seen without the desert, which is its unrelated substratum, so also the universe cannot exist without Brahman.

A Vedantist who has come to perceive his identity with Brahman's essence will also plainly perceive the nature of maya as the "world show" conjured up by the Great Magician. This applies to the ever-changing mirage-like phenomena of life which yet exist in the unalterable "Truth" that sustains them. Moksha (release) is not the dissolution of the world but rather "the displacement of a false outlook (*avidya*) by the right outlook, wisdom (*vidya*)."

While educated Hindus have involved themselves in some aspect or degree of philosophic Hinduism, the Indian people have been instructed and entertained by a prodigious, largely anonymous, collection of tales called the Puranas ("Ancient Stories"), dating from the fifth to the eighteenth centuries. The Puranas have been instruments of mass education, for they have brought to the illiterates of India, by way of stirring romance and lively legend, Hindu philosophy, ideals, customs and manners. It is the Puranas that contain the main body of fantastic and contradictory myths from which the various sects and cults—rising like islands from the central sea of Hinduism—have drawn the richly detailed anecdotes of their favorite personal deities.

All Indians on all levels of life know the tales from the Ramayana and the Mahabharata, those two celebrated epics which are often compared to the Iliad and the Odyssey. For centuries storytellers have been sitting in the village square at twilight, in "the sacred hour of cowdust," relating episodes from the former about the hero Rama, who is one of the incarnations of Vishnu in human form. Rama's many earthly tribulations include unjust banishment to a forest and the abduction by the demon king of Lanka (Ceylon) of his ineffably pure wife, Sita. Sita, in due course, was rescued by that notable monkey, Hanuman, friend and servant of Prince Rama, with the help of an army of brother monkeys who built a causeway from the tip of India to the island of Ceylon and crossed over to rout the demon king. Until fairly recent times, thanks to the wandering storytellers, hardly any Indian girl or boy grew up without knowing the story of the Ramayana, and the hero and heroine of this very old legend were the ideal Hindu husband and wife. Although the book is full of violence and grotesque humor, it also stresses tenderness, morality and chivalric behavior. In its attitude toward the animal world it gives expression to the Indian intuition of kinship with his animal brothers which scholars like Coomaraswamy and Zimmer find of particular significance. In *Myths of the Hindus and Buddhists,* speaking of Hanuman, Coomaraswamy has written: "When he bows to touch the foot of Rama, that Prince who is also a divine incarnation, we witness the meeting point of early nature-worships with the great systems that are to sway the future of religion."

The Mahabharata, an epic of even more immense dimension than the Ramayana, almost eight times as long as the Iliad and the Odyssey combined, has been appraised as the greatest of all efforts ever made to conserve in a single collected form the most ancient beliefs and traditions of a race. In agreement with an old Bengali saying, "Whatever is not in the Mahabharata is not to be found in the land of Bharata [India]," Coomaraswamy finds in this enduring creation from the timeless past a complete revelation of the Indian mind. The leading subject of this longest poem in the world is the painful internecine strife between the royal Kauravas and Pandavas, but it also contains many stories within its own story and, most importantly, in a section of eighteen chapters, India's best-loved devotional book, the Bhagavad-Gita.

The Gita, the Song Celestial, or Song of the Divine One, is a metrical dialogue between the god Krishna and a troubled human hero named Arjuna, who has been reluctantly forced to engage in righteous battle against his own kinsmen. Krishna, disguised as a charioteer, attends Arjuna in order to bolster his faltering will with wise discourse, and this "sermon on a battlefield" has become the favorite text and enduring inspiration of many modern Indians (among them the late Mahatma Gandhi) who have been forced, against their true natures, to participate actively in stirring events. (The battlefield for Gandhi was, however, the human heart, the real sphere of human action where only weapons of understanding and compassion are truly viable.)

Although the Gita's dates are given by some scholars as early as 200 B.C. and by none as later than A.D. 200, this heartening dialogue from India's remote past has been more frequently translated into English than any other Hindu sacred writing. Many Western people who had never heard of the Gita learned of its existence at the time of the first experimental nuclear blast on the New Mexico desert when Dr. Robert Oppenheimer related, in a widely read interview, that the awesome spectacle of nuclear explosion brought into his mind apocalyptic words from the pages of this ancient text: "Suppose a thousand suns should rise together in the sky; such is the splendor of the Shape of Infinite God." (In the Gita, needless to say, the light of a thousand suns was not the light generated by man, the experimental creator and possible destroyer of his own kind, but of God himself.)

The charioteer-philosopher, Krishna, of this battlefield sermon, may seem a far cry from the young pastoral Krishna, whose mischievous and amorous exploits in his sportive days among the cows and *gopis* (milkmaids) are so beloved of Indian artists and romantic poets, and whose worship has obviously fulfilled some deep requirement of sexual-religious ecstasy in the Indian nature. Both Krishnas are, however, the same god in different guises: the many-lived Vishnu. The preserving and restoring powers of this remarkable deity, Vishnu—often depicted riding an enormous bird, the Garuda—have led him to make nine descents to earth, with a tenth yet to come. At times of worldly stress or crisis, Vishnu can be counted on to put in an appearance. He came once as a fish to tow the Hindu ark (for the Hindus also have a legend of a great flood); again he came, as a boar of cosmic dimensions, to raise the tiny young goddess Earth from the overwhelming primeval waters. Once he appeared as a dwarf who, by a clever ruse, defeated the tyrannical monarch of a prehistoric era.

Among his most popular incarnations are his embodiments as Rama, the noble human hero of the epic Ramayana, and as the adored, indigo-hued Krishna, mentioned above, whose youthful pranks and exploits provide the themes of innumerable Indian dances, poems, and works of art. Images of this beguiling young Krishna (before he turned philosopher in the Gita) have a special charm and gaiety. As a precocious infant, whose divinity is not yet recognized, he is shown at the crawling stage, holding up a sweet cake. Grown somewhat older, he is seen dancing for joy with a pat of stolen butter in his hand. As an irresistible youth, he appears in the classic "three-bend pose" of the amorous flutist calling to his rustic love, Radha. Krishna, as a joyful herdsman, fascinating lover, fickle Don Juan, queller of serpents, princeling hero and all-around charmer, became the subject matter for delightful paintings—rapturous, vigorous and delicate—that were a product of the Hindu courts of the Punjab Hills and Rajasthan during the sixteenth to eighteenth centuries. (These graceful sensual paintings have become of increasing interest to Western collectors.)

The emphasis that began to be placed in the Krishna cult on the romance between this lovable god and the beautiful gopi, Radha, found expression also in passionate love poems. These poems, however, are not intended to be descriptive merely of the joys of earthly love between a man and a woman. They are intended rather, as in the Biblical Song of Solomon, the poems of St. John of the Cross, or a number of rather startling Protestant hymns written in terms of the relationship between a lover and a beloved, to express symbolically the struggle of the individual soul in search of fulfillment and the eventual transports of blissful union with the Divine One.

There is still another manifestation of the composite hero-god of many incarnations, Vishnu, perhaps the most mysterious and provocative of them all. Depicted as a child, he is seen floating on the primal ocean, reclining on a banyan leaf, toe in mouth; again as an older, ineffably serene cosmic dreamer, he lies asleep on the coils of Sesha, the primeval serpent, also afloat on the primal waters, "the resting place of all the worlds to be."

In general Vishnu's cosmic role is Preserver of the Universe. Down the ages, however, in the inexplicable ebb and flow of Hindu mythological conceptions, he has also played the role of Creator, a function primarily attributed to Brahma, the first member of the syncretic Hindu triad: Brahma-

Vishnu-Shiva. Brahma is a far more shadowy god than Vishnu or Shiva, or the powerful Divine Mother of many aspects. No sect stems from his worship, and, puzzlingly enough, he is often seen as a small figure in the center of the mystic lotus that emerges from the sleeping Vishnu's navel. Joseph Campbell has described Brahma as essentially a "theologian's god" whose worship never struck vital roots in the popular folk soil. That he was used to lend support to a man-made system of social organization seems implicit in the myth which tells us that the four castes sprang from his body: Brahmins, priestly interpreters, from his mouth; Kshatriyas, the warrior-rulers and aristocrats, from his arms; the Vaisyas, supporters of commerce and agriculture, from his thighs; the Shudras, or laborers, from his legs; merely a metaphoric way, according to one authority, of representing the "four human functions: cogitation, protection, sustenance and service." Today Brahma is so relatively unimportant that only one or two temples in all India are reserved for his exclusive worship.

Although Shiva, the third member of the godly triumvirate, is designated as the Destroyer of the Universe, it must be kept in mind that as Destroyer he is also a Creator in the cyclic Hindu system of thought, where all life is seen as part of a great rhythmic process aptly reflected in the world of nature in which the pattern of continual death and rebirth expresses itself in the very turn of the seasons. And here one thinks of the violence of India's seasonal changes, so unlike the gentler gradations of the temperate zone; the tempestuous, often disastrous force, for instance, of the desperately awaited monsoons which—by their effect on nature—exemplify that very benefi-cence-in-destruction principle that underlies the paradoxical substance of India's major deities.

Lord Shiva is a more fearsome and complex god than Vishnu. His worship, in many of its elements, is believed, as already mentioned, to date back to Dravidian times and India's pre-Aryan cultures. Some scholars go so far as to suggest a possible proto-Shiva in one of the famous seals excavated from the ruins of Mohenjo-Daro. This seal shows a godlike human creature seated among animals—a tiger, an elephant, a rhinoceros and a buffalo—in the ritualistic cross-legged, heel-touching posture associated with later forms of yoga meditations. Whether the origins of Shiva's worship go back that far is not easily determined, but it does seem clear that his cult has its roots in pre-Vedic India, even though its written texts postdate the Aryan Vedas by many centuries.

Shiva can assume many roles for his devotees. He is an ascetic, a fertility god, a ghoul, a divine hermit delighting in solitary meditation high in the Himalayas, a scholar, a supremely devoted spouse. Among his many titles are the Lord of the Creatures, the Lord of Sacrifice, the Divine Hermaphrodite, the Great Ascetic, the Divine Yogi, the Cosmic Musician. Above all, however, he is the King of Dancers, whose movements signify the eternal life-death rhythm of the universe, a concept given superb form in the sculptured dancing figures already referred to. The animal particularly associated with Shiva is Nandi, the bull, whose image is usually found in Shiva temples along with the carved stone symbol signifying the creative male energy of the universe.

It was Shiva, in one myth, who brought the mighty River Ganges to earth, breaking its first torrential fall from Heaven in the curling locks of his hair, permitting it thus to descend gently to the waiting plains from the high Himalayas, where the god had been seated in profound meditation. The Descent of the Ganges is the subject of one of the most awe-inspiring Indian sculptures—claimed as the world's largest bas-relief—carved on an immense seashore monolith at Mahabalipuram, near Madras in southern India, some-time during the seventh century A.D. Shiva also played a vital role, as did Vishnu, in another great event of an even more distant age, the Churning of the Milk Ocean, or the Cosmic Sea, to extract from it the elixir of immor-tality. This titanic theme of struggle for power among gods, demons and serpents is superbly portrayed on a gigantic wall relief at Angkor Wat in Cambodia—where Hinduism once prevailed as the transplanted religion of its kings and rulers.

Shiva is associated, too, with what is sometimes called the "left-hand side" of esoteric Hinduism—a term originating from the traditional sculptured position, on the god's left side, of his consort or "female essence" (*Shakti*). Left-hand cults, mystical-erotic worship of feminine divinities, belong to the Shaktic or Tantric sects that developed during India's medieval period. Tantrism has its own independent body of literature, the Tantras, parts of which are claimed as shruti, or "revealed" texts, given by Shiva himself as the proper spiritual guidance for man during the present world age, just as the ancient Vedas—also termed sruti, it will be recalled—were intended for man's direction in an earlier era. Some teachings found in the Tantras deal with sexual practices, and it is these texts, more rumored about than read, in conjunction with frank expressions of sexual love in certain temple art, that shock many Indians as well as travelers from abroad.

Although Tantrism has often been criticized as a debasement of Hindu-

ism, a religious degeneracy infinitely far removed from original Vedic practices, there have also been favorable interpretations of these Indian teachings
that developed outside the strict Vedic heritage. Heinrich Zimmer saw in
Tantrism a very special, even "heroic," affirmation of the deepest natural
forces of life, for it taught that man must rise "through and by means of
nature, not by the rejection of nature." Every idea of "guilt," or "sin," had to
be surmounted on the way to the life of a guru—since all expressions of the
life force were equally holy, all beings and things were "members of a single
mystic 'family' (*kula*)."

Certain Tantric mystery rites, conducted in the name of the Great Mother
Goddess by special initiates, expressed deliberate, bold defiance of long-
established tabus of orthodox Hinduism. Groups of Shaktic adepts who
secretly met together put aside all bars of caste distinction. As equals seated
in a circle around a specially drawn magic diagram called a *yantra* or
mandala, they ate the meat and fish forbidden by Vedic orthodoxy, drank
intoxicants from the same cup and took part in sexual intercourse. (These
medieval mysteries—sometimes compared to the European Black Masses—
had also a violent and morbid side that found expression in Indian art and
literature even as, near the end of the Middle Ages in Europe, such
unpalatable subjects as Dances of Death and tomb art—showing bodies
consumed by worms—made their appearance.)

Although it is probably true that a number of Tantric rites were degraded
to a level of gross sensualism, there is also little doubt that many Tantric
practices were profoundly mystical, strictly disciplined and conducted on the
highest yoga plane. Today organized Tantric communal rites are believed to
have died out altogether; perhaps they have merely gone underground. In
any event, they are presumed to belong to the past, along with temple
courtesans and other customs and expressions of a passionate people who
were—in certain geographic areas more than others—extraordinarily frank
and free about the life of the senses.

Incorporated in the design of many Indian temples a candid sensuality
finds expression in figures of amorous couples (*maithuna* or *mithuna*)
locked in a variety of ingenious, perverse, tender, torrid and frequently
acrobatic embraces. These figures are, in a sense, an aesthetic embodiment of
a Tantric concept that sensual bliss (*bhoga*) could be a form of yoga or a
way to enlightenment. As found in the still-remarkable ruins of the Sun
Temple near the sea at Konarak in Orissa, these emblematic sculptured
figures, depicting union both physical and cosmic, are undoubtedly related

to an ancient cult of sun worship. Both here and elsewhere—notably at Khajuraho—they were also, however, a specific manifestation of the great Tantric mystery "in which each is both," further exemplified in the divine embrace of the god Shiva and his wife Shakti. This particular sculptural concept, born of medieval Hindu mysticism, eventually made its way to distant Tibet and Nepal, where the figure known as *yab-yum* came to represent, in its own special and sometimes fearsome way, the Buddhist doctrine of "transcendental monism."

The often magnificent temple sculptures of medieval Hinduism were, in general, intended as more than an exercise in the turning of resistant stone to the uses of unabashed eroticism. The all-seeing eye that calmly accepts life in its manifold manifestations may be a prerogative as much of the artist as of the scientist, and certainly to look dispassionately at the best of these sculptures, even to see them reproduced in photographs, is to be aware of a deep significance in the free flood of energy that flows connectedly through them like an invisible current, infusing them in the moment of fulfillment, waiting gently or subsiding softly—but never entirely disappearing—in the tender exchange of breath and glance that follows, or precedes, the ultimate embrace. It is not too difficult to read in these maithuna a human metaphor of the desired philosophic fusion of contrasting principles, a union expressed on the mythological plane in the conjunction of a god and a goddess and, on the highest plane of all, by the joining of the individual soul, atman, and the Universal Spirit of life, Brahman. In one of the Upanishads, which preceded the famous erotic temple sculptures by about two thousand years, one reads:

> In the embrace of his beloved a man forgets the whole world—everything both within and without; in the same way he who embraces the Self knows neither within nor without.

(It should be remarked, however, that the Vedic Upanishads, in general, transcend the physical plane and are almost wholly dedicated to spiritual and contemplative states of mind.)

The question of whether reaction to Indian temple art may not lie wholly in the eye of the beholder strongly presents itself also on viewing one of the silent dignified "holy of holies," empty of all ornament, where Shiva's lingam, that ancient symbol of divine creativity, rises from the stone floor, sometimes in conjunction with the feminine *yoni*, often adorned with wreaths of flowers and anointed with sanctified *ghee* (butter). Such a quiet enclosure, the "womb room" or "germ cell," is the very life center of certain sanctuaries, intended to symbolize the inmost chamber of the heart where the god's pure essence should have its eternal serene abode. Although it is said that even in earliest times the Aryans "abhorred" the veneration of this explicit symbol of creativity and scorned the conquered early Indians as "phallus worshipers," the lingam has endured nonetheless as a part of a deep mystery of prehistoric worship. It plainly seeks to give expression to a concept of cosmic generation far more profound than the merely sexual connotation so easily ascribed to it.

The third of the three most widely worshiped divinities in India today is the Divine Mother, or Shakti, the personification of the female energy of the universe. Conceived in both destructive and creative forms, Shakti, like her male counterparts, manifests herself in many guises and under many names. As Shiva's wife Kali, already referred to, she sometimes appears as an unattractive, fierce and violent symbol of power—an appearance which can also convey, however, a poetic intensity—at once awesome and revealing, which (as in the Kangra painting illustrated) defies adequate interpretation, though its unfamiliar iconographic elements may strongly affect the imagination. These fearful Kalis are of relatively late origin. They represent an important Dravidian contribution to Vedic Hinduism, for by giving expression to the negative aspect of the maternal principle, i.e., by showing the Mother Goddess as the tomb as well as the womb of all life, they enunciate in unique terms the mysterious concept—now so much a part of the abstract thought of Hinduism—that destruction and production arise from the same source. Kali represents another of syncretic Hinduism's most compelling paradoxes. Though sometimes garlanded with serpents, hung round with skulls, brandishing a sword, holding a severed demon's head, she may also be making, with one or more hands, a mudra of reassurance or even a gift-giving gesture. In some images she is shown dancing on the supine body of her consort Shiva, a symbolic stance which leads the mind into unfamiliar channels of speculation. By using Great Time or Eternity (other names of Shiva) as her dancing platform, is the Mother, or lesser "time," here implying the rise and fall, appearance and disappearance, of all phenomena from an eternal cosmogonic substratum?

Sometimes the embodiment of feminine cosmic energy is depicted in the form of Durga, a sort of feminine St. George, an imperious dignified goddess often portrayed as serenely remote and detached even when in the act of slaying a buffalo-headed demon. Zimmer has seen in this particular aspect of the goddess a symbol of the reascendance to power of the timeless neolithic Divine Mother, triumphing over the long-entrenched patriarchal masculine

Aryans. This transformation, more than a millennium in the making, has now—also in Zimmer's view—found significant, open expression in the national anthem of the New India, which begins, "I praise and adore the Mother." (Zimmer has also, however, drawn attention to a passage from the Kena Upanishad dating probably from the seventh century B.C., which shows the Aryans of that distant time already making a place for the Divine Mother in their evolving spiritual hierarchy. The scripture recounts how, during one of the periodic cosmic crises that mark Hindu mythology, Indra—an early Aryan god—was visited by a beautiful and awesome apparition of the Mother Goddess. She came to reveal to Indra the true nature of all-powerful Brahman, the Immutable Absolute, source of even his, Indra's, power. With this startling act of revelation, Zimmer suggests, we see the phenomenon of "womanhood incarnate" serving as a "guru of the male gods," an early portent of the eventual attainment of supremacy in the Hindu cosmogony of this timeless archetype, the Great Mother.)

Shiva's consort of many aspects is not always a figure of overt power. She may appear in tenderly appealing aspects like that of his loving, ingratiating bride Parvati (or Uma), daughter of Himalaya, a personification of the towering mountains that guard India's northern boundaries.

Vishnu's female counterpart, far less complex than Shiva's, takes form as Lakshmi, goddess of prosperity and good fortune. There is also the divine Sarasvati, associated with both Brahma and Vishnu, who symbolizes wisdom and music as she rides a swan or peacock, while holding a lute and a manuscript. Altogether Hinduism offers an almost endless diversity of female deities, extending down to simple local goddesses whose crude colorful images can be found in the shrines of thousands of Indian hamlets.

Before leaving the engrossing subject of the place of Shakti in Hinduism, we should take note of the fact that Shri Ramakrishna, perhaps the most remarkable of modern Indian mystics, took as his object of personal devotion the Divine Mother in the form of Kali, a choice that may be related to another of his significant acts, the choosing of a woman for one of his early gurus. Such a procedure is relatively rare in the later annals of Indian religious history in which, for centuries, orthodox Hindu women, along with outcasts and Shudras, were not permitted to hear the reading of the most sacred sections of the Vedas. (All three categories were classified as "laboring under certain disabilities.") The introduction of such essentially primitive and unspiritual laws as those forbidding the inclusion of women in the holiest religious circles is another part of a little-understood decadence that developed in certain sections of the complex Hindu social structure. Scholars have pointed out that not only was there no similar disbarment of women in the Vedic and Upanishadic period but, on the contrary, any number of noted feminine saints and spiritual leaders are to be found in early annals. The exclusion of women from the inmost mysteries of spiritual instruction was not true either of the Tantric sects of the Middle Ages. As we have just seen, not only did they worship Divinity in female form; they allowed women full participation in all types of religious activity including the organization of groups of female ascetics or temple dancers. Much earlier, too, the greatest of all "reformers" of Hinduism, the "historic Buddha," born in present-day Nepal in the sixth century B.C., made a place for nuns in his Order. In short, women's place in India has so many contradictory aspects that generalizations cannot be safely indulged in. Certainly their original position in this part of the world is known to have been far from subservient. Virtual systems of matriarchy still survive in the Dravidian south (the "real" India, one often hears modern Indians say), a circumstance attributed by some authorities to the fact that neither strict Aryan orthodoxy, nor the invader Muslims' insistence on woman's submission, managed to penetrate this far geographically. Today the educated women of India serenely occupy—on the international as well as the national scene—places of public influence and power that many ambitious Western women might well envy.

On a level slightly less elevated than Shakti, Shiva or Vishnu, there exist innumerable lesser deities who also receive ardent worship from devoted followers and continue to provide—as they have for aeons—Hindu artists in all media with a marvelous and unique range of subject matter. One of the most popular of folk gods is the jolly, fat-bellied, elephant-headed Ganesh, the symbol of good luck and prosperity, an icon whose source, in all probability, lies in the remote Indian past, when man, through almost unimaginable feats of skill and courage, tamed and trained the dangerous jungle creature, the elephant, to become a valuable ally in work, war and pageantry. Ganesh's somewhat incongruous attendant is a rat, whose presence signifies the overcoming of obstacles different in kind from those the huge elephant so easily surmounts. Together the powerful beast and the small clever rodent constitute a symbolic team devoted to promoting good fortune through a combination of force and cunning.

The legendary patriarch and sage, Manu, is also widely venerated, though not worshiped in any cult way. Perhaps an actual historical personage, he is the supposed progenitor of the present human race and survivor of that Great Flood of prehistory in which the Hindus also believe. To Manu is sometimes ascribed authorship of an ancient lawbook known as the Code of Manu, said to have "fixed Indian conduct for all time." There also survive in Indian mythology deities connected with early Nature worship, prototypes common to the primitive rites of more familiar cultural groups from Greece to Scandinavia; a Sun God, a Dawn Goddess, the Wind, Fire, Moon and Planets. In addition, countless demons, imps, snake gods, tree and water nymphs, "guardians of the world," divine musicians and so on create endless variety and diversion.

In a sense Hinduism is like an enormous repository of the mythmaking proclivities of the human race, with this significant difference: that India's repository is not a mere storehouse of dead or repressed elements, but a still-vital force in the daily existence of hundreds of millions of people.

Anachronistic as this labyrinthine mythology may appear to the foreign mind, many of India's ancient theories about the universe are startlingly modern in scope and worthy of a people who are credited with the invention of the zero, as well as algebra and its application to astronomy and geometry; a people who so carefully observed the heavens that, in the opinion of Monier-Williams, they determined the moon's synodical revolution much more correctly than the Greeks. India's President, Dr. Radhakrishnan, has written of his early countrymen:

> They measured the land, divided the year, mapped out the heavens, traced the course of sun and planets through the zodiacal belt, analyzed the constitution of matter, and studied the nature of birds and beasts, plants and seeds.

Many hundreds of years before those great European pioneers, Galileo and Copernicus, had to pay heavy prices in ridicule and excommunication for their daring theories, a section of the Vedas known as the Brahmanas contained this astounding statement:

> The sun never sets or rises. When people think the sun is setting, he only changes about after reaching the end of the day and makes night below and day to what is on the other side. Then, when people think he rises in the morning, he only shifts himself about after reaching the end of the night, and makes day below and night to what is on the other side. In truth, he does not set at all.

The Indians, whose theory of time, as already noted, is not linear like ours—that is, not proceeding consecutively from past to present to future—

have always been able to accept, seemingly without anxiety, the notion of an alternately expanding and contracting universe, an idea recently advanced by certain Western scientists. In Hindu cosmology, immutable Brahman, at fixed intervals, draws back into his beginningless, endless Being the whole substance of the living world. There then takes place the long "sleep" of Brahman from which, in the course of countless aeons, there is an awakening, and another universe or "dream" emerges. This notion of the sleeping and waking, or contracting and expanding, of the Life Force, so long a part of Hindu cosmology, has recently been expressed in relevant terms in an article written for a British scientific journal by Professor Fred Hoyle, Britain's foremost astronomer. In October, 1965, an American front-page newspaper account of this article spoke of Dr. Hoyle's having "dropped a scientific bombshell" by admitting that he had been wrong for twenty years in his theory about the nature of the universe. Long the chief proponent of the so-called "steady-state" theory, which holds that the universe has always been much the same as it now is, Dr. Hoyle says that he has come instead to believe that "the universe probably is in a state of flux, expanding for billions of years, then contracting to what amounts to a dense ball of matter, then expanding again."

Plainly, contemporary Western science's description of an astronomical universe of such vast magnitude that distances must be measured in terms as abstract as light-years is not new to Hinduism whose wise men, millennia ago, came up with the term *kalpa* to signify the inconceivable duration of the period elapsing between the beginning and end of a world system. These world systems of ancient Indian thought—following one another in endless succession as Brahman sleeps or wakes—consisted of a conglomeration of many suns, stars, planets and moons, again suggesting modern astronomy's "island universes," of which more than a million have now been discovered, some of them at least two million light-years distant.

We reckon a light-year as the distance light travels in a year's time, or 5,878,000,000,000 miles. The number is, of course, almost unimaginable; the mind cannot grasp it. To pictorialize a kalpa—that is, the time between the initial condensation to the final conflagration of a world system—an Indian sage of the sixth century B.C., Siddhartha Gautama, who became the Buddha, reduced this immense concept to singularly vivid terms. Imagine, he said, a mountain of the very hardest rock, a mountain much larger than any peak in the Himalayas, and suppose that a man, with a piece of the very finest, sheerest silk gauze from Benares comes just once every hundred years to touch that great mountain with the gauze ever so slightly. The time it would take him to wear away the entire mountain would be about the length of a kalpa.

Each kalpa is divided in Indian reckoning into four *yugas,* or ages, of which mankind is now said to be living in the fourth, the last and darkest, the Kali yuga, at the end of which inevitable recurrent dissolution will take place. There are a number of descriptions in classic Indian scriptures of the conditions characteristic of the Kali yuga. A particularly fulsome picture of the general decline is provided in the Matsya Purana:

> There is no one, any more, in whom enlightening goodness (*sattva*) prevails; no real wise man, no saint, no one uttering truth and standing by his sacred word. The seemingly holy Brahmin is no better than a fool. Old people, destitute of the true wisdom of old age, try to behave like the young, and the young lack the candor of youth. The social classes have lost their distinguishing, dignifying virtues; teachers, princes, tradespeople and servants sprawl alike in a general vulgarity. The will to rise to supreme heights has failed; the bonds of sympathy and love have dissolved; narrow egotism rules. Indistinguishable ninnies conglomerate to form a sticky, unpalatable dough. When this calamity has befallen the once harmoniously ordered City of Man, the substance of the world-organism has deteriorated beyond salvage, and the universe is ripe for dissolution.

Although this state of affairs may sound ominously contemporary, the present Kali yuga is dated with startling certitude by some Indian sages as having begun as long ago as Friday, February 18, 3102 B.C. Sometimes this date is also claimed to mark the beginning of the great Mahabharata War, that fratricidal struggle in which the god Krishna (Vishnu) came to guide the chariot of the worried human hero, Arjuna, and advise him on matters both spiritual and temporal, as described in the Bhagavad-Gita. Another tradition places this great conflict—the theme of one of India's two major epics—as late as 900 B.C., and this latter date, taken in conjunction with other reckonings that make the years of the present yuga "man years" rather than the much longer "god years," would suggest that the Kali yuga might be drawing alarmingly near its end.

It is clear that Indian religious cosmology is sharply at variance with that inherited by Western peoples from the Semites. On the highest level, when stripped of mythological embroidery, Hinduism's conceptions of space, time and multiple universes approximate in range and abstraction the most advanced scientific thought. This is a fact which could prove helpful in making Hindu philosophy somewhat more acceptable to Western minds now stretched by the findings of contemporary astronomy, just as Hinduism's vast treasury of still-living myth, if reappraised in modern psychoanalytic terms, or through the new "science of mythology," might provide useful insights into the singular activity of that part of human consciousness which Carl Jung called "the collective."

The long dynamic history of Hinduism has been marked by periodic renascences and—after the entrance of England on the Indian national scene—by significant surges of feeling for and against the West. Details of this rising and ebbing wave cannot be gone into at any length here, but some aspects of Hinduism's most recent upsurgence must at least be mentioned. The movement known as the Brahmo Samaj is generally cited as ushering in the modern period in Hinduism. The Brahmo Samaj looks for its inspiration to a noted Bengali, Ram Mohun Roy (1772–1833). Roy heralded the coming changes born of the impact of the world-colonizing British on the then relatively isolated and self-contained India. He became a close friend of many noted Englishmen and admired many aspects of the Christian-Western heritage even while he worked vigorously to restore what he believed to be the true original spirit of Hinduism and to rid it of an accretion of decadent customs such as *sati* (the immolation of widows on their husbands' funeral pyres), child marriages, abuse of the caste system and primitive types of idol worship. He deplored narrow and ignorant orthodoxy alike in Hinduism and in Christianity. He clearly foresaw the national danger that would result if English-educated Indians threw overboard, out of ignorance or as a matter of expediency, their own rich philosophic heritage and unique cultural traditions.

Somewhat later, the Arya Samaj was founded by Swami Dayananda Saraswati (1824–1883). It, too, sought and brought about long-needed socioreligious reforms even as it upheld classic Vedic teachings and encouraged pride in the ancient philosophic achievements of the motherland. The impassioned emphasis in the Arya Samaj on "a return to the Vedas" became a slogan that, in time, related itself to the rising tide of Indian nationalism. The movement acquired a strong political cast. In spite of advocating a return to "pure" Vedic roots, the Arya Samaj has been accused of paying surprisingly scant attention to the profound philosophy embodied in the

Upanishads and, thereby, in the opinion of at least one outstanding authority, deliberately cutting itself off from "the perennial sources of Hindu religious thought."

Shri Ramakrishna, already described in these pages, and his disciple, Vivekananda, were also directly involved in Hinduism's modern renascence. Vivekananda's first revolutionary trip to the West in 1893 created a sensation in America. In that year, he turned up, an unknown and unheralded swami, at a conference on world religions held in Chicago. Here his striking presence, profound learning, and personal magnetism took his eminent confreres by storm. His courageous journey overseas (orthodox Hindus, and, above all, highborn Brahmins, were not supposed in those days to travel outside India) led to the establishment of still-flourishing Vedanta Society centers in the United States and Europe. On his return home, his Western experiences led also to the founding of Indian groups where—along with Ramakrishna's "universal religion"—there were also taught types of social service, new then to India.

It was inevitable that Great Britain's involvement in India would bring Hinduism more directly to the attention of Western people and create among them a number of fervent supporters of its ancient truths and mysteries. One of the most ardent converts and proselytizers was a remarkable Englishwoman, Annie Besant (1847–1933). A one-time freethinker, a dynamic and eloquent lecturer, Mrs. Besant—who, after her conversion, made India her home—was instrumental in gaining an intelligent Western audience for certain aspects of Hinduism's often misinterpreted philosophy. She is also credited with arousing new interest among modern Indian intellectuals in their country's ancient metaphysical and cultural heritage. In his autobiography written in 1948—a book of consummate and exemplary candor—Mohandas K. Gandhi, most famous of all modern Hindus, frankly admits that during his stay in England as a young man it was the reading of a book on Theosophy, written by Mrs. Besant's Theosophical guru, the controversial figure, Mme. Helena Petrovna Blavatsky, that stimulated him to re-evaluate the classic religious literature of his own land, hitherto neglected, even ignored by him in common with many educated Indians of that period. Blavatsky's *Key to Theosophy*, lent him by British friends, was responsible, so he asserted, for first disabusing him of the "notion fostered by the missionaries that Hinduism was rife with superstition." Gandhi never, however, joined any Theosophical group either in England or India.

Theosophy, known to its followers as "The Ancient Wisdom," claims to be an amalgam of the fundamental teachings of East and West, a synthesis, so to speak, comprising all of what has been termed "the perennial philosophy" common to all mankind. It is also rooted in the Vedantist concept of One Divine Reality and its followers believe in the cyclic Hindu rhythm of the cosmos and accept as true the Asian law of karma.

The influential Annie Besant's many activities in India included the founding of a Hindu college in Benares which has grown into the present Benares Hindu University. She played an active part in the fight for Home Rule for India and was even imprisoned by the British along with many prominent Indian patriots. Gandhi once referred to her as one of India's most "valiant warriors" and upon one occasion wrote a strong letter to the British Viceroy protesting her exclusion from an important conference between the British Government and Indian representatives. Although some unfortunate publicity, brought on by the aberrant activities of certain members of the Theosophical Society, tended in time to dim Mrs. Besant's original luster, she is still honored in India as a great pioneer in Hinduism's modern renascence and a true friend of the Indian people.

It was Mrs. Besant's close associate and fellow Theosophist, the Reverend Charles Leadbeater, a former Anglican clergyman, who, in 1909, personally "discovered" the contemporary Indian teacher, Krishnamurti. Mrs. Besant shared Leadbeater's firm belief that a fourteen-year-old boy from Madras was none other than this age's World Teacher, an incarnation of Divinity in human form. She spread far and wide the word of the amazing young twentieth-century avatar. When, however, in due course, Krishnamurti had been highly educated in England, Europe and India and prepared in every possible way for his messianic work on a world scale, he repudiated the exalted role into which he had been thrust by Mrs. Besant. While he has continued up to the present time to be an influential and impressive teacher, with a large and devoted following of eminent Europeans, Americans and fellow Indians, he has adopted a detached, uncompromising, almost iconoclastic tone that has sometimes led people to compare his methods to those of Zen Buddhism:

> I maintain that Truth is a pathless land and you cannot approach it by any path whatsoever, by any religion, by any sect. . . . I do not want followers, and I mean this. The moment you follow someone you cease to follow Truth. . . . I am concerning myself with only one essential thing: to set man free. I desire to free him from all cages, from all fears,

and not to found religions, new sects, nor to establish new theories and new philosophies.

And yet a true Hindu, on the highest plane of total life-acceptance, speaks forth in other words of his: "Truth is what *is*—and that is the beauty of it."

In the present century, four other exceptional Hindu teachers and leaders have achieved worldwide fame: Rabindranath Tagore, Shri Aurobindo Ghose, Mahatma Gandhi and Vinoba Bhave.

Tagore (1861–1941), a Bengal aristocrat of extraordinary beauty and presence, and a mystic poet who won the Nobel Prize for Literature in 1913, was also a distinguished educator whom Gandhi called "the Great Teacher." Like Vivekananda, Ram Mohun Roy, and other courageous spirits before him, Tagore broke the Hindu tabu about travel abroad and went all over the world teaching and exchanging ideas. He gave the Hibbert lectures at Oxford in 1930 and, in his several trips out of India, engaged in lively dialectic with famous Western intellectuals and authors, including William Butler Yeats, G. B. Shaw, Romain Rolland, Robert Frost, John Dewey, Helen Keller, Thomas Mann and Albert Einstein. In recent years, the attendance at Santiniketan—the school Tagore founded not far from Calcutta—of a daughter of the American ambassador, Chester Bowles, restimulated American interest in Tagore as a personality and in his unremitting work for international understanding and peace.

Quite different in method and impact were the teachings of the most mysterious and reclusive of all latter-day Indian gurus, the "silent sage" of Tiruvannamalai in Southern India, Shri Ramana Maharshi (1879–1950). Shri Ramana was capable of sustained periods of religious trance (samadhi) comparable to those of Ramakrishna, whom, however, physically, and one might even say emotionally, he in no way resembled for he had none of Ramakrishna's volatility and childlike playfulness. He was a man of exceptional dignity and presence, with eyes of almost hypnotic power. His physique seemed, to many Europeans, more Western than Indian. Shri Ramana believed in the power of silent communication. It seems obvious from the record of his life that he possessed telepathic powers, for there are many accounts of how those who came to see him found their deepest questions answered in his silent presence. He also often appeared to disciples in very vivid dreams that served to focus their strivings toward the goal of Selfhood—something altogether different from fulfillment of the ego or the

"I"—which was the basis of Shri Ramana's teaching. Many educators, scholars, philosophers and psychologists were fascinated by this God-engrossed soul, notably Heinrich Zimmer for whose still untranslated book about Shri Ramana, *Der Weg zum Selbst* (The Way to the Self) Carl Jung wrote the introduction. In this introduction Jung expressed the fear that this embodiment of the "thousands' years old spiritual culture of India" might be one of the last of his kind to appear in a world more and more involved in technological advance, less able to provide, anywhere on earth even in India, the silence, peace and detachment necessary for seeking "the liberalizing Original Source" of life itself.

To Shri Ramana the man who found the true Self found God, discovered indeed that he was God himself—a teaching which might strike Westerners as sacrilegious although it is consonant with certain clear, yet cryptic, words of Jesus—"I and my Father are one," or "I am in my Father and my Father is in me." (There are a number of Western mystics of the past who have also stressed God-identification, notably Meister Eckhart who once wrote, "God expects but one thing of you, and that is that you should come out of yourself in so far as you are a created being, and let God be God in you.") Shri Ramana believed in total equality; when very young he divested himself of the sacred Brahmin thread which serves to set this caste apart from all other Hindus. He welcomed at his ashram all who wished to come—regardless of caste, creed, sex, race or personal history. At his death (of cancer—like Ramakrishna before him) he said to a grieving disciple, "I am not going away. Where could I go? I am here."—words that again remind one of Meister Eckhart, and his reply to the question of where a soul went at death, "Why should it go anywhere?"

Shri Aurobindo Ghose (1872–1950), next to Shri Ramana Maharshi the least known to the general Western public of India's latter-day gurus, was at one time an anti-Colonial agitator who, while imprisoned for violence, underwent a tremendous spiritual conversion and emerged to become one of his country's most illustrious sages. He founded a noted ashram in the old French-Indian city of Pondicherry, a hermitage designed to attract people who believed, as he did, that the manifold problems of modern life could be solved only by the creation of individuals of a "higher order." Shri Aurobindo taught, and wrote about, a type of training whereby the "supermind" is brought down to "irradiate the mind and body of the individual," thus creating a kind of spiritual superman who could affect the life around him as did the seers of old. Many remarkable people from his own country, and from Europe and America as well, were drawn to Pondicherry, where they relinquished all their worldly ties and possessions to live a dedicated, simplified, but strenuous communal existence.

While Ghose and Shri Ramana in their remote ashrams were hoping to achieve, on the highest individual plane, an amelioration of the world's increasing troubles, tensions and confusions, Mahatma Gandhi (1869–1948) was going actively into life to help bring independence to the Indian people after a century and a half of British rule. Gandhi had a great affection and admiration for the British people, and many of them—including Lord Louis Mountbatten, the last viceroy of India, and his wife—returned the warmest feelings of respect and love for him. In his autobiography, in recounting the fact referred to earlier that it was British friends who first led him to the serious reading of Hinduism's sacred scriptures, he also described how he turned at the same time to the study of the sacred documents of all other religious faiths. It was then that his young mind began to seek and find the unifying threads of thought in the Gita, the Christian Sermon on the Mount and in the life and teachings of the Buddha as recounted in Sir Edwin Arnold's long poem about the Buddha's life, *The Light of Asia*. This quiet emphasis on the unifying elements in all world faiths was to grow stronger in Gandhi with each passing year and to lead him to constant repetition of such basic beliefs as "All gods are good and all men are brothers."

Gandhi knew and enjoyed many Americans. He numbered among his most devoted disciples and attendants—his ashram "family," as he called them—a daughter of President Woodrow Wilson. Worldly journalists like Louis Fischer and Vincent Sheean became his close friends. They both wrote best sellers about their interviews and experiences with the Mahatma. Sheean was present at the very moment of Gandhi's assassination, standing only a few feet from him. He has vividly described in *Lead Kindly Light* (a title from Gandhi's favorite Christian hymn) the personal mystical experience that came to him, an onlooker, under these stunning and deeply tragic circumstances.

His friendship, even his love, for many Westerners and for many of the ways and works of the West did not, however, deflect Gandhi from his conviction that India's eventual salvation must come to her through national independence; there was no other way, and he was willing to endure repeated prison terms, fasts to the verge of death and, finally, death itself, to pursue this end. He never wished to be considered an incarnation of Deity.

"The woes of mahatmas," he said sadly, even ironically, on more than one occasion, "are known to mahatmas alone." But there was no avoiding his destiny. The total selflessness of his life constrained the Indian people to worship him as a veritable god.

During the dark and tragic days of the partition of India into the Indian Republic and Pakistan, Gandhi went fearlessly, often on foot, into the most dangerous trouble spots. His extreme impartiality in this time of unprecedented Muslim-Hindu antipathy led to his assassination by a fellow Hindu who found his behavior traitorous. Many eminent Christian theologians have described Gandhi as the "most Christlike" modern man. Because of his great following among the masses and his influence on such outstanding political figures as Nehru, Gandhi was unquestionably the leading spirit in founding the "New India" where such ancient folkways as child marriages, ban on intercaste matings, the subservience of women, and "untouchability" began to disappear. He lived and died by a philosophy (Satyagraha) which insisted that the truth as realized in one's own inner heart should be expressed outwardly in direct action of a nonviolent social nature.

This kind of dynamic spiritual-social realism also underlies the land-reform movement known as Bhoodan, the creation of another dedicated, practical "saint," Vinoba Bhave (1895–   ). Bhave—who, like Gandhi, has also drawn to his movement a number of interested Westerners—travels the Indian countryside, walking great distances daily with a band of devoted followers, engaged in a campaign to persuade those who have land to give up some portion of it to those who have none.

In bringing to a conclusion this all too brief survey of a vast subject it might be wise to emphasize the simple truth that even a cursory study of Hinduism lays unusual, though rewarding, demands on the mind and imagination of Western people. To acquire the most superficial grasp of its subtleties and complexities demands relinquishment of the usual exoteric viewpoint most Westerners seem able to maintain even in the presence of the most ancient and magnificent mysteries of their own Judeo-Christian tradition. In understanding Hinduism's vast range of belief and practice it is necessary not only to yield oneself to a prodigious mythology still vitally alive among the simple people, but to come to grips also with the challenging Hindu concept that there is nothing permanent in life, that existence is rather a relentlessly dynamic ebb and flow of energies forever growing, dying, appearing and disappearing. This concept of the total dynamism of the cosmos, maintained by Hinduism down the centuries, is one of its powerful possible connections with contemporary scientific thought, particularly in the field of physics.

Yet it must be remembered that Hinduism also teaches that from the position of the Ultimate itself, there is no ebb or flow, no this or that, no polarities or opposites. The indescribable Absolute One, the metaphysical, *not* mythological, concept of Brahman, though containing all manifestations, essentially stands beyond paradox, polarity, and phenomenology. It is toward the attainment of an eternal still center of union with this nameless and formless Spirit (sometimes referred to as the "Great Within") that the yogi aims in his search for release from maya: that illusion of reality which is not Reality itself, *though embodied in it*. The answer to the question of "why" this necessity for the constant bewildering play of maya in the universe and for man's subjection to it remains hidden, or at least inexplicable, though Hinduism on its highest metaphysical plane would assert that some men have, through specific practices, found the truth for themselves and made the effort to pass on to others a methodology for its attainment. (The cosmic riddle as to why the Absolute subjects one of its manifestations—man—to the frustrating "conflict of opposites" is also projected, as Ananda Coomaraswamy once pointed out, in the Biblical story of the fall of man from a state of grace and bliss to a condition in which Adam had to face the necessity of acquiring knowledge of good and evil, life and death, male and female and all the rest of human existence's unceasing dualism. Here one could also justifiably ask: Why should Biblical man have "fallen" in the first place? What was "gained" thereby?)

Hinduism has seemed singularly able to accept the dispassionate impersonality of the All in One without crying out against it in despair, rage or rebellion. Perhaps this is because the many-sided genius of this paradoxical land of so many blended cultures and peoples knew how to soften—even, one might say, to warm—the utter detachment of an unimaginable Absolute Power by lively popular tales, legends, and art forms involving the behavior of a prolific hierarchy of gods and goddesses who were themselves subject to fateful powers and influences. Over and over again in the rich, profuse mythology of Hinduism one encounters the story of a particular demon, or even of a human ascetic, who by the practice of supreme control of all his energies created a state of being so irresistibly powerful that even gods of the high order of Vishnu, Shiva, Brahma or the Great Mother must pay heed. The force, the *heat* (*tapas*), generated by a superhuman godlike mastering of energy made it necessary for the supplicated god, whatever his identity, to pay attention and grant the suppliant's wish. If, as sometimes happened, the wish was a demonic one, involving destructive activity on Earth, then the gods found it necessary to pool their divine resources in order to circumvent great peril to all existence.

Hinduism—not only in philosophy and literature but also in art—has the capacity for immense conceptions, profound and subtle apprehensions, that can entice the imagination and stun the mind with their depth, range and boldness. The many masks of the many gods, their various appearances and incarnations, have been employed to suggest the infinitely possible variations of one supreme essence. In seeking to give expression to that almost inexpressible idea of a unity which admits also of polarities, a "union beyond the opposites," Hinduism created such arresting icons as the divine two-in-one embrace of Shiva and his Shakti; or Shiva alone, presented in androgynous aspect, half male, half female, or the two-sided figure of Hari-Hara, an expression of the seemingly "opposite" creative-destructive forces of Vishnu and Shiva embodied in one being. The triple activity of the members of the two classic godly triads of Shiva, Vishnu and the Mother, or Shiva, Vishnu and Brahma—who give life, foster life and annihilate it—is the Hindu way of representing the mystery that lies at the very heart of existence itself, where mutually contradictory elements must, perforce, be recognized, understood and accepted before there can be the possibility of transcendence.

More importantly Hinduism's profusion of theories, rites, philosophies, practices and points of view indicates an exceptional spirit of free speculation—even, one might say, of free "research"—into metaphysical matters. For centuries Hinduism has lent tacit support to a bold concept: the idea that the ultimate meaning of the universe, the secret of its single permeating Principle, is within man's power to grasp. Although the path to Brahman lies through knowledge, this does not imply knowledge limited only to narrow mental or intellectual content. Since Brahman is All and One, possessed of both form and formlessness, the way to this ultimate Reality may even include the simplest form of *bhakti*, childlike worship of any of life's multiple manifestations. Single-hearted devotion to a personalized aspect of a god is therefore but one of a number of possible approaches to the eventual goal of divine knowledge. Although a Westerner might be inclined to ask to what "use" this attainment of divine knowledge will be put, to the Hindu such a question would be essentially meaningless because to him divine knowledge is an end in itself, a state of being which represents the culmination and significance of the universe.

There is among Hindus in general, and in spite of the deep timeless sadness one so often feels in their presence, a capacity for joyful, even euphoric, participation in life that is one of their most arresting qualities. No Westerner who has ever shared a dawn with the simple country people of India is likely to forget the moving sight, the reassuring experience of men, women, and children—often carrying flowers—greeting the new day with song and homage; walking to temple tanks for the morning purification bath, to the fields with bullocks, to and from the wells with water. In the midst of the poverty, deprivation, sadness, ignorance, superstition and even, one might fairly say, neurosis of this very old people, there endures a vital living force among them, a capacity for the worshipful acceptance of life itself—quite apart from all theological dogma and religious constructions— that is without parallel in the modern world. The most restrictive caste discriminations have never been able to destroy an immemorial nonpersonal inclusiveness that frequently expresses itself in awesomely large mass gatherings to worship, pay respect, or merely to share some invisible, perhaps imaginary but nonetheless powerful emanations from a place, a time, or a person: the enduring, energizing mystery of the *darshan*. The Hindus' restorative power to feel and express ecstasy, to share personally in the quintessential rhythmic *lila* of the universe, is dramatically exemplified in stories of Shri Ramakrishna getting down from his carriage on occasion to dance with drunkards in the street because the sight of their reeling joy transported him to a state of divine bliss, quite different in source and nature but nonetheless related to his own recurrent God-transported raptures.

Down the millennia of its existence, Hinduism has made a priceless contribution to the collective religious life of mankind through the remarkable findings of her many brilliant mystics and philosophers, as set forth in a voluminous literature. Perhaps, however, her most significant contribution to the universal body of religious inquiry is the persistent, unshakable belief that union with the Divine is attainable while one is still on earth. Moreover, any man in India is at liberty to pursue salvation after his own fashion with no danger of finding himself at some point branded a heretic. Indeed, heresy in Hinduism is virtually impossible, for as the authoritative Upanishads firmly state: "Reality is One though sages call it by different names."

BUDDHISM

As a fletcher makes straight his arrow, a wise man makes straight his trembling and unsteady thought, which is difficult to guard, difficult to hold back. . . .

It is good to tame the mind, which is often difficult to hold in and flighty, rushing wherever it listeth; a tamed mind brings happiness. . . .

Not a mother, not a father, will do so much, nor any other relatives; a well-directed mind will do us greater service. . . .

If one man conquer in battle a thousand times a thousand men, and if another conquer himself, he is the greatest of conquerors.

One's own self conquered is better than all other people conquered; not even a god could change into defeat the victory of a man who has vanquished himself. . . .

—from the *Dhammapada*

May all living things be happy and at their ease! May they be joyous and live in safety! All beings, whether weak or strong—omitting none—in high, middle, or low realms of existence, small or great, visible or invisible, near or far away, born or to be born—may all beings be happy and at their ease! Let none deceive another, or despise any being in any state; let none by anger or ill will wish harm to another! Even as a mother watches over and protects her only child, so with a boundless mind should one cherish all living beings, radiating friendliness over the entire world, above, below and all around without limit; so let him cultivate a boundless good will toward the entire world, uncramped, free from ill will or enmity.

—the *Metta Sutra*

B UDDHISM, the religion of reason and meditation and the faith of approximately one fifth of humanity, was founded by the so-called "historic" Buddha, Siddhartha Gautama, a unique spiritual genius born in northeastern India at a date generally accepted as 563 B.C. Although in the land of its origin Buddhism was in time reabsorbed into the all-embracing Hinduism from which it sprang, it was destined to become and remain the dominant influence in vast sections of Asia, including Ceylon, Burma, Cambodia, Thailand, Vietnam, Laos, as well as Nepal, Sikkim, Tibet, Mongolia, China, Korea and Japan. In all these countries it has had an almost incalculable effect on art, thought, literature and ways of life.

As happens with all world religions, there have accrued to Buddhism, with the passing of the two and a half millennia since its founding, the usual elaborate deification cults, superstitious rites and even, to some degree, fixed authoritative dogma. These developments bear little relation to the original precepts of the strongly pragmatic, down-to-earth, compassionate yet tough-minded aristocrat who established this religious philosophy almost six centuries before the beginning of the Christian era. During the more than forty years of active ministry that followed Siddhartha Gautama's attainment of Supreme Enlightenment while seated in deep meditation under a sacred fig tree—a scene frequently depicted in Asian art—this gifted teacher took special pains to emphasize to his many devoted followers that none of them was to look upon or rely upon him as a Divine Savior or Intercessor. He had, to be sure, become a "Buddha," but this simply meant an Enlightened or Awakened Being. In his opinion, not he, nor any other great Master or

World Teacher, could do more for those who sought help about attaining salvation than merely to "show the way"; each man must find the path to final peace and knowledge through his own efforts.

Said the Buddha: "Within this very body, mortal as it is and only six feet in length, I do declare to you are the world and the origin of the world, and the ceasing of the world and the path that leads to cessation."

Another of his challenging sayings—"Look *within, thou* art the Buddha" —clearly indicates his psychological emphasis on humanity as the instrument of its own fate.

The Buddha made very few concessions to his fellow Indians' love of mythmaking, or to the common human desire to dwell on the miraculous and the supernatural. The world as it was seemed enough of a miracle for him, offering, as it did, the one road immediately at hand for attaining the final goal of Nirvana—release from blind appetites and the limiting sense of a "separate self." Over and over again, with tireless patience, the Buddha— using the repetitive teaching style of the Far East in the days before written literature—expressed his belief that final illumination required only determination and ardent desire, a quickened "awareness" (a favorite Buddhist word) in thought and deed, and a sincere wish to compose human experience after more meaningful, less ego-centered patterns. Although the Buddha went forth personally to teach his doctrine of "mindfulness" as the way to enlightenment, he never failed to stress the necessity for freedom from all sacrosanct religious authority. "Believe nothing," he said to his followers, "just because you have been told it, or it is commonly believed, or because it is traditional or because you yourselves have imagined it. Do not believe what your Teacher tells you merely out of respect for the Teacher. But whatsoever, after due examination and analysis, you find to be conducive to the good, the benefit, the welfare of all beings—that doctrine believe and cling to, and take as your guide."

Buddhism is sometimes described as a reform movement within an already calcifying Hinduism—comparable to Lutheranism and the European Christian Reformation many centuries later. This is an oversimplification, but it is possible to agree that millennia before Martin Luther, Siddhartha Gautama was, in effect, promulgating the principle of the "priesthood of all believers." He took a firm stand against the growing strictures of the Indian caste system and the acceptance of inherent superiority, or inferiority, because of the circumstances of individual birth. Brahmins, he declared, did not deserve their exalted title simply because of hereditary status, but only if they lived lives that were virtuous and exemplary.

"It is not the knotted hair and the sprinkling of ashes that make a Brahmin but the practice of truth and love. . . . Neither abstinence, nor going naked, nor shaving the head, nor a rough garment, neither offerings to priests, nor sacrifices to gods will cleanse a man who is not free from delusions."

Anyone from a king to a barber who wished to listen to the Buddha's teachings, or follow him in his missionary wanderings, or join the Sangha, the formal fellowship of Buddhist disciples, was free to do so. Even women —after some hesitation—were admitted to the Sangha, whose establishment is often counted as one of the Buddha's most practical achievements, in large measure responsible for the eventual spread and continuity of Buddhist doctrine in the Asian world. The founding of an Order appears also to illustrate still further the Buddha's psychological acumen, for although he taught that each human being must tread the path to "awakening" or "deliverance" alone, he also realized what sustainment there could be in daily association with others working toward a common goal. Of the establishment of the Buddhist Sangha, Arnold Toynbee has said that it was a greater social achievement then the founding of the Platonist academy in Greece.

There are many stories illustrating the human warmth and loving-kindness of the radiant personality whose sculptured image—usually in a pose of meditation—is to the Eastern world what the Christ figure is to the Western. The Buddha's compassion was accompanied, however, by an unflinching realism whenever he addressed himself to the laws that govern earthly life. He once said, "I teach only two things, O disciples, the fact of suffering and the possibility of escape from suffering." How could one deny the first of these "truths," as he called them? Did not suffering begin with the very agony of birth itself, and continue through all the unavoidable complexities of human life: illness, disappointments, decrepitude, decay, death? Even love and happiness carried the dark shadow, for separation from or loss of what one loved brought suffering, as did the inability to get what one desired. There was just one escape from the meaningless maze. One must learn to conquer *tanha* (in Sanskrit, *trishna*, literally "thirst"), the ego's craving for satisfactions that could only lead to frustration, anxiety, sorrow, in face of the further indisputable truth that "impermanence is the law of all existence." Since change and flux are a universal part of nature, does it not behoove human beings to take their emphasis off having, holding, possessing, even *being* this or that, and to concentrate instead on "extinguishing" the troublemaking greedy ego?

The Buddha went so far as to declare that an individual's seeming individuality, his self, was not "real" in any fixed sense, but was actually only a succession of instants of consciousness. As he lay dying peacefully in his eightieth year, fully aware that his end was near, he did not alter this uncompromising viewpoint. He was, he stated calmly to those gathered about him, soon to disappear. Ananda, his favorite and grieving disciple, must wipe away his tears and accept this irrevocable fact. The members of the Sangha were not to mourn his passing but just get on with the work of spreading knowledge about the cause and cure of suffering and the attainment of enlightenment. The obligations of personal effort and self-reliance shine through these deathbed exhortations:

"Therefore, be ye lamps unto yourselves. Betake yourselves to no external refuge. Look not for refuge to anyone beside yourselves. Hold fast to the Truth as a lamp."

His final words are quite in character: "Decay is inherent in all compound things" and "Work out your own salvation with diligence."

So saying, there passed from the earthly scene a transcendent human being who, though born to an existence of ease and luxury, had spent half of his lifetime wandering the Indian roads, preaching a doctrine about a Middle Way of knowledge that all were welcome to follow who would, or could, regardless of past experiences or present status in society.

Immediately after the Great Demise, according to Buddhist history, a First Great Council of five hundred leading monks was held, at which the entire teaching was recited aloud, the most venerable monk repeating the rules of discipline, another giving the sermons, a third dealing with what could be called the psychology and philosophy of the Buddha's doctrine. This was the first authoritative formulation by Buddhist elders of the Great Teaching, a procedure some Buddhists have averred the Buddha himself might have deplored as apt to lead to profitless dogmatizing and to the very binding traditionalism he had criticized in Hinduism.

One hundred years after his death a Second Great Council was held in an attempt to settle certain doctrinal and interpretational differences that had grown up in the brotherhood. The third of the Great Councils was called by the most worldly and powerful early Buddhist convert, the Indian Emperor Ashoka, who ruled almost the whole of the vast Indian subcontinent during forty years of the third century B.C. This Third Council, tradition tells us, was held to "purify" the teaching and exclude certain fanciful theories that had been introduced by adherents improperly versed in the original tenets. At this Council, one thousand monks recited the entire canon during a period of nine months, and from this restating of basic principles there was laid the foundation for intensified missionary effort following one of the Buddha's injunctions to his disciples:

"Fare ye forth, brethren, on the mission that is for the good of the many, the happiness of the many; to take compassion to the world; to work for the profit and the good and happiness of . . . men."

The Fourth Council, in the first century A.D.,* was held on the island of Ceylon, off the southern tip of India, indicating the spread of the doctrine southward. At this momentous Fourth Council the memorized scriptures— handed down for centuries by word of mouth in the classic teaching tradition of Asia—were first recorded in writing. This record, in the Pali tongue, constitutes to this day the orthodox Buddhist canon. The Fifth Council was not held until almost two thousand years later in Mandalay, Burma, in the year 1871, at which time these same Pali texts were inscribed on seven hundred and twenty-nine marble slabs placed at the foot of Mandalay Hill. The last council, mentioned further on, was held in the 1950's in Rangoon, Burma.

In addition to the Pali Canon, other sources of Buddhist doctrine lie in writings from ancient Sanskrit, the tongue of early Northern (Mahayana) Buddhism. Some southern Buddhists, however, claim that the Pali Canon should alone be considered authoritative. They contend that the Buddha spoke in a language approximating Pali, and they even go so far as to declare that he deliberately avoided the use of Sanskrit in preaching or teaching as he "wished to use the speech of the people." These claims and views concern the average Buddhist as little as scholarly disputations about the relative accuracy and merit of Aramaic, Hebrew or Greek in translations of early Biblical literature concern the average Christian. The point is that the Pali Canon and other accepted scriptures represent to Buddhists a record of what

---

* There is some disagreement in the numbering of the various Great Councils. For example, another first-century gathering, convened, so it is claimed, by the powerful Northern Indian monarch Kanishka, is not recognized by Southern or Theravada Buddhists, although it was a very important council in the Mahayana development and had wide influence on the Buddhism of Tibet, Central Asia and China.

the earliest disciples and later followers of the Great Teacher first remembered and, in due course, recorded, just as the disciples of Jesus left accounts—by no means similar in all respects—of their Savior's life and sayings in the Christian Bible.

Almost from the beginning of Buddhist history there have been two main schools of Buddhist teaching. One branch, the Theravada, or School of the Elders (less correctly known as the Hinayana or Small Vehicle of Buddhism), is the Buddhism of such countries as Ceylon, Burma, Thailand and Cambodia. The other, the Mahayana, or Large Vehicle—which became, down the centuries, the majority sect—spread to the north and east, finally reaching China, Korea and Japan. The words "large" and "small" have reference to the respective latitudes or restrictions of doctrinal approach and the interpretations and practice of Buddhist principles. The Mahayana does not object to its designation as Large Vehicle, but the Hinayana Buddhists consider it preferable to refer to themselves as the Theravada School, or School of the Elders. In general, and briefly, the authoritarian Theravada School inclines toward a strict, even austere, personal adherence to established rules and doctrines, while the Mahayana holds that a more flexible and permissive attitude comes nearer the Buddha's true aims. As a consequence, the countries in which Mahayana Buddhism has flourished have created a far wider diversity in ways of Buddhist worship and art. Buddhism's diversity, however, rests on a basic unity comparable to the underlying unifying principles of Christianity that exist in spite of many denominational differences in interpretation and practice.

The personal life story of the world-shaking "sage of the Shakya clan" or Shakyamuni (another of the Buddha's several titles), when presented in straightforward biographical terms, has not only the ring of veracity, it also serves to shed significant light on some of the social roots of a dynamic religious philosophy that rose in the sixth century B.C. to challenge an already entrenched Hinduism. On the other hand, when told with the inevitable overlay of poetic and legendary embellishment—which mankind seems unable to omit from its religious chronicles—the Buddha saga also provides valuable insights into the workings of man's myth-making mind, something we have already seen lavishly illustrated in the chapter on Hinduism.

Legendary accounts of the Buddha begin with the usual miraculous birth common to all world heroes, especially spiritual ones. The Buddha's mother,

Lady Maya, was impregnated "immaculately" by a sacred white elephant who, visiting her in a dream, touched her left side with a white lotus. Court soothsayers predicted a divine event. At the birth of her son (from his mother's right side as she stood in a garden under a sal tree), the entire world of nature gave evidence of the arrival of a supreme being. The child at once talked, declared himself a future Buddha, and took seven steps in each of the four directions. Wherever he stopped, lotus blooms appeared beneath his footprints.

Putting miracles aside, Siddhartha Gautama (also spelled Gotama), the Buddha-to-be, was the son of a rajah who reigned in a minor but rich principality on the southern border of present-day Nepal during the sixth century B.C. Gautama belonged to the second of the four major Indian castes, the princely or ruling subdivision known as the Kshatriya, which occupied a strategic position between the priestly and merchant classes. When the local astrologers cast the newborn baby's horoscope—today still a common practice over much of Asia—his father was given a somewhat disturbing prophecy about this eagerly awaited son. The court seers announced that a choice between two very different destinies lay before the rajah's heir. He could become the greatest of sovereigns or an equally famed ascetic.

This latter possibility made little appeal to the young prince's worldly father. Fear of such an end to his fond hopes of succession, coupled with love for his beautiful and brilliant son, determined the rajah to prevent Siddhartha at all costs from coming in contact with misery or unhappiness in any form. No shadows were to fall on his carefree and gracious existence—shadows that might lead to awkward questions or to painful speculations on life's inequities.

Young Siddhartha, however, possessed of an eager spirit and inquiring mind, found it impossible to remain forever confined within the palace grounds. After he reached adolescence he secretly disobeyed his father's loving but firm injunctions and, accompanied by his faithful servant, Channa, went forth into the nearby villages to see for himself what life was like beyond the palace compound.

On these several fateful journeys he came in turn upon four sights which forever altered the pattern of his thinking. These four sights, known in the literature of Buddhism as the Four Signs, were an old man, a sick man, a corpse, and a mendicant holy man, a *sadhu*.

When Siddhartha first looked upon old age, with its attendant physical deterioration, caught his first glimpse of hopeless disease, saw a lifeless body surrounded by weeping mourners, he turned in consternation to his servant Channa, who could only reply sadly to his shocked questionings, "Yes, my prince, these things must come to all men." How then, Siddhartha wondered, did human beings endure their fate, inextricably bound up as it was with physical decay and mental wretchedness for so many, with inescapable deterioration and death for all? This was his initial perception of humanity's *dukkha*, that dislocation and suffering to whose diagnosis and cure the Buddha subsequently devoted his lifetime, following methods that have led Western writers to refer to him as a great spiritual physician who first discovered the cause of man's obvious sickness and then offered a possible, though rigorous, cure. More than two millennia ago this perceptive analyst had indeed looked unflinchingly at certain mysterious psychophysical conditions common to all men. In describing these "psychic injuries" sustained by every human being on his way through life, Gerald Heard has used, to illuminating effect, a contemporary vocabulary. What the Buddha, as a young man, first perceived in an intuitional flash, sought later to clarify through years of metaphysical search and finally found deliverance from were: "the trauma of birth, the pathology of sickness, the morbidity of decrepitude and the phobia of death."

Siddhartha's first perception of life's grim realities—so clearly to be seen on every side when once he traveled away from the sheltered palace compound of his father—left the sensitive prince miserable and puzzled. What, he asked himself, was life's possible meaning? What reason was there to be born at all? While wandering one day, reflecting on these and other seemingly unanswerable conundrums, he chanced to look into the face of a passing holy man, one who had chosen, so Channa told him, to "wander homeless." In the serene face and calm eyes of this recluse Siddhartha thought he saw the only hope for his growing pain and bewilderment.

At last Siddhartha's inner turmoil became so great that he was impelled to abandon forever his sheltered, luxurious life, to leave his beautiful young wife and first-born son and go forth alone on a desperate quest for truth. Not daring to bid farewell to any member of the household, not even his wife and child, lest they influence him to stay, he stole away in the middle of the night knowing that he could have no rest until he found for himself the cause and cure of man's suffering, wrongdoings and mortality. This silent leave-taking from a beloved family is known in Buddhist lore as the Great

Renunciation. As a part of the several episodes of the Great Departure it is a favorite theme in Buddhist art, depicted in many charming scenes, such as the arrival on the fateful night of supernatural beings who bore aloft on the palms of their hands the hoofs of the future Buddha's horse so that no sound would be made until he and the faithful Channa had reached the outer gates where other divinities waited to make it possible for them to depart undetected by the watchmen. Once well away, Siddhartha took leave of the weeping Channa after making the sacrificial gesture of cutting off his long aristocratic locks and flinging them into the air. He was soon able to exchange his princely robes for a poor man's garments and thus attired set off alone on the first stage of his long search for truth.

In this part of the world, at the time Siddhartha came to manhood, metaphysical speculation was flourishing with an almost tropical exuberance. It was, indeed, a time of intellectual ferment over the face of the known world—a curiously yeasty period that gave birth to such geniuses as Confucius and Lao-tzu in China, Zoroaster in Persia, to Pythagoras and other noted thinkers in Greece, and, in India, to the future Buddha. There were any number of famous Hindu teachers to whom the restless young nobleman could turn for the services of a *guru*. But nothing of what he was taught seemed to fill his needs, for he found too much metaphysical speculation and philosophic hairsplitting, too many elaborate rites, too great a reliance on one viewpoint or another. It has been suggested by no less an authority than Ananda Coomaraswamy that had the most noted of Siddhartha's several gurus, a teacher named Alara, been equal to the eager reach of this young man's deeply probing inquiries, the sect called Buddhism might never have been founded; Gautama would merely have become another of the great individual teachers, or even avatars, of Hinduism—which, as a matter of fact, many Hindus do today consider him. This particular opinion is, however, debatable, and, as the record stands, Siddhartha, dissatisfied with his various teachers, went forth once more on his own.

In spite of the Buddha's dissent from certain methods of religious practice and pedagogy common at the time, it should be borne in mind that there are rooted in Buddhism a number of ancient Indian beliefs expressed in terms like *karma, Nirvana, dharma* (the law), *samsara* (the endless round of existences), *maya*—and others. The Buddha took some of these immemorial Indian doctrines and reassayed them, seeking to give them a more direct relevance and new dynamism. Here Buddhism presents an interesting comparison with Christianity, which drew first on native roots—Judaism—and later, though losing out in the land of its origin, went forth to conquer the Western world just as Buddhism conquered the Eastern.

When, after some years of search, Siddhartha had decided that no guru could provide him with the answers he sought, that his earnest efforts appeared only to be stifling his hope of reaching living truth, he determined to take up the life of a solitary ascetic. For seven more years he lived alone as a forest hermit, practicing the most extreme yoga disciplines. He succeeded in subduing physical appetites and in acquiring a stricter control over his mind, yet he seemed no nearer the final enlightenment that he believed must lie within a man's reach. Finally he came to the very depth of personal discouragement and weakness. From prolonged austerities and virtual starvation—self-imposed—he lay at death's door. At this point, when all seemed hopeless, he had a most remarkable illumination, one that was to prove of particular significance in the later history of Buddhism, setting it apart from many of the most traditional and revered Hindu spiritual procedures. The human body, Gautama saw, was the one instrument man had through which to attain enlightenment. Why, then, was he subjecting his once-excellent physical instrument to abnormal and extreme self-mortification? In this moment of blinding insight, the emaciated hermit, who had by now reached the age of thirty-five, at once decided to return to a more natural life.

His first symbolic act after this momentous decision was to accept a dish of fresh curds from a village maiden, brought to him on the Full Moon Day of the month of May—subsequently the greatest of all Buddhist festive days. At the startling sight of acceptance of food by their noted fellow ascetic, whose incomparable self-denial had become a local legend, the five hermits who dwelt nearby left the neighborhood in shocked dismay. As for Siddhartha, he quietly finished his meal and, when he had done so, placed the empty bowl in a nearby river, where—again a symbolic occurrence—it floated *upstream against the current* to the hidden dwelling of a Serpent King, a personification of nature's wisdom. Siddhartha then bathed, changed his garments and, greatly refreshed in body and spirit and with a new insight and determination, took up once more the familiar cross-legged lotus posture of meditation, under a nearby fig tree destined to become the Bodhi Tree (Tree of Wisdom or Enlightenment). This sacred spot is today a pilgrimage center for many devout Buddhists. It lies near the city of Gaya, and the original tree that sheltered the Buddha is also said still to survive here.

No man can explain "enlightenment" to another, and the Buddha was no exception. But whatever he experienced during his time under the Bodhi Tree was, for him, a final and unarguable clarification of all his wonderings and searches. The fetters that had bound him to the unrealities of human existence were severed forever, and he gave voice to a triumphant song of victory—a song built on the theme of reincarnation, that pattern of "eternal recurrence" that the new Buddha had now overcome through his attainment of a higher, truer consciousness than that of his limited personal ego.

> *Many a house of life*
> *Hath held me—seeking ever him who wrought*
> *These prisons of the senses. . . .*
> *Sore was my ceaseless strife!*
> *But now*
> *Thou builder of this dwelling—Thou!*
> *I know Thee! Never shall thou build again*
> *These walls of pain. . . .*
> *Broken Thy house is, and the ridge-pole split. . . .*

There are various versions of the length of time and the kind of experiences that came to the Buddha immediately following his enlightenment. Some of the books tell of the various types and degrees of contemplation, his recollection, in detail, of all his former lives, his review of the essential points of his future teaching as he moved seven times, for periods of seven days each (making forty-nine days in all), from various trees and even to and from a "God-wrought pavilion," savoring the sweetness of the attainment of Nirvana and perfecting the doctrine he was soon going forth to share with his fellow men. During this period, Mara the Tempter (who had frequently come to trouble Siddhartha as Satan troubled Jesus in the wilderness) made his last desperate attempts to divert the Buddha from his path—offering, in one version, the distraction of his most beautiful daughters. Also at one point during this post-enlightenment period, the meditating Buddha was assailed by wild storms during which he was protected by a serpent king, Mucalinda, for in Buddhism, as in Hinduism, unlike Christianity, mythological serpents play kindly, not evil, roles. Mucalinda issued forth from the roots of the tree where the new World Savior was seated, wound his coils seven times under the meditating figure, raised his cobra head protectively over the Great Teacher and so remained for seven days until the raging floods subsided.

This scene of the Buddha and the protective serpent, "Lord of the Earth," is a favorite theme in Buddhist sculpture. Sometimes the Buddha is shown seated on the coils of a serpent genie as if on a throne, the cobra's hood hovering over him like an imperial canopy. In all this part of Buddhist iconography there may be sensed a profound symbolic meaning: the recognition and acceptance of the instinctive world of nature yet also the triumph over it by way of a higher development of man's mind, will and spirit as exemplified in the meditating figure of the fully enlightened Buddha.

Now that the Buddha had attained Nirvana, or freedom from all earthly ties, he might—by virtue of this supreme detachment—have left the physical plane altogether. He chose not to do so, and this choice became the nexus of certain developments of "responsibility to others" in later Buddhist teaching. The decision the Buddha made is not presented as altogether an easy one. Indeed, certain Buddhist paintings from China and Japan show him "descending" into the world again with the look of a man who has had his struggles, struggles that have taught him how far from simple it will be to teach others the true way to self-discovery and release. No matter how great his effort, would his endeavors not prove in vain? He hesitated, and the very earth, we are told, "trembled" as it waited on the fateful answer to his troubled question: Could he possibly communicate the marvel of his discovery, a truth "going against the stream, deep, intimate, delicate, hidden, not to be reached only by mere reasoning"? In the end, "the great Buddha heart of infinite compassion" prevailed. (Some Hindus assert that the Buddha became a World Teacher at the behest of none other than "Highest Brahma" himself.) The newly All-Enlightened took pity on the plight of mankind. Declaring, "I will beat the drum of the Immortal in the darkness of the world," he arose from his seat under the Tree of Wisdom and went forth on the initial stage of a long and selfless ministry.

Arnold Toynbee, who has been quoted on his opinion of the social significance of the founding of the first Order of Buddhist monks, the Sangha, has said of the Buddha's return to the world—which was in "logical contradiction" to his basic doctrine and against his personal inclination—that it marked a high point in humanity's development. It symbolized the personal sacrifice of a sentient being who, although he has attained salvation, or Nirvana, for himself, turns back from "the open door" in order to help his fellow creatures reach the point to which he, by unflagging effort, has already come on their common path.

The first converts he made were the five hermits, his recent neighbors in the forest solitude, who had so deplored his fall from fanatical asceticism. They had gone to Benares, the holy Indian city, and taken up residence in the Deer Park on the city's outskirts (now Sarnath). The Buddha followed them there, and when they saw him approaching, they realized from his appearance that he had, during their absence, attained some remarkable glorification. They bowed before him in awe and respect and gladly sat down to listen with attention to the words of his first revolutionary sermon on the Wheel of the Law. The wheel (*chakra*) is an ancient Indian symbol. Originally probably a sun sign, and later one of the identifying marks of the Hindu god, Vishnu, it denotes in yoga a "center" of physical and psychic energy. Today it appears on India's national flag, where it also symbolizes the "return to the spinning wheel" that played such a vital part in Gandhi's program of economic independence for his countrymen. The Buddha, drawing the wheel on the ground in a pattern of rice grains, employed this old, already familiar Indian symbol to exemplify the eternal karmic round of existence (samsara) kept going by man's unceasing desires, his tanha, or thirst, for ego satisfactions.

From the outset of his ministry the Buddha emphasized a Middle Way of conduct lying between self-indulgence on one hand and extremes of asceticism on the other. His doctrine was based on the incontrovertible, undeniable truth about humanity's suffering, a truth that he embodied in a formula of four parts to which he gave the adjective "noble." These Four Noble Truths, constituting what might be termed the Buddha's diagnosis of humanity's sickness, took a simple form: 1) No one can deny that existence involves a great deal of suffering for all human creatures. 2) This suffering and general dissatisfaction come to human beings because they are possessive, greedy and, above all, self-centered. 3) Egocentricism, possessiveness and greed can, however, be understood, overcome and rooted out. 4) This rooting out can be brought about by following a rational Eightfold Path of behavior in thought, word and deed that will create a salutary change in viewpoint.

This Eightfold Path is the Buddha's basic formula for deliverance from the kind of crippling invalidism that comes with having a "body-identified mind," as Gerald Heard has described mankind's general state. The eight requirements that will eliminate suffering by correcting false values and giving true knowledge of life's meaning have been summed up as follows: "(I) First, you must see clearly what is wrong. (II) Next decide to be cured. (III) You must act and (IV) speak so as to aim at being cured. (V) Your livelihood must not conflict with your therapy. (VI) That therapy must go forward at the 'staying speed,' the critical velocity that can be sustained. (VII) You must think about it incessantly, and (VIII) learn how to contemplate *with the deep mind.*"

This same procedure for the cure, or relief, of mankind's obvious un-happiness, his dislocation (dukkha) can also be presented more succinctly in a simple list of eight steps:

Right views (or understanding)
Right purpose (or aspiration)
Right speech
Right conduct
Right means of livelihood (or vocation)
Right effort
Right kind of awareness or mind control
Right concentration or meditation

Even a novice could, in the Buddha's opinion, practice the first six steps. He could learn to think and speak with care and truthfulness, abide by basic moral laws, earn his living in ways that were not deleterious to himself or others, and maintain consistently the pursuit of the goal indicated in the last two steps. With the achievement of awareness and mind control, through ever deeper contemplative practices, there was bound to come a calm freedom from the unpredictable vagaries of ego drives and willful appetites. When ultimate freedom from every kind of egocentric thought and wish had been gained, the aspirant would also, inevitably, be through with the endless wheel of "becoming." Nirvana, the supreme goal, the selfless "peace that passeth all understanding," would then be within his reach.

Apart from the major precepts involved in following the Eightfold Path, the Buddha took scant interest in precise rules for his adherents. When asked on one occasion whether a true disciple should not live a hermit's existence, he simply replied, "Whoever wishes may dwell in the forest and whoever wishes may dwell in a village." What mattered was not where an aspirant chose to live but how well he could concentrate on the search for truth. Even on his deathbed, the Buddha gave his disciples permission to alter the lesser precepts of the Order if they saw fit, for it was not organiza-tional regulations but individual effort that truly counted. He also warned members of the Sangha against setting up the fundamentals of his teaching with any undue or excessive authority. Buddhist doctrines were to be considered merely as a means to an end. Imagine, he said, a man who has used a raft to cross a river. Would anyone consider him wise if he then went on carrying the raft of his passage around with him? The raft is not the important thing. The real aim is to get across the river. Although there are any number of examples that indicate the Buddha's freedom from canonical authority, today almost all Buddhists to some extent or other make use of scriptures, differing only from country to country and sect to sect as to which are considered the most reliable sources of original doctrine.

It has been said that ignorance is to Buddhism what original sin is to Christianity. By ignorance, the Buddha did not mean merely absence of knowledge, but an erroneous point of view. He particularly urged a new approach to the question of the nature of the self. To the Buddha the idea of a separate self was a mere intellectual invention, corresponding to no reality at all. The self, he argued, was plainly "a process in time," not a single solid "thing" or "fact." One of the homely examples which he used to clarify his ideas on this difficult subject was that of a chariot. The word "chariot" is merely a descriptive term for a number of constituent parts placed in a certain relation to each other, and just as no part of this aggregate can be separated off and called "the chariot," so no part of the human creature can be separated into something called "I." The term "I" is merely a convenience for designating an ever-changing combination, or bundle, of attributes known in Buddhism as *skandhas*. Skandhas consist of the body, sensations, perceptions, mental formulations (ideas, wishes, dreams) and consciousness. There is a constant interplay and interconnection among the skandhas, which may give a sense of personal continuity and identity but which, in truth, preclude the possibility of a definite "I" existing by itself, totally independent of and unconnected with the constantly shifting relation between physical and psychic forces.

The teaching of the principle of non-ego is known in Hinayana Buddhist terms as *anatta* (in the Sanskrit of Mahayana sources as *anatman*). In speaking of this basic Buddhist teaching that life is "nothing but a series of manifestations of becomings and extinctions," Hajime Nakamura, writing in Kenneth W. Morgan's *The Path of Buddhism*, has this to say:

"It is quite wrong to think that there is no self at all according to Buddhism. The Buddha was not a mere materialist. As *body* is a name for a system of qualities, even so *soul* is a name for the sum of the states which constitute our mental existence. The Buddha did not deny the soul, but was silent concerning it. . . . The Buddha did not want to assume the existence of souls as metaphysical substances, but he admitted the existence of the self as the subject of action in a practical and moral sense."

Christian emphasis on the "redemption of souls" and general Western emphasis on individuality and the cult of the personality have made Buddhism's repudiation of the idea of specific definite egos perhaps the hardest of all its concepts to grasp. Yet many Western philosophers have reached similar conclusions, among them William James, Bertrand Russell, Schopenhauer and David Hume, the father of Western empiricism. Abraham Kaplan, in his chapter on Buddhism in *The New World of Philosophy*, has quoted Hume as expressing true Buddhist doctrine when he wrote: "For my part, when I enter most intimately into what I call *myself*, I always stumble on some particular perception or other, of heat or cold, light or shade, love or hatred, pain or pleasure. I never can catch myself at any time without a perception and never can observe anything but the perception."

Hume's conclusion was, therefore: "What we call the mind is nothing but a heap or bundle of different perceptions united together by certain relations."

Between certain Western thinkers and the philosophers of Buddhism there may exist a number of interesting similarities, but there is also a significant difference worthy of mention. In the West, a philosopher's theories and beliefs can be accepted as valid even though they remain entirely unrelated to his personal way of life. In Buddhist opinion, mere theoretical notions are considered useless, representing only sterile mental exercises. A man must act and live by what he has discovered to be true. Said the Buddha: "The man who talks much of his teaching but does not practice it himself is like a cowman counting another's cattle." And: "Like beautiful flowers full of color but without scent are the well-chosen words of the man who does not act accordingly."

Although the charge of atheism has often been laid at the door of Buddhism, the Buddha's doctrine is actually no more atheistic than it is theistic or pantheistic. To be sure, in Buddhism salvation is in no way dependent on some supermundane Deity sitting in inexorable judgment, doling out rewards and punishments even beyond the grave. The Buddha would have found it impossible, from his intellectual position, to conceive of a God in terms of a human image or "personality," yet it is hardly fair to accuse of atheism a teacher who could state about an inconceivable Power well beyond human imagination or speculation: "There is an unborn, an unoriginated, an unmade, an uncompounded; were there not, O mendicants, there would be no escape from the world of the born, the originated, the made and the compounded."

THE ART OF BUDDHISM

The importance of the Buddha image in any study of the philosophy and art of Asia can hardly be overemphasized. The changing types of the Buddha icon as it was created in various parts of India, Ceylon, Burma, Cambodia, Thailand, Java, Laos, Vietnam, Tibet, Nepal, Gandhara (between present-day Afghanistan and Pakistan), Mongolia, China, Korea, and Japan provide many clues to the nature, development and interchange of philosophic and aesthetic ideals in these widely scattered cultures. Over a great part of the Eastern world the Buddha image is the equivalent of the Christ image in the West, but it has a more varied range of representation. The icon of Christ, which was, so to say, "invented" early in the Christian era and subsequently perfected by gifted European artists of the Middle Ages and the Renaissance, follows a fairly consistent physical typology—that of a slender, long-haired and bearded man, usually portrayed with a simple halo over his head. The Buddha image, although it developed specific iconographic stereotypes, was also created in many different forms along whatever stylistic lines the artists of the country which received the teaching chose to use in representing this World Savior. Most often the aim was to indicate the supernatural qualities of a supreme divinity, but sometimes it was to emphasize the earthly and human aspects of this Sage of the Shakya clan who, like Jesus of Nazareth five hundred years later, was born as a man. For many years following the Buddha's demise no Buddha images were made. It was considered illogical that a truly Enlightened Being "who had gone beyond the fetters of the body" could ever be represented in human form, and so the Buddha's presence in early narrative sculptures was merely indicated by an empty throne, a footprint, a royal umbrella or other symbols of his non-physical presence.

As in the section on Hinduism no strict pattern of chronological sequence has been followed. The intention has been simply to give some sense of the wide range of Buddhist art. Interested readers are referred to the bibliography for books dealing at greater length with this engrossing subject.

This figure of the Teaching Buddha (5th century A.D.) in the familiar "lotus posture" used in Asian meditation, his hands in the *mudra* known as "turning the wheel of the law," is a masterpiece from Sarnath near Benares, a famous site in the early annals of Buddhism since it was the scene of the Buddha's first sermon. Artists from this noted sanctuary and pilgrimage center created some of the most beautiful of all Buddha figures, destined to shed their stylistic influence on many distant parts of the Asian world. Although only 5 feet 3 inches in height—including pedestal and halo—the figure has, along with an intrinsic grace and balanced symmetry, the superb monumentality of the best art of the Gupta period (320–600 A.D.), generally considered the golden age of Indian art. The triangulation of the figure necessitated by the yoga posture of *padmasana* is part of its serene charm, and although the rules of a strict aesthetic canon have been observed—an ovoid face, expanded chest, wide shoulders, slim waist, lotus lips, raised eyebrows, an inward-turning gaze—they in no way distract from the figure's innate calmness and clarity. The fingers are touching each other in a pattern representing "the circle of the chain of causes," a specific *mudra* or sign of the Buddhist theory of "coming into existence by being conditioned by a preceding cause" or, one might say, being born into a certain kind of life by the force of the law of karma. Buddhism's aim was to eradicate emphasis on the individual ego and on weak human desires which keep the ever-moving "wheel" of cause and effect in motion. Beneath the pedestal on which the Buddha sits are small figures of his first five converts and a woman and child.

42

43

The sculptured panels on the four richly carved gates and the encircling railing of the Great Stupa (burial or relic mound) at Sanchi in central India are—with those at Bharhut, a little to the north (see illustration 46)—the earliest known examples of the Buddhist theme in art. In general, the narrative carvings at Sanchi as (43) north gate, early 1st century A.D. are concerned with the previous lives, both human and animal, of Siddhartha Gautama, the prince who became the Buddha. His actual presence after his Enlightenment is indicated, however, only by some abstract symbol (see text, page 125). The designs from Sanchi are rich sources of information about the folk religion of the period, since many of the deities pictured belong to pre-Buddhist forms of worship. The stupa itself (44), a mound of earth faced with stone, was originally covered with white and gold stucco. It is surmounted by an umbrella in three parts signifying the Buddha, the Dharma (the "Teaching," or the "Law"), and the Sangha or religious order the Buddha founded. The monument was designed for the circumambulation of pilgrims who took a ritual walk—never counterclockwise—on "the Path of Life around the World Mountain"; thus the stupa might be said to represent a cosmic diagram.

44

45   16

In accordance with the view that one who has achieved supreme Enlightenment and passed beyond the physical fetters of existence could not be represented by a human body (see text, page 125), the sculptured narrative relief from Amaravati (45), the so-called Great Departure—showing Buddha leaving his princely palace for the life of a homeless mendicant—indicates the holy presence only by an umbrella borne aloft above a prancing riderless horse, *circa* 100 A.D. (46) Relic mound (Bharhut, early 2nd century B.C.) symbolizing the Buddha's attainment of final Nirvana. In later art the Buddha's departure from earth and attainment of Parinirvana is represented by his recumbent figure. (47) The Buddha preaching his first sermon in the deer park at Benares is indicated only by a cushioned throne. (Note the swastika on the empty throne, an ancient solar symbol.) From Nagarjunakonda, 3rd century A.D.

47

48

It is generally accepted that the earliest
Buddha images were made near the end
of the 1st century A.D. in the ancient
northwestern province of Gandhara,
which now lies on either side of the
Afghanistan-Pakistan frontier. This section of India was colonized by officers
and men from the armies of Alexander
the Great, and traders from the Roman
world. The Gandhara Buddhas made by
journeyman craftsmen of the Mediter-
ranean area often resemble Hellenistic
or Roman Imperial art of the early Christian era. (48) Stucco head of the Buddha.
The *ushnisha* or cranial protrusion that is one of the Buddha's thirty-two "marks" of
divinity (symbolizing his attainment of higher wisdom) was treated by Gandharan
sculptors simply as an extra topknot of hair. (49) Seated Buddha. Typical Hellenistic
drapery is used for the Buddha's robe. (50) Gandharan artists even went so far as to
create a realistic likeness of the starving Buddha during his period of extreme asceticism. All Gandhara, 2nd–3rd centuries A.D.

49

50

51

52

Scenes of the Buddha's birth. In Buddhist legend the Buddha's mother, Queen Maya, was "immaculately" impregnated by a white elephant—always an augur of great events—who visited her in a dream, touching her side with a white lotus (51). Bharhut, 1st century B.C. (52) Buddha seen emerging from his mother's side as she stands beneath the sal tree where he was born. Below in the same scene the new World Savior is seen taking his first steps and declaring, according to legend, his future destiny. Gandhara, 2nd century A.D. (53) A charming Nepalese version (11th century A.D.) of the birth of the Buddha from his mother's side as she stands leaning on a blossoming tree. Already emerged, the future World Savior is standing on a lotus pedestal at his mother's knee. The deities pouring water on the young Buddha are the gods Brahma and Indra who signify by their act acceptance of the Buddha by the Vedic, or early Hindu world.

53

54

55

With the expansion of the permissive Mahayana school of Buddhism (see text, page 84), came widespread breaking of the original tabu against representation of the Buddha's physical being. Certain classic image types—almost stereotypes—were developed in India with, however, some diversity in pose and garments. (54) Draped standing figure from Mathura, a section about 100 miles south of modern Delhi, where some scholars aver the making of Buddha images may have begun as early as at Gandhara. This one, 5th century A.D. (55) Seated figure from Amaravati, *circa* 3rd century A.D. Note the circular wheel design (*chakra*) on the sole of the exposed foot. (56) Torso from Sarnath, Gupta (320–600 A.D.). Here all drapery gone, the torso is clothed in a transparent sheath intended to reveal the pure immortal body of the Transcendent Being. (57) Buddha seated in so-called "European style" as part of an ornamental stupa, Cave 10, Ellora, early 7th century. The statue is illumined by natural light from above. Early pilgrims circumambulated the figure; their chanting reverberating from the vaulted ceiling suggested the sacred "first sound," *om* or *aum.*

56

57

58 59 60

The converted Indian Emperor Ashoka (3rd century B.C.), who erected many stone columns inscribed with Buddhist edicts urging brotherhood and kindness to all—as in (58) a lion-crowned column which still stands at Lauriya Nandangarh—is also believed to have sent his son and daughter as missionaries to Ceylon. Today's traveler to this lovely island, which lies near India's southern tip, comes on many ruins of once glorious monasteries and some of the world's most impressive statues of the Great Teacher. (59) A monumental standing figure (Ceylon, 3rd century A.D.), interestingly contemporary in feeling, expresses the best of the Theravada ideal. Free of all suggestions of the evanescent or supernatural, it stands firmly on the bare ground like lesser mortals who have been adjured by the founder of their faith: "Look within, *thou* art the Buddha." (60) A seated figure of·noble symmetry, at once dynamic and serene, its hands in the *mudra* of "inward absorption," a supreme model of the Buddhist spiritual superman who has by will and determination won through to final victory. (12th century A.D.) (61) The Great Demise of the Buddha does not represent death in simple human terms but rather a final freedom from all future births. This gigantic figure at the hour of his attainment of Parinirvana lies in a quiet open countryside. (Note human figure near feet to indicate scale.) Not included here is an upright statue of the Buddha's most devoted disciple, Ananda, which stands near the Buddha's head. (12th century A.D.)

61

63

As Buddhism spread triumphantly throughout Asia, Buddhist images and icons took on many different aspects. (62) At Angkor Wat the gifted Khmers of Cambodia made an enormous representation of the Buddha's foot, rich in iconography with the significant wheel in the center of the sole. (63) They also often represented the Buddha's hand, all its fingers of prescribed equal length, the symbol of the lotus within the wheel in the palm. They were fond, too, of images of the Buddha (during the storms that were hurled against him at the time of his Enlightenment) seated in the lotus posture, lifted out of the floods by the coils of a protective cobra who also sheltered the new World Savior with his canopied hood. (64) This one, probably Siamese, Lopburi, 11th–14th centuries A.D. (65) An 11th-century Burmese artist produced a serene, flame-encircled Buddha figure.

62

64

65

The old kingdom of Dvaravati (6th–12th centuries A.D.) now a part of Thailand, produced Buddha images which seem to have been inspired by the Gupta art of northern India, as in this so-called Mon-Gupta head (66) which is at once magnificently natural and yet ineffably spiritual. (6th–7th centuries A.D.) In the kingdom of Sukhodhaya (Sukhothai), 13th–15th centuries, now also a part of modern Thailand, some artists attempted realistic representations of the Buddha's legendary "marks of divinity" (as set forth in imported Ceylonese scriptures), exemplified here in rare "Walking Buddhas" (67, 68, 69) with arms like a young elephant's trunk, projecting heels, parrot-beak noses, lotus mouths and so on. In a rare monograph on *Indian Artistic Anatomy* Abanindranath Tagore has shown how the seemingly farfetched physical attributes of the Buddha represented an attempt to establish relationships between man and the world of nature: eyebrows like leaves, necks with the spiral turns of a conch shell and so on. (See text, page 126.) The Walking Buddhas, with their gliding and undulant movement, represented to the artists of the period the Buddha as wanderer and missionary teacher.

66

67

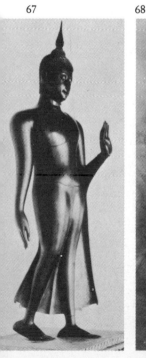

68

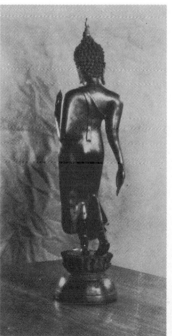

69

70

71

In Mahayana Buddhism symmetrical diagrammatic paintings, often extremely complicated, were designed to serve as aids in meditation (70), or for use in the worship
or invocation of deities, as in (73), Lha-mo. This flame-encircled Kali-like figure from
Tibet represents the patron goddess of the Dalai Lama. Himalayan artists did not
hesitate to create even Buddhist deities in violent poses. (71) Nepalese version of the
Tantric "union of the opposites" (*yab-yum*), a dynamic, even fearsome, deity and his
shakti or "female essence." (72) The Buddha's half-open eyes look out from four sides
of this stupa (near Katmandu, Nepal), which is meant to suggest a human figure
hidden in the structure in the posture
of meditation, crossed legs in the base,
body up to the shoulders in the hemi-
sphere, the head in the kiosk whose
tiered form implies ascending states of
consciousness. (8th or 9th century A.D.)

72

74

75

Across the vast reaches of the Asian world countless ruins, sad and magnificent, some deserted, some reclaimed and restored in modern times, testify eloquently to the quiet infiltration down the centuries of the non-crusading faith of Buddhism. (74) High in the cliffs of Afghanistan, at Bamiyan, stand the colossal remains of a Buddha, one of many rock-hewn images in this region lying along the old trade routes that brought not only merchants and traders, but, from the 4th century on, awestruck Chinese pilgrims visiting holy India, the Buddha's homeland. (4th–5th centuries A.D.) In Burma's ancient city of Pagan the Ananda Temple still shines with frosty brilliance (76) but there are many haunting remains (75) of its once 5,000 pagodas.

76

77

(77) One of the architectural wonders of the world, the Great Stupa at Borobudur in Java (from 800 A.D.), a magnificent complicated mandala in stone, terraced and galleried in a ritualistic pattern of squares and circles. More than ten miles of sculptured reliefs, designed for the education and edification of circumambulating pilgrims, tell a legend and point a way no longer clear in all details even to scholars, although the monument in its entirety is known to represent a microcosmic diagram of the universe in Mahayana Buddhist terms. (78) Buddhas of infinite compassion gaze out on the green landscape of Java, some in the open, some hidden within the intricate stone network of the multiple dome-shaped smaller stupas of the upper terrace.

78

79

80

According to tradition Buddhism entered China in 68 A.D., but important image-making came later in large measure due to the influence of Central Asian nomads who took control over much of northern China and, as devout Buddhists, encouraged —from 386 to 535 A.D.—works of Buddhist art. (79) Maitreya, the "Buddha of the Future," Wei dynasty, dated 477 A.D., generally considered one of the most important dated Buddhist bronzes now in the Western world. (80) A graceful bodhisattva, perhaps Kuan-yin, T'ang dynasty (618–917 A.D.), undeniably sensuous with its curving lines and clinging draperies. The on-moving wave of Buddhist faith produced beautiful Korean figures as in (81), again Maitreya, with a beguilingly solemn yet youthful air (7th century A.D.). Some hundreds of years later the wave of image-making reached a climax of a kind in the erection at Kamakura, Japan, of (82) the 37-foot-high Amida Buddha (1253 A.D.).

82

81

83

84

The Mahayana theory of the bodhisattva, the enlightened being who postpones his own Nirvana until he has aided all creation to reach a state of enlightenment, became a favorite subject for Buddhist artists everywhere. The mysterious, enigmatic, "Gothic" smile of the bodhisattvas is seen on a noble cross-legged figure of Maitreya (83) from Yun-kang, Wei dynasty, China (second half of the 5th century A.D.), and (84) a Khmer head of the late 12th century wears a similar subtle smile, characteristic of many Cambodian images. (85) One of the most ineffably beautiful bodhisattva images is that of Avalokiteshvara Padmapani ("lotus in hand"), painted on a cave wall at Ajanta, India (*circa* 600–642 A.D.), a tender but detached princely figure holding a long-stemmed flower. (86) Again an Indian Avalokiteshvara in the pose of "kingly ease," *circa* 1100 A.D.

85

86

87

88

With the ever-wider spreading of Mahayana Buddhism there inevitably came many picturesque ramifications and extensions of Buddhist mythology and teaching. Special types of bodhisattvas put in their appearance, including, in Japan, bodhisattvas of the Moon as in (87) a painting from 1191. A humanistic emphasis also appeared as seen in (88), Liang Kai's 12th-century painting of the Buddha, a worn figure of a man leaving his mountain retreat, returning—with some quite obvious doubts—to the world and the great task of spreading enlightenment that he had set himself. Rather far removed from the Buddha's original rules about self-help came faith in Amida (or Amitabha), the Buddha who dwelt in a glorious Western Paradise, the Pure Land, to which all might go who merely worshiped by uttering his holy name; here seen (89) descending to earth together with 25 protective bodhisattvas bound on a journey to aid the souls of men. Japan, 13th–14th centuries A.D.

89

The Chugu-ji temple at Nara, Japan, contains a suavely contoured wooden image about 4 feet 3 inches in height, dating from 650 A.D., now generally identified as a representation of Maitreya (Miroku in Japanese), "The Buddha of the Future." Sometimes identified as Kuan Yin (in Japanese, Kwannon). In this noble figure there may be traced many waves of stylistic influence that accompanied the flow of Buddhist philosophy across Asia. The melting roundness of the torso is reminiscent of the golden age of Gupta India, and the tranquil, wavelike drapery speaks strongly of certain Chinese sculptural modes. The calm face and subtle gesture of the fingers suggest quiet wisdom and infinite compassion.

He had a peculiarly effective way of indicating the futility of trying, with man's limited finite mind, to solve the question of an unlimited and infinite Being. When large abstract queries were put to him—the kind that are essentially unanswerable—he either maintained a pointed silence or attempted to shift the interrogator away from metaphysical speculation onto the more exacting if less exciting subject of how best to live one's daily life.

The Buddha's characteristic attitude toward those who overindulged themselves in speculating, theorizing and debating comes through most effectively in the story of a follower named Malunkyaputta. This monk, who had a restless, overactive mind, announced to the Buddha on one occasion that if he did not get some specific straightforward answers to his inquiries about First Causes, and in particular as to whether life was eternal or not eternal, he intended to give up the Sangha for good. The Buddha replied that such an attitude reminded him strongly of a man who, having been struck by a poisoned arrow, refuses to accept the services of a physician, or even to have the arrow removed, until he has made a lengthy detailed inquiry about who shot the arrow and how and why; or again, of a man in a burning house who refuses to put out the blaze, or even to leave the doomed edifice, until he has discovered who started the conflagration.

"Whether the dogma obtains, Malunkyaputta, that the world is eternal, or that the world is not eternal, there still remain birth, old age, death, sorrow, lamentations, misery, grief and despair—all the grim facts of human existence—for the extinction of which in the present life I am prescribing."

In other words, theological disputations would never promote that spirit of calm, unflagging personal endeavor so necessary for the attainment of final understanding about the "true nature of the self," and release, thereby, from the invidious delusion of separateness.

Other world faiths have often charged that Buddhism is a philosophy of pessimism and despair, an accusation that has sprung, in part, from misinterpretations of the old Sanskrit word Nirvana which occupies such an important place in the Buddhist vocabulary. Etymologically Nirvana means "extinction," and this definition was long taken by Western scholars as proof of the negative emphasis in the Buddha's doctrine. Many Buddhists, however, interpret the term rather differently. What is "extinguished" when Nirvana is attained, they claim, is merely that self-centered, self-assertive life to which unenlightened men tend to cling as to the highest good. Nirvana should be taken to mean the extinction of everything which obstructs the "real life"; at the same time it implies "boundless expansion," and, indeed, emphasis should fall not on the image of the "drop of water which merges into the ocean," but rather on "the ocean which enters into the drop."

Perhaps the best answer to the charge of Buddhism's pessimism and fatalism can be found among the cheerful and kindly people of predominantly Buddhist countries like Burma, Thailand and Tibet, where alien influences were kept at a minimum until comparatively recent times. Here there would seem to be little despair in the concept that man's life is not an enduring entity, that it is, instead, merely a part of a "process."

The repeated emphasis on humanity's suffering, the frequent repetition of the word "dukkha" in Buddhist literature, has also contributed to charges of fatalism and hopelessness. Closer examination of this word so central to Buddhist teaching has cast new light on its meaning, and the intention behind its usage. Dukkha literally refers to an ill-made axle and, by indirection, implies a wheel that is awry. Dukkha, therefore, might be said to stand for awryness, out-of-kilterness, dislocation, and in this interpretation clearly implies the possibility of correction.

Although the Buddha was not deficient in human sympathy or human understanding, he never retreated from his uncompromising presentation of the truth as he saw it. "All that we are is the result of our thoughts; it is founded on our thoughts; made up of our thoughts." So spoke the unflinching psychologist. Again and again there comes the familiar refrain: "By one's self the evil is done, by one's self one suffers; by one's self the evil is left undone, by one's self one is purified. The pure and the impure stand and fall by themselves, no one can purify another."

Life, in his view, followed certain fixed laws of cause and effect and the sooner one learned this hard truth the better. "I will teach you the law," said the Buddha to his disciples; "*that* being present, *this* happens; from the arising of *that, this* arises; *that* being absent, *this* does not happen; from the cessation of *that, this* ceases." And so one comes to karma:

That which ye sow, ye reap. See yonder fields!
The sesamum was sesamum, the corn
Was corn. The Silence and the Darkness knew!
So is a man's fate born.
He cometh, reaper of the things he sowed. . . .

Yet the Buddha taught no merely mechanical form of predestination, for he believed in a way of escape from the inherited karma of family, race, caste, and the results of deeds performed in former existences. The way to transcend karma lay in the proper use of the mind and the will. In Buddhist teaching, therefore, karma takes on almost the tone of opportunity, although because of the Buddha's penetrating analysis of the "illusion" of a separate self, the highest Buddhist thought does not interpret karma in a purely personal way. In an influential Buddhist scripture written in the first or second century B.C., *The Questions of King Milinda* (the Indian name for the Greco-Bactrian monarch Menander), the sage Nagasena answers the king's queries as to whether he who is reborn "remains the same or becomes another." "Neither the same nor another," replies Nagasena. To illustrate his statement, he uses first the example of a flame which, though seemingly the same as it burns, is, in reality, always different, though without any break in continuity. Again he takes as illustration milk, which in the guise of curds, butter, then clarified ghee, remains nonetheless milk, though totally different in appearance. Thirdly, Nagasena uses an ocean wave to make his point. Seen on the shore, a specific wave when followed with the eye appears to be the same though in reality it is a continuously different mass of water.

Certain Buddhist sects, notably those in Tibet, have placed special emphasis on the state of consciousness at the time of death as a determinant of an individual's rebirth pattern. In Tibetan belief, pre-death hours can directly affect subsequent experiences in a dreamlike realm, known as the Bardo, that lies between death and a new life. Experiences during the sojourn in this intermediate world can be influenced, it is believed, not only by the dying man's degree of enlightenment—or his lack of it—but also through assistance from lamas (Tibetan priests) who attend his demise.

As described in Dr. Evans-Wentz's scholarly translation of, and commentary on, *The Tibetan Book of the Dead* (the *Bardo Thödol*), monks are specially trained to assist in guiding the departing "aggregate of energies" toward a higher rebirth, if, that is, the recently dead finds himself unable to check the karmic pull back toward an earthly existence. The supreme goal lies in final escape from earth lives, in release into a "consciousness free of all limitations" symbolized by the "clear light of the void." On this clear and particularly bright light—visible at some point to all the dying, it is claimed —the dying man is exhorted to concentrate every possible psychic and mental force.

Detailed accounts of the kinds of experiences natural to the post-death state—brought back, according to Tibetan legend, by one or more highly trained lamas who "died" and later returned to report their findings—have been kept for centuries in the sacred lore of Tibetan Buddhism. As recorded by Dr. Evans-Wentz and a famous Tibetan scholar and linguist, Kazi Dawa-Samdup, the "forty-nine symbolic days" spent by the psyche in the Bardo afford an interesting comparison with the forty-nine days of testing common to world teachers like Jesus in the desert and the Buddha under the Bodhi Tree. There are also a number of provocative connections with the doctrine of purgatory, certain long-neglected Christian books on the art of dying, the ancient Greek mystery rites and even more recent records kept by the British Society for Psychic Research and other accredited groups investigating so-called "spiritualism." The Tibetan Buddhist "science of dying" stresses, however, with typical Buddhist psychological insight, the reminder that all the Bardo experiences—similar to dreams and nightmares—are in reality merely the dead man's own thought forms. The phenomena he experiences in the after-death state are related to his own development, tastes, habits, desires and thoughts during his lifetime. "The deceased human being," writes Dr. Evans-Wentz, "becomes the sole spectator of a marvelous panorama of hallucinatory visions; each seed of thought in his consciousness-content *karmically* revives; and he, like a wonder-struck child watching moving pictures cast upon a screen, looks on," unaware of the source of the phenomena unless he has been previously prepared, through training and contemplative exercises, to understand the "non-reality of what he sees." (It is understood, of course, that not all human beings will experience exactly the same phenomena in the after-death state any more than the living do in their real life or in their dreams. One is reminded here of the widespread belief that a drowning man relives his whole life in mere seconds.)

A particularly arresting Freudian touch is provided in this ancient book on the after-death state by a description of what happens if and when the departed psyche, or "aggregate of energies," fails to resist the strong karmic down-pull and is about to enter a new womb and return to the human state once more. If the Bardo-wandering psyche is about to be born a male, "a feeling of intense hatred toward the father and of jealousy and attraction toward the mother is begotten." If it is about to be born as a female, "a feeling of intense hatred toward the mother and of intense attraction and fondness toward the father is begotten."

Many other aspects of this remarkable document, which—in common with other Buddhist teachings—has its exoteric as well as its esoteric side and interpretations both commonplace and sublime, are of particular interest to modern minds. Since contributors to *The Tibetan Book of the Dead* (or *The Art of Liberation by Hearing on the After-Death Plane,* as the Tibetans also describe it) were highly evolved Buddhists—similar in many respects to Hindu "adepts," or masters of occult science—they were by no means held within the narrow kind of world cosmology which is today giving Christian and Jewish theologians their problems in the face of Space Age discoveries. Buddhists could—and can—readily accept not only the notion of the existence of life in many worlds other than that of Earth; they also believe in, and teach, the interpenetration of numberless "world systems" both ethereal and visible. The universal as well as personal importance of the disciplining and refining of man's nature through training in the eight Buddhist ways of thinking and acting, the very real significance to the *total universe* of the curbing of all base human appetites (tanha or trishna) become apparent as the reader follows in the Bardo text the procedures whereby a specific human body is relinquished, a new one taken on, or final "liberation" into Nirvana achieved. Several English poets, among them Francis Thompson, William Blake, John Donne, have sounded a Buddhist note in lines they have written expressing their own personal sense of the totality or the interrelated oneness of the universe. There is Thompson's

> . . . *thou canst not stir a flower*
> *without troubling of a star.*

Blake's

> *To see a world in a grain of sand*
> *And a Heaven in a wild flower,*
> *Hold Infinity in the palm of your hand*
> *And Eternity in an hour.*

and Donne's lines from one of his sermons: "God is so omnipresent . . . that God is an angel in an angel, and a stone in a stone and a straw in a straw."

Finally, very much as a Buddhist would perceive the "fruitful Void" (on which we shall have more to say later), Leonardo da Vinci wrote in one of his notebooks: "Among the great things which are to be found among us, the Being of Nothingness is the greatest."

In his illuminating introduction to *The Tibetan Book of the Dead,* Dr. Evans-Wentz also sheds some interesting light on the difficult matter of Buddhism's true position on the widely held Asian theories of karma and reincarnation. In this context, he quotes a surprising—and, to his mind, pertinent—passage on "karma and heredity" by the nineteenth-century British scientist Thomas Huxley. In his *Evolution and Ethics* Huxley wrote:

> Everyday experience familiarizes us with the facts which are grouped under the name of heredity. Every one of us bears upon him obvious marks of his parentage, perhaps of remoter relationships. More particularly, the sum of tendencies to act in a certain way, which we call "character," is often to be traced through a long series of progenitors and collaterals. So we may justly say that this "character"—this moral and intellectual essence of a man—does veritably pass over from one fleshly tabernacle to another, and does really transmigrate from generation to generation. In the new-born infant, the character of the stock lies latent, and the Ego is little more than a bundle of potentialities. But, very early, these become actualities; from childhood to age they manifest themselves in dullness or brightness, weakness or strength, viciousness or uprightness; and with each feature modified by confluence with another character, if by nothing else, the character passes on to its incarnation in new bodies. The Indian philosophers called character, as thus defined, "karma." . . . In the theory of evolution, the tendency of a germ to develop according to a certain specific type, e.g., of the kidney bean seed to grow into a plant having all the characters of *Phaseolus vulgaris,* is its "karma." It is the last inheritor and the last result of all the conditions that have affected a line of ancestry which goes back for many millions of years, to the time when life first appeared on the earth.

Then, quoting Professor T. W. Rhys Davids, Huxley ends:

> . . . the snowdrop is a snowdrop and not an oak, and just that kind of snowdrop, because it is the outcome of the *karma* of an endless series of past experiences.

(It might be said that the Buddha's constant insistence on the proper use of the mind and the will, his endless patient repetition of the psychological view that all that happens to us is fundamentally determined by our thoughts, gives Buddhist teaching on karma a hopeful and positive rather than a fatalistic and negative aspect; for thoughts *are* subject to control, and the mental attitude toward one's life *makes* that life.)

In Tibet, a rich mixture of indigenous Himalayan mysticism and trans-planted Indian Buddhism, with some overlay of Tantrism (all of this possible to the permissive Mahayana), tended also to produce examples of what might be called a kind of super-yoga. A number of firsthand accounts that we would consider supernatural are described in the books of Mme. Alexandra David-Neel, a redoubtable French scholar and explorer who managed over forty years ago to penetrate "forbidden" Tibet disguised as a Buddhist lama. She has described a scene she inadvertently witnessed between two lamas who were practicing—not however in the presence of a corpse—the techniques of actual physical assistance to the dying by which the "spirit" would be enabled to leave a body by the proper aperture at the top of the cranium. The two lamas, on whom she eavesdropped in a forest clearing, were seated in postures of meditation and were taking turns uttering an eerie, unfamiliar cry of *Hik!* that seemed lifted from their very bowels. When, after a number of repetitions of this strange word, one monk turned aside and spat a stream of blood, Mme. David-Neel saw, to her surprise, standing upright in the top of his skull a long straw. Later she learned from her Sikkimese guide and interpreter that the two men were practicing one of the esoteric sounds or magic syllables with which officiating lamas of certain sects, at the moment of a man's death, tried to assist the spirit to de-part through the cranial channel corresponding to the soft spot on a newborn baby's head—an opening that Tibetan lamas believe can be physically enlarged through the proper practice of meditation and the utterance of certain magic sounds.

In further explaining the practice of the ritualistic cries she had overheard by chance, Mme. David-Neel's interpreter told her:

> Only a lama who has received, from a competent master, the power of uttering that *hik!* with the right intonation and required force is capable of success. After *hik* he shouts *phat!* But he must be careful not to articulate *phat* when he is only practicing like the monks you over-heard. The combination of these two sounds invariably leads to the separation of body and spirit, so that the lama who pronounced them correctly over himself would immediately die. This danger does not

exist when he is officiating, because he acts by proxy in place of the dead—lending him his voice, so that the effect of the magic words is felt by the dead man, not by the lama.

Once the psychic power of drawing the spirit out of its corporeal envelope has been conferred, by a competent master, upon a disciple, the latter must practice the uttering of *hik!* in the right tone. It is known that this has been attained when a straw stuck in the skull stands up straight as long as desired. For by shouting *hik* a slight opening in the skull is produced and the straw is placed in it. In the case of a dead man the opening is much larger. It is sometimes large enough to introduce the little finger.

There have always been devotees of Buddhism who, contrary to the example set by the Great Teacher, experimented in the occult, just as others have engaged in philosophic and metaphysical theorizing of an abstract order. Some of the speculative thought of early Buddhism, particularly that pertaining to the essential dynamism of the universe and the delusion of permanent substance, comes very close to modern Western scientific theory. Original Buddhism, as already noted, strongly emphasized the impermanence of all things (*anicca*) and the absence of substance in all things (*anatta*). It taught that only by grasping the basic truths embodied in these two terms could the way to deliverance be found. Through profound meditation it was possible for a man to gain insight into the true nature of existence—that it is impermanent and substanceless and thus capable of causing man to suffer because in his blindness he does not perceive these great truths and attaches himself to things, persons, life itself. When freedom from this basic illusion was gained—as the Buddha gained it under the Bodhi Tree—a man was rid of the power of karma and thus was also freed of the recurrent cycle of birth and death.

A formula known as Dependent Origination was devised to guide a disciple seeking to comprehend the difference between the seeming reality of the physical world and its *true* reality. Understanding of this vital formula became central to the attainment of Buddhist enlightenment in the Southern (Hinayana) School of Buddhism which flourished in Ceylon and Burma. The chain of relationships by which one life is endlessly linked to a succeeding life is described as follows:

From ignorance there arise karma formations.

From karma formations there arises the moment of consciousness that links one birth with another.

From that moment of consciousness there arises psychophysical (mind-body) existence.

From psychophysical existence there arise the six organs of sense. (The Buddhists add the mind to the five sense organs.)

From the six organs of sense there arises contact.

From contact there arise feelings.

From feelings there arises desire.

From desire there arises grasping.

From grasping arise the processes of life.

From life processes arises birth.

From birth arise old age, sickness, death, sorrow, lamentation, pain, grief and despair.

With the overcoming of ignorance about the nature of one's illusory self, the entire chain would be presumed to cease, bringing freedom from any further compulsion to "become."

The principle of Dependent Origination related itself also to the Buddhist teaching about the Void or Emptiness (Shunyata) referred to above in relation to the proper after-death goal. The Buddhist Void is far from being a nihilistic doctrine. The Void is not nothingness or annihilation but the very source of all life. In speaking of this theory as taught in the Buddhism of China and Japan (where it has influenced the creation of a very subtle aesthetic, as we shall see in the chapter on Zen), Hajime Nakamura, the Japanese Buddhist scholar, says:

"Voidness . . . is . . . that which stands right in the middle between affirmation and negation, existence and nonexistence. . . . The void is all-inclusive; having no opposite, there is nothing which it excludes or opposes. It is living void, because all forms come out of it, and whoever realizes the void is filled with life and power and the . . . love of all beings."

This subtle doctrine is, by its very nature—expressed in the term "Void" itself—not a matter that readily lends itself to brief or simple exposition. Perhaps, however, modern science can again be brought to our aid if we remind ourselves that in this century the nonmaterial nature of the universe has been widely accepted since Eddington in *The Nature of the Physical World* presented his two famous tables: one a seemingly solid "symbol," the other a mysteriously balanced group of invisible energies and forces. Still, though accepted as scientific fact, such knowledge as the nonsubstantiality of substance plays little part in the living of our everyday lives or the thinking of our everyday thoughts. The early Buddhists, being Indians, perhaps found less difficulty than Westerners in acceptance of the world as maya, or a kind of magical show in which what is seen is both true and not true. Buddhism would say this is not to argue that what is seen is non-existent, but only that we take it for what it essentially is not.

The Buddha, in spite of his profound mind, tended in general to keep his teachings within the bounds of simple human understanding, holding fast to the necessity for acquiring that non-egocentric nonpersonal viewpoint which alone, in his opinion, could mitigate life's inevitable suffering and widen the individual perspective. There is one story among many that particularly well illustrates the Buddha's doctrinal emphasis on overcoming the astigmatism of a too personal viewpoint. A distraught mother came to the Buddha carrying a dead child in her arms. She had been unable to accept its death and, almost insane with grief, had traveled a long distance to speak to the Great Teacher of whom she had heard. When, hoping for a miracle, she appeared before the Buddha with the little corpse in her arms, he did not say to her that he could or could not bring back the dead, nor did he deliver any sermon on the universality of her experience. Instead, he suggested very quietly that she go forth and find for him a single mustard seed—but one of a very special kind; it must come from a household in which there had never been a death. During the mother's fruitless search for a household that had never known death, she was able at last to relate her own loss to that of others and therein to find eventual cure for her grief.

The Buddha had an astute way of cutting the cloth of his teaching according to his followers' needs. For aspirant monks, who had difficulty in removing their thoughts from the world's distractions and attractions, he did not hesitate to prescribe meditations on dead bodies, decaying corpses, piles of human bones or the least pleasant of the body's processes. But uncompromising as was his stand about the way to truth, he was never unaware of individual needs. There is a story of a monk, dying of dysentery, who lay neglected in one of the resting places of the Buddha's disciples. When the Buddha discovered the sufferer, he himself took over his care, bathing and tending him as if he were his child. In chiding the neglectful fellow monks, he spoke words that have a Biblical ring: "He who would wait on me let him wait on the sick."

Buddhism, though often described as a religion for rationalists and intellectuals, plainly developed not only along the line of wisdom, *prajna*, but also along that of compassion, *karuna*. In the type of Buddhism followed in the southern countries of Ceylon, Thailand and Burma, a meditation on *metta*, or the sending forth of loving-kindness to the whole world, is practiced daily by the monks. This practice has its origin in an early scripture known as *The Discourse on Universal Love* in which the Buddha is quoted as saying:

> As a mother, even at the risk of her own life, protects and loves her child, her only child, so let a man cultivate love without measure toward the whole world, above, below, and around, unstinted, unmixed with any feeling of differing or opposing interests. Let a man remain steadfastly in this state of mind all the while he is awake, whether he be standing, walking, sitting or lying down. This state of mind is the best in the world.

Among the most significant and, to some people, most appealing of the various Buddhist doctrines that appeared after the Master's death is that of the *bodhisattva*, a Mahayana development. Bodhisattvas are highly evolved beings, on their way to Buddhahood, who have voluntarily chosen to lend their special powers to help mankind achieve illumination. The difference between a Buddha and a bodhisattva might be said to be that the former is truly "awake," often, indeed, referred to as "the Awakened One," whereas the latter is a being of a "wakeful nature" or one who is "awakening." These sublimely compassionate beings, destined to become future Buddhas, are a natural mythological outgrowth of the teaching of universal loving-kindness. The distinguishing traits—known as the Ten Perfections—characteristic of bodhisattvas vary in some essentials from sect to sect, but the following list may be taken as representative: liberality, morality, renunciation, wisdom, energy, forbearance, truthfulness, resolution, good will and equanimity. Bodhisattvas have inspired some of the most distinctive creations in the entire field of Asian art. Sometimes these Buddhas-to-be are presented with feminine countenances, as in the Chinese Kuan Yin (Kwannon in Japan) —an appearance considered suitable for the conveyance of an impression of boundless compassion. Frequently, their entire aspect is androgynous.

The bodhisattva ideal exemplifies another of the differences between the two chief branches of world Buddhism, Hinayana and Mahayana. Hinayana or Theravada Buddhism, the conservative Buddhism of countries like Ceylon, Burma and Thailand, tends to emphasize the ideal of the *arhat,* an individual who through unremitting meditative effort attains release from the "round of becoming" for himself alone. The Mahayana branch, which belongs to Tibet, China, Korea and Japan, places stronger emphasis on all creation's sharing a common karma to which every individual contributes either for good or ill. To the Mahayanists the Buddha's own decision to go forth into the world and share his enlightenment was the highest proof of his spiritual attainment.

If, as the Buddha taught, the universe is "mind only," it would follow in Mahayana doctrine that whoever does a good deed or a bad one unavoidably affects all life. This theory of universal, indissoluble interdependence is taught today in the Japanese Kegon School of Buddhism in the image of a great web which is to be pictured, during meditation, as extending throughout the whole universe, its vertical lines representing time, its horizontal ones space. Wherever the threads of this vast imaginary net cross one another, there should be imagined a crystal bead symbolizing a single existence. Each of these crystal beads reflects on its bright surface not only every other bead in the vast net but also every reflection of every other reflection—countless, endless reflections, each in a sense independent, and yet all bound together in a single related totality.

As Buddhism was, down the years, inevitably influenced by Hinduism, there developed concepts of the Buddha himself as a cosmic deity, one in a long line of spiritual beings who appear on earth in successive eons to serve as man's guides and helpers. (Hinduism, it will be remembered, finally accepted the Buddha as merely another appearance of its often incarnated god Vishnu.) In other parts of Asia where Buddhism penetrated, the concept of Buddhist incarnations led to further elaborations which specifically claim Siddhartha Gautama as the seventh in a line of past and future Buddhas of which Maitreya, now waiting as a bodhisattva somewhere outside the earth's space-time, will be the next. That the Buddha, who was born in the sixth century B.C., may have accepted the Indian theory of avatars is suggested in one of the sayings attributed to him:

"I have seen the Ancient Way, the old Road that was taken by the formerly All-Awakened, and that is the path I follow."

From the various theories that developed about the Buddha's former lives there grew a delightful collection of Indian tales called the Jatakas. These charming folk stories, which the fables of the Greek Aesop resemble in many interesting respects, are accounts of the Buddha's former incarnations in various human and animal forms. They might be said to represent, after a fashion, an allegorical expression of the theory of evolution from lower to higher forms. In the Jatakas one sees the Buddha wisdom shining forth in each of a long chain of animal and human existences, and this ever-present wisdom forms a connecting thread of increasing "awareness" which finally produced the historic Buddha of the present eon, who, legend says, related these lively yet always moral tales for the edification of his simpler followers.

The Jataka stories have lent themselves most attractively to the work of many Asian artists. In general, the importance to Asian art of the Buddha story—coming in the wake of the inevitable development of Buddhist mythology—can hardly be overestimated. The image of Shakyamuni, whether seated in meditation or standing (the two most common types of images), walking, or reclining in the hour of death, represents for the whole Asian world, as already stated, the equivalent of the Christ image for the West. Yet, interestingly enough, centuries passed after the Buddha's death before any representations of him as an actual physical being were conceived or executed. This was in keeping with an old scripture that states, "The Buddha, who has gone beyond the fetters of the body, cannot be endowed by art with the likeness of a body." When an artist, in telling stories of the Master's life and teaching, found it necessary to indicate the Buddha's presence, he used only specific symbols: an empty throne, an umbrella (symbol of sovereignty), a *stupa* (mound for relics) the wheel of his first sermon, footprints. Even in such lively scenes as the future Buddha's departure from his father's palace, the horse—whose hoofs are being lifted up by divine beings to prevent all telltale sounds—departs riderless through the palace gates.

It was in Gandhara, a section of northwestern India settled by Greeks of the invading armies of Alexander the Great, that the earliest Buddha images were created—as far as we now know.* The making of these icons followed on the conversion of this region to Buddhism by the greatest of all Indian monarchs, Ashoka, who inherited the Indian throne about 270 B.C. It was quite natural for the anthropomorphic-minded descendants of Greeks to represent their new god in the form of a divine man, but the sudden appearance of the Buddha image also indicates a change in Buddhist doctrine, a certain relaxation of strict orthodoxy under the influence of new

---

* There is today a growing belief that the making of Buddha images was taking place in Mathura (near modern Agra) contemporaneously with the Gandhara school. Mathura was the summer capital of the Kushans, whose greatest king, Kanishka, was, like Ashoka before him, an ardent Buddhist convert.

Mahayana interpretations of Buddhism's message. This early Buddhist art, representing the Buddha as a divine man, is commonly known as Gandharan, also as Greco-Buddhist or Greco-Roman. Although interesting for many reasons, historical as well as doctrinal, it often lacks the subtle beauty of later Indian work. Some of the Gandhara sculptures have an awkward stocky appearance and an unnatural stiffness of pose; others have an almost foppish air; some even go so far as to present the Buddha in the guise of a worldly princeling. Later, in the high period of Indian art, the Gupta (A.D. 300–600), the Buddha image flowered into greater grace, while still continuing occasionally to show certain Hellenistic and even Roman influences.

The Buddha's image, although that of a human being, was traditionally depicted with unusual physical characteristics to indicate his exalted state or supernatural anatomy. At the top of the head (sometimes concealed by a conventional headdress of round curls) was the *ushnisha*, a protuberance suggesting the presence of a sort of superbrain or intuitive intelligence, even sometimes a "flame of invisible light," believed to stream forth from the "lotus center" in the skull, or as part of a conception of "the Buddha all aflame." In the center of the forehead appeared another protuberance, small, round and beadlike, variously described as "soft like cotton," resembling a jasmine flower or a hoarfrost blossom. This was the *urna*, interpreted as the "third eye of spiritual vision." The hands on Buddha images were engaged in classic Indian *mudras*: reassurance, giving blessings, calling the earth to witness the Buddha's right to his title. Later a halo or nimbus appeared, often enormous and elaborately decorated. The exaggerated elongation of the earlobes indicated the fact of royal birth, since, as a prince, the Buddha would have worn very heavy earrings.

At certain times and in certain places an even more extreme iconography developed from old literature pertaining to the thirty-two major and eighty minor marks said to signify Buddhahood. Preposterous descriptions of the Buddha's physical being were taken literally: arms like a young elephant's trunk, a skin of gold, lotus-petal fingers, nose like a parrot's beak and projecting heels. The marvel is that many of these images—notably the rare walking Buddhas of the ancient Sukhodaya (Sukothai) kingdom (in modern Thailand), with their long full arms, deep chests, narrow waists, downcast eyes and inscrutable smiles—can triumph so luminously over the incongruities to which the image makers felt obliged to conform.

Although any making of icons was counter to original Buddhist teachings and certainly quite far from the viewpoint of the founder himself, the whole world has cause to be grateful to Buddhist artists. In all parts of Asia they have provided mankind with some of the most remarkable and beautiful creations in the field of art, including not only sculpture but paintings, frescoes, mystic diagrams, even architecture. Buddhist art includes the great temple compound at Borobudur in Java—an enormous *mandala* in stone, almost indescribable in its scale and grandeur; in central India the marvelous stupa and carved gates at Sanchi and the subtly sensuous frescoes and sculpture at Ajanta; the ineffably serene celestial scenes of Buddhas and Buddhas-to-be produced by the gifted painters of China, Korea and Japan; and innumerable icons in bronze, gold and ivory from every Eastern country. In general, Buddha images, as well as the attendant figures of saints and bodhisattvas, possess a mysterious quality of dynamic serenity. They often seem to be subtly breathing and in their ineffable quality of aliveness offer tangible proof of their creator's identification with the Great Master's teachings.

A vigorous spreading of Buddhism began definitively, as already stated, with the reign of Ashoka, "Buddhism's Constantine," as he is sometimes called. Ashoka, "the amiably glancing," inherited the throne of India from his grandfather, Chandragupta, a brilliant opportunist who, having learned of the death of Alexander in far-off Babylon, attacked the Greek forces left behind in India, conquered them and proceeded to set up a kingdom for himself and his remarkable grandson. In the beginning of his long and extraordinary career, Ashoka, outdoing his grandfather, established a record of useless slaughter and cruel behavior hardly equaled by any other monarch in history. After the destruction by the most barbaric means of many thousands of people, Ashoka was, however, converted to Buddhism. He spent the rest of his life not only attempting to make up for his years of outrageous conduct, but to spread the word of the religion that had so drastically altered his own life.

Ashoka extended his concern to the animal world by abolishing the royal hunt and establishing hospitals for sick animals and birds. In his zeal to proselytize for Buddhism, Ashoka erected many stone columns throughout the vast dominion over which he ruled, to act as spiritual guideposts for his people. Some of these pillars survive to this day, and the words carved on them express the purest Buddhist thought:

Not superstitious rites but kindness to servants and underlings, respect for those deserving respect, self-control coupled with kindness in dealing with living creatures, these and virtuous deeds of like nature are verily the rites that are everywhere to be performed.

Ashoka sent missionaries far and wide to preach the new religion. Legend says he even sent his only son as a monk to Ceylon, repaying a gift of splendid pearls from the monarch of this distant island by a return offering of "the Jewel of Truth." Some stories say that Ashoka's daughter also went as a missionary nun to Ceylon in order to teach the Buddha's wisdom to the women there. She is credited with taking with her a slip from the famous original Bodhi Tree. It was planted at Anuradhapura, and the enormous old tree still growing at this pilgrimage spot is said to be the very same one the princess brought with her. Whether or not this story is true, certainly Ceylon became, and has remained, one of the most powerful centers of Hinayana Buddhism. In addition to the Buddha's tooth, a relic stored in the temple at Kandy, the island has many remarkable Buddhist sculptures, some in caves, some in deserted open plazas beside the imposing remains of once-glorious monasteries, palaces and libraries. One of the most moving of these sculptures is a figure of the Buddha, many times life size, depicted in the hour of his death. He lies serenely on his side in a silent and deserted landscape with his favorite disciple, Ananda, standing quietly near his master's head. It was also in Ceylon, sometime in the first century A.D., that the scriptures of Buddhism—orally transmitted for centuries in the immemorial Asian manner—were first put into writing. This was done, according to the *Mahavamsa, The Great Chronicle*, of Ceylon, because the wisest monks had come to feel that the people were less righteous than in former times, and so they called an assembly to write down the teachings "in order that the doctrine might endure." These ancient written scriptures are the Three Baskets or *Tipitaka* (in the Pali tongue of Ceylonese Buddhism; *Tripitaka* in Sanskrit). The term refers to the containers in which the long palm-leaf scrolls were stored.

During the centuries of Buddhism's dominance in India, the Sangha was responsible for the founding of many universities and study centers to which came thousands of eager disciples from all over India and other Asian lands. Some of the most valuable descriptions we possess today of the size, beauty and influence of these great centers of study and art were written in the early fifth and mid-seventh centuries A.D. by intrepid Chinese travelers like Fa-

Hsien and Hsuan-Tsang, who endured almost inconceivable hardships on journeys to and from China in their desire to visit in person the original sites of the Buddha's ministry and return with scriptures and images.

There are a number of explanations for the final complete decline of Buddhism in the land of its birth, none of them entirely satisfactory. It is claimed that gradually, as a result of powerful patronage in high places and the ever-ready temptation of easy living on the part of those whom society supports, a certain softness and divisiveness had begun to creep into the Buddhist Sangha. This subtle decline was also accompanied by an upsurge of theistic Hinduism, due to the ever-increasing influence throughout India of new forms of devotional worship (*bhakti*) which stressed love of a god (in particular such Vishnu incarnations as Rama and Krishna) and emotional self-surrender. Slow-moving changes in the status of Buddhism were further quickened by the arrival on the Indian scene of invading Muslim peoples who, out of their fixed fanatical belief in Allah as the one and only God, made ruthless attacks on Buddhist schools, monasteries, shrines and works of art. Historians have recorded that in the systematic destruction of the great Buddhist universities of Nalanda and Bihar, thousands of monks were burned alive and many more beheaded. The actual burning of the Nalanda library, said to have been the greatest in the world at one time, went on slowly for several months, an incalculable loss to future scholars. The richness of the many jewel bedecked golden images (so alien to the Buddha's early teaching) further roused the image-hating—and probably also covetous—Muslims to heights of destructive vandalism.

There is a subtle irony in the fact that the Muslims were able to rout Buddhism more readily than Hinduism because of the formal organization of the Sangha and such differentiating marks of Buddhist dedication as shaved heads and yellow robes. In reference to the wearing of this distinctive robe, the Buddha once remarked in humorously mocking phrases, "If the mere wearing of the robe could banish greed, malice, etc., then as soon as a child was born, his friends and kinsfolk would make him wear the robe and would press him to wear it, saying, 'Come, thou favored of fortune! Come wear the robe; for by the mere wearing of it, the greedy will put from them their greed, the malicious their malice and so on.' "

Islamic fanaticism and direct attacks on Buddhist monasteries and teaching centers appear to have left the pacifist wearers of the yellow robe leaderless and disoriented. Many monks fled northward to Nepal and Tibet;

many died. This disruption and violence from the outside are not, however, the whole story of Buddhism's decline in India. There had already been, for some time before the Muslim invasions, absorptive action on the part of the ever-assimilative and flexible Hinduism. It is difficult to determine at just what point the two religions, in certain areas, began to share places of worship and teaching, but it is plain from surviving records that they did. Some writers dwell on the theory that Hinduism had long secretly resented Buddhism because of its criticism of the caste system and its denial of sacrosanct status to the Brahmins. This idea probably has some truth in it, although there is another and more tolerant view which describes Hinduism as merely acting true to character, ignoring the differences in conduct and teaching principles and assimilating Buddhism as just another "view of life."

It has not been possible within the range of this short introduction to a very large subject to do justice to the many branches and sub-branches of doctrine and practice that grew from the original teaching. Buddhism's long, rich and generally honorable history has been affected not only by its travels up and down and across Asia but by the confused and turbulent history of the many lands in which it settled. In Burma, for instance, where legend has Buddhism coming with Ashoka's missionaries, there were many subsequent vicissitudes and such drastic interruptions as the military incursions of Kublai Khan. In other lands, like Cambodia, Thailand, Java, Malaya, Sumatra, and Bali, Buddhism periodically had to contend with Hindu rulership, and at these times it came inevitably to some degree under the influence of Hindu mythology and iconography. In Vietnam, where Mahayana Buddhism was first brought, it is said, by way of China, there took place in the last century a countermovement—stemming from nearby Cambodia—for a revival of the Hinayana, or Theravada. Vietnam is, therefore, a country in which both the classic traditions may be said to exist, though in what state of "purity" is not easily determined.

During Buddhism's centuries of travel across Asia, it was inevitable that many concessions—far removed from the original rational and psychological teachings—were made to the folk mind. This can be clearly seen in China, where, however, a strong emphasis on concrete reality, or the Is-ness of the Is (quite in keeping with another aspect of the Chinese character), also played its part. One of the significant developments of doctrine that appeared in this part of the Asian world and moved on to Korea and Japan was an outgrowth of the teaching of the Indian missionary monk Bodhidharma, who came West, tradition says, to restore Buddhism's original directness and to teach his followers that "the finger pointing at the moon was not the moon (Enlightenment) itself." Bodhidharma's followers—trained in dynamic meditative practices—served as therapeutic agents clearing away a long incrustation of mythology and uncharacteristic ways of worship. This might be said to mark the beginning of a fresh approach to Buddhist religious instruction and religious experience, which will be taken up in the chapter on Zen.

In general the art forms and rituals stemming from the various ethical, psychological, mystical and philosophical interpretations possible to Buddhism have an enormous range. The bodhisattva doctrine that grew up in Mahayana led to the concept of a number of Divine Beings, among them Manjusri, the bodhisattva of Meditation or Wisdom; Kuan Yin (in Japanese, Kwannon), the Goddess of Mercy already mentioned, who is the Chinese female version of the Indian male bodhisattva, Avalokiteshvara; and Amida, or Amitabha, Buddha, worshiped by the Pure Realm sect who believe that a concentrated recital of his name is enough to ensure salvation. (This particular Buddha conception is represented in the enormous—and world-famous—statue at Kamakura in Japan.) There is also a widely held belief in Maitreya, the Buddha of the future, mentioned before, who is waiting now in some celestial sphere to make his appearance on the world scene; a theory that may conceivably indicate the influence of Christianity's Second Coming of Christ, as is sometimes claimed, although it would more logically appear to suggest Hinduism's theory of avatars, the periodic incarnations of divinity. One sees in these Mahayana developments that the "historic Buddha" has now become a transcendent cosmic reality who, in the words of E. A. Burtt, "is working in all ages and in innumerable worlds for the salvation of all sentient beings."

In Himalayan Buddhism, along with the highest kind of intellectualism and abstraction, one finds influences that are frankly and strongly Tantric, particularly exemplified in figures often seen in Buddhist shrines showing a male divinity with his Shakti or female essence locked in a close embrace (yab-yum)—rather a far cry from the uncompromising restraint of the earliest Buddhist images of northern India. In Tibet and the neighboring Buddhist kingdoms of Bhutan, Sikkim and Nepal, many colorful customs form a part of daily devotions. Followers of Buddha in the Himalayan lands turn prayer wheels by hand and even by water power, paint prayers on flags to blow in the mountain winds (the idea being to use the messengers of the air to convey sacred words into the atmosphere—no stranger perhaps than the idea of messages sent by radio). In these high mountain countries to the north of India—Nepal, Sikkim, Bhutan, Tibet—monks, and laymen also, meditate on intricate sacred diagrams called *mandalas, thankas* and *patas*. They paint the holy words *Om Mani Padme Hum* (Hail to the Jewel in the Lotus) on special *mani* walls throughout their lands. The now exiled Dalai Lama, the former temporal and spiritual head of their country, represents for Tibetans the highest possible concentration of divine power in human form. In the Hinayana countries of Ceylon, Thailand and Burma, where the great monasteries have been for centuries the real focus of national life, it is still considered a part of a young layman's education to spend a certain period of time in the cloistered atmosphere of those who have formally assumed the life of a monk. It is also taken for granted that laymen come to a monastery for a "refresher course" in mindfulness, and it is quite common, particularly in Burma, for politicians and businessmen to interrupt their lives and go away for a period of meditation practice usually lasting not less than six weeks. A British admiral, E. H. Shattock, who took a course in what is known as Satipatthana a few years ago in a monastery outside Rangoon, found among his fellow "monks" the chief of the Rangoon police and the owner of a flourishing chain of sterilized-milk factories. Admiral Shattock's concise, clear and remarkable little book, *An Experiment in Mindfulness*, is one of the valuable records of a Westerner's experience in an unfamiliar meditative praxis of Buddhism. The admiral was given only two basic exercises to do, but he did them all day, alternately. One was to walk back and forth a given short distance for a given period of time, with his consciousness totally fixed on the separate actions involved in taking a step: "up, forward, down; intending stopping, intending turning, intending starting; up, forward, down." The object was to "break the apparent continuity of the mind," and this seemingly simple exercise—along with the second one, which required a fixed awareness of the gentle rise and fall of the abdomen in breathing—served, in a few weeks, to make forever clear to the admiral the essentially undisciplined nature of his highly "trained" mind, which he found at the mercy of innumerable intrusive, seemingly uncontrollable, darting and fluttering "butterfly thoughts." At the end of some weeks of work in Satipatthana, the admiral was left with several surprising conclusions, among them that rather too much of Western mind-training was equivalent "to the stuffing of geese to produce pâté de foie gras," whereas the most highly trained Buddhists, in his experience, started by first "tackling the mind itself and training it to allow access to insight."

One could write at great length on the diversity of Buddhist worship and related Buddhist art. In summation here one can only repeat that no matter how many peripheral differences one finds in Buddhism, there does exist a basic unity of teaching founded on the Four Noble Truths about human suffering and the Eightfold Path of Deliverance that brings an end to suffering, chiefly through conquest of the ego. Buddhism is able to contain within itself the same wide range of viewpoint and practice as Christianity, which has managed to hold inside its loose compass such contrasting institutions, philosophies, sects and people as the Vatican, the Quakers, the Inquisition, Holy Rollers, image-worshiping Italian and French peasants, the "heresies" of Meister Eckhart and Teilhard de Chardin, the miracles of St. Theresa, the "communism" of Simone Weil, the intellectual thrust of Tillich, the "old-fashioned" fundamentalism of Billy Graham—just to select at random a sampling of Christian paradoxes. At the heart of the manifold efflorescences of Buddhism there remains a calm center; an intuitive yet rational, compassionate yet uncompromising focus of psychological teaching concerning man as "the creator of his own world."

Today the Buddhists of all countries have joined in the formation of a World Buddhist Fellowship, aimed at aiding Buddhism to fulfill more successfully a modern role in relation to contemporary problems. As part of this movement, the momentous Sixth Buddhist Council, composed of scholars, monks and eminent laymen, was held in Burma's capital city, Rangoon, in the 1950's. A series of conferences, extending over many months, came to a climax in May, 1956, with a large-scale commemoration of the 2,500th anniversary of the Buddha's Enlightenment. Part of the goal of this diligent Council was the production of a revised and complete edition of old canonical scriptures. While this somewhat conventional approach to missionizing was going on in the Theravada countries, that very different type of practice and teaching just referred to, originating in China with Bodhidharma and perfected later in Japan, was beginning to attract increasing interest among the artists and intellectuals of the Western world under its Japanese name of Zen.

Well before Zen, however, Buddhist doctrine had attracted groups of disciples in the Western world, many drawn to it by its lofty thought, its emphasis on the reflective doctrine of "mind only," a conception about the universe toward which the most advanced Western thinking would seem now to be steadily moving. Buddhism in Europe was, to begin with, the exclusive province of scholars—German, Hungarian, French, British. The

German philosopher, Schopenhauer, is generally credited with first acquainting Europe with Buddhism as a living faith. Toward the end of the nineteenth century the enormous success of Sir Edwin Arnold's long poem about the Buddha's life, *The Light of Asia*, aroused widespread interest and attracted new types of Western people to Buddhism's Middle Way. The English Buddhist Society, an active and distinguished organization, has been in existence for over forty years and has been responsible for the publication of a number of important Buddhist texts. England has hospitably received various Buddhist missions from different parts of Asia, and within the last few years a *vihara*, or Theravada teaching center and home for visiting monks, has been established in London by *bhikkus* from Ceylon. In other parts of Europe—Holland, Belgium, Finland, Sweden and Switzerland—Buddhist groups also flourish.

In his comprehensive general book on Buddhism, Christmas Humphreys, the eminent British lawyer and founder of the English Buddhist Society, states that there are more than a hundred American Buddhist Societies in existence at the present time. In a recent printed opinion from the United States Supreme Court dealing with new interpretations of the rights of conscientious objectors, the Honorable William O. Douglas pointed out that the major religious denomination of our fiftieth state, Hawaii, is Buddhism, that the latest (1961) Yearbook of American Churches lists for one American Buddhist sect alone 55 churches, 89 church schools and an exclusive membership of 60,000. The total number of all Buddhists in North America is 171,000, according to the 1965 World Almanac.

In referring to Buddhism's growing Western influence, Dr. Graham Howe has said in his *Invisible Anatomy*: "In the course of their work, many psychologists have found, as the pioneer work of C. G. Jung has shown, that we are all near-Buddhists on our hidden side. . . . To read a little Buddhism is to realize that the Buddhists knew, two thousand five hundred years ago, far more about modern psychology than they have yet been given credit for. . . . We are now rediscovering the Ancient Wisdom of the East."

India, the land of the Buddha's birth, is today showing an unquestioned revival of Buddhist influence, largely because of the rising strength of the Untouchables. Like the original Buddha, no true Buddhist could respect the strictures of caste, and therefore Buddhists from earliest days accepted Untouchables in their midst. Today, an Indian Untouchable who becomes a Buddhist tacitly steps outside the ancient, still slowly changing forms of the Hindu caste system.

In bringing to a close this necessarily brief account of Buddhism it might be added that in place of the moral imperative "Thou shalt not"—so much a part of Judeo-Christian precepts—Buddhism in general offers a perhaps sounder psychological counsel, "It would be better if you refrained from." This attitude is basic to both Mahayana and Theravada, much as they may differ in other matters—like Mahayana's use of intercessory rites versus the almost puritanic self-reliance of the Theravada, or the former's belief in the efficacy of prayers versus the stress on "works" in the latter, and other significant differences on which there has not been space to dwell at any length.

But although interpretations of Buddhist doctrine may vary, the teaching that life is One is emphasized by all sects and branches of this vital religious philosophy, followed by so many hundreds of millions of people. The Oneness of all life is a truth, Buddhism asserts, that can be fully realized only when false notions of a separate self—whose destiny can be considered apart from the whole—are forever annihilated. When the individual seeker has finally acquired this supreme sense of the Oneness of all life, he has, indeed, reached the bliss of Nirvana. Freed completely of the limiting conditions connected with the sense of a personal ego, he has come to "the end of separateness."

ZEN

The Perfect Way knows no difficulties
Except that it refuses to make preference:
Only when freed from hate and love,
It reveals itself fully and without disguise.
A tenth of an inch's difference,
And heaven and earth are set apart:
If you want to see it manifest,
Take no thought either for or against it.
To set up what you like against what you dislike—
This is the disease of the mind:
When the deep meaning [of the Way] is not understood
Peace of mind is disturbed and nothing is gained.
[The Way] is perfect like unto vast space,
With nothing wanting, nothing superfluous:
It is indeed due to making choices
That its suchness is lost sight of.

. . . .

When the mind rests serene in the oneness of things
. . . dualism vanishes by itself.

               —beginning of the *Hsin-hsin-ming* by Seng-ts'an
               as translated by D T. Suzuki in *Essays in Zen*
               Buddhism, First Series

A dunce once searched for a fire
With a lighted lantern
Had he known what fire was
He could have cooked his rice much sooner.
                    —from *The Gateless Gate*

My storehouse having
Burnt down
Nothing obscures the view
Of the bright moon.
                    —Masahide

The great path has no gates
Thousands of roads enter it.
When one passes through this gateless gate
He walks freely between heaven and earth.
                    —from *Zen Flesh, Zen Bones*

As the India-born religion of Buddhism moved slowly across Asia, century after century like a mighty river, it began—as described in the previous chapter—to reflect on its placid surface influences from the different countries through which it passed. Buddhism reached China certainly as early as the first century A.D., perhaps earlier, and in due course passed on from China to Korea and Japan. During these travels and transitions Buddhism developed several divergent forms of teaching, among them one in particular which, under its Japanese name of Zen, was destined to create an unusual stir in the twentieth-century West and even to find itself acclaimed (not very accurately, Zenists aver) as a type of Far Eastern existentialism.

In the simplest terms Zen might be described as a unique blend of Indian mysticism and Chinese naturalism sieved through the rather special mesh of the Japanese character. The origins of its name indicate its historical genesis. Zen is the Japanese way of writing and speaking the Chinese word *Ch'an*, and *Ch'an* is a transliteration of the Sanskrit word *dhyana* meaning meditation or, more fully, "contemplation leading to a higher state of consciousness," "union with Reality." The ancient Indian mystical root, along with strong humanistic and pragmatic influences from the land of Confucius and Lao-tzu, are evident in this enduring "way of life" that has lately caught the attention of many American and European psychoanalysts, artists, philosophers and theologians.

Although Zen may be classified as one of the branches belonging to the permissive, many-sided Mahayana School of Buddhism, described in the preceding chapter, its inclusion here as a separate Way of Wisdom seems justified because of its special teaching methods, the significant influence on it of Chinese philosophy, and, in particular, the place it has made for itself in recent Western thought.

Before we take up, very briefly, the effect of the philosophies of Confucianism and Taoism on this branch of Buddhism during its years in China, it should be stressed (since it is so often overlooked by contemporary writers on the subject) that Zen's stated aim is none other than the aim of the Indian Buddha himself, the attainment of an absolute or ultimate knowledge lying beyond all change and the "sway of the opposites." The state of consciousness, known in the Zen vocabulary as *satori*, is held to be comparable to that special level of insight attained by the Buddha while seated in deep meditation under the sacred Tree of Enlightenment in the sixth century before the birth of Christ. Zen is firmly grounded in specific exhortations of the Buddha, notably his trenchant suggestion, "Look within, *thou* art the Buddha" and his deathbed injunction to his disciples, "Be a lamp unto yourselves. . . . Work out your own salvation with diligence." In the centuries following Buddhism's first appearance in China—an event of imprecise date—there took place, however, a vital exchange of ideas between this transplanted teaching and the two classic Chinese philosophies, Taoism and Confucianism. Together, in time, these three philosophies might be said to have created a fourth, a subtle blend of them all: Indian metaphysical abstraction, Taoistic paradox and Confucian pragmatism—Zen.

Both Confucianism and Taoism—the two philosophies that are said to represent the two sides of the Chinese character, the practical and the mystical—preached trust in human beings and in humanness. Basic to the teachings of the Master Confucius (born in the same century B.C. as the Indian Buddha) was a common Chinese virtue, *jen*, which meant being human, but human in the very best sense. Each of the two Chinese philosophies voiced—often in familiar and homely terms—belief in man's innate good sense, his possession of an "intuitive wisdom" that only needed awakening to serve as support and guide. Like the Buddha in sixth-century India, Confucius in sixth-century China also made a strong case for keeping one's mind on the here and now:

"The path of duty lies in what is near and men seek for it in what is remote. The work of duty lies in what is easy and men seek for it in what is difficult."

Confucius too had little patience with speculation on the unsolvable mysteries of the supernatural, or things outside the range of sight and sound: "While you cannot serve men, how can you serve the gods? While you do not understand life, what can you understand of death?"

Taoism emphasized an elusive concept, *wu-wei,* nonaction, or, better, noninvolvement, or perhaps more precisely, triumphing over one's insistent ego, letting things "happen" in accordance with their own innate laws, instead of attempting to impose one's wishes as if *they* were the very laws of life. "Everything is what it is . . . is all One . . . the Tao," said Lao-tzu. In dwelling on this abstraction, the Tao (which might be compared to the Buddhist Void, or even to Hinduism's Absolute, the indescribable essence of all life, Brahman), Lao-tzu wrote:

"How unfathomable is Tao—like unto the emptiness of a vessel, yet, as it were, the honored Ancestor of us all. Using it we find it inexhaustible, deep and unfathomable. How pure and still is the Way! I do not know who generated it. It may appear to have preceded God."

The pith of Taoistic doctrine is set forth in a small controversial book called the *Tao Te Ching,* usually translated as *The Way and Its Power.* Not long ago an American author, Holmes Welch, at work on this often-dissected masterpiece of wisdom and paradox, came up with the startling fact that no other book except the Bible had been translated into English as often as the *Tao Te Ching.* In part, he surmised, this might be due to the many amazing parallels that have been found between New Testament sayings of Jesus Christ and certain aphorisms of Lao-tzu written centuries before the Christian era.

Though Lao-tzu made use of aphorisms and simple metaphors, the philosophy he propounded was far more esoteric and paradoxical than the teaching of his fellow countryman, Confucius. The *Tao Te Ching* utilized a kind of contradictory, seemingly illogical style in an obvious attempt to rouse the mind from familiar ruts. Even in translation Lao-tzu has a way of so successfully jolting the reader into attention that someone has remarked of the *Tao Te Ching's* train of thought, "It is like an express on a bad roadbed," adding, "Like Zen Buddhism, Taoism seems to be trying to shake sense into us." This approach to teaching "enlightenment" or "awareness" certainly has points of comparison with the Japanese Zen method of instruction by way of the *koan,* or riddle—which will be taken up at some length further on in this chapter.

In speaking of the necessity for non-striving, and for overcoming the spirit of competition, Lao-tzu expounded subtle laws of "alternation" and the paradoxical power of the weak over the strong:

"If you would breathe deeply, the lungs must first be emptied. Desiring strength, you must first weaken. If you will overthrow, you must first exalt. If you would take, you must first give. This is called 'Hiding the Light.' This is how the soft vanquishes the hard and the weak the strong."

Such psychological-physiological riddles as these came in time—directly or indirectly—to find embodiment in Zen-rooted activities like judo and archery, which Japan has taught to the modern world. Even Zen's "happy idiots," Han-shan and Shih-te (Kanzan and Jittoku)—those joyously care-free poet-recluses of the Chinese T'ang dynasty who so often appear in Zen legend and art—and much of the zany humor which characterizes Zen (serving to set it apart from all other religions)—can be traced to Taoism. The great Master Lao-tzu himself once made the unequivocal statement: "If it were not laughed at, it would not be the Tao."

All the foregoing is, of necessity, a mere brushing of the surface of profound, often ambiguous yet also practical teachings that first developed in the highly cultivated and complex social world of China more than half a millennium before the words of the Buddha were brought by missionary monks from distant parts of Buddhist-converted Asia. On its arrival Buddhism took immediate and firm root in Chinese soil, where it had a lasting effect on culture in general and in particular on Chinese art. That Buddhism could effect such significant interchange with indigenous philosophies suggests an inner kinship between the thought processes native to the Chinese and this transplanted philosophy from India. Today it is Zen's deliberate lack of strict boundaries and fixed beliefs that has enabled it to make creative use of other systems of thought, according to Dr. Daisetz Suzuki, the noted Japanese scholar to whom must go the largest share of credit for bringing Zen to the attention of the West. In his book, *Zen and Japanese Culture*, he has pointed out that since Zen's teaching is concentrated on an "intuitive experience," a Zenist may be ostensibly a "Taoist, a Confucian, even a Shintoist"—which is the original "nature religion" of the Japanese people. He has added significantly, "Zen experience can also be explained by Western philosophy," and herein lies, perhaps, the kernel of its present Occidental status and the reason it seems to offer so many Westerners a fresh outlook on the human dilemma.

Zen was not formally established in Japan until the thirteenth century. Prior to this date, however, there had been a significant exchange of Buddhist monks and teachers between Japan and China, a traffic of inestimable importance not only to Japanese culture but to the history of Zen philosophy and the world's art, for Buddhist emissaries acted, in effect, as disseminators of Chinese civilization. Japanese monks returning from China brought back with them the new Zen ways of teaching enlightenment. They also returned with treatises on art and examples of the exquisite paintings of the great Sung era, a period of unparalleled flowering that lasted in China from the tenth to the thirteenth centuries. When the Mongolian invaders finally brought the Sung idyll to an end, the Japanese—who escaped the Mongols by a miraculous wind—were able to preserve some of the greatest Chinese art and artifacts, as well as the new-old, India-born, Chinese-influenced Buddhist teaching. To this day it is impossible to separate Zen philosophy as taught in Japan from the various arts, disciplines, and precepts it has preserved, encouraged and practiced in an amazingly pure stream of transmission right up to modern times.

Before the current Americanization of Japan almost the entire culture of this island country owed its uniqueness to Zen principles translated into a very special aesthetic. Qualities like simplicity, naturalness, stillness, tranquility, asymmetry, emptiness have been given expression for centuries in types of Japanese architecture, in ways of designing interiors and gardens, as well as in writing plays, poetry and music, serving ceremonial tea, arranging flowers, making pottery (a high art in Japan), handling the brush in painting and calligraphy, and performing in the theater. The precise disciplines of judo (jujitsu), archery and ceremonial swordsmanship (*kendo*) are also rooted in Zen principles.

All these arts and techniques constitute various Zen "ways" known as *do*, considered to be expressions of Zen enlightenment in daily life. Those who can perform one, or several, of these *do* have the opportunity to manifest thereby the inner essence of Zen; to keep themselves constantly alive to Zen's deeper meaning. Even those who have merely mastered the skills of judo, kendo, "tea," flower arrangement, archery or the style of performance in a No drama are demonstrating at least the outer forms of what on the inner plane (where techniques are transcended and where mind, body and spirit have become truly one) may be said to represent a type of satori or awakening.

Since Zen's fundamental viewpoint is not easily grasped—depending as it does more on intuition than on explication, and stressing experience rather than doctrine—it might be helpful to take a familiar *do* like judo (now increasingly taught in the West as a form of self-defense) to illustrate one of the ways in which Zen "works." Whether the fact is realized or not by all its modern Western practitioners and teachers (many of whom seem to be ex-Marines), judo's roots lie deep in Zen philosophy, for it teaches "the instinctive—or intuitive—wisdom of the body," the secret power that lies in "nonresistance," the meaning of "awareness without tension." In judo, emphasis falls (as also in kendo and archery) not on carefully thought-out and calculated moves, not on physical strength or the competitive spirit. There is another kind of "knowing" that does not come from learning the individual tricks (the *ji*) but rather in assimilating the underlying principles or *ri*. One of the early, perhaps Taoist-influenced, exponents of this singular science, or art, is said to have developed its inner laws through observing how, in winter, the strong resistant fir boughs broke under the weight of snow while more yielding and supple weeds and branches were seen to bend, relax and thus lightly drop their burden. (*Ju* means "gentle" or to "give way"; *jutsu* means "art" or "practice.")

A Westerner, Trevor Leggett, who studied judo for many years with Japanese masters, has written, in *A First Zen Reader*, that in classical judo training one is expected to discover the profound Zen truth expressed in the Taoist classic *Saikondan:* "The stillness in stillness is not the real stillness; only when there is stillness in movement can the spiritual rhythm appear which pervades heaven and earth."

Other Zen precepts like "Throw away the body to find the spirit" or "Enter at one stroke" are specifically exemplified on the physical plane, says Leggett, in the marvelous feats of technique to be seen in contests between classically trained experts, opponents who have long since mastered such principles as "no holding back" but also "no aggression."

Zen would readily admit that such paradoxical "laws" as those just mentioned cannot be grasped with the mind alone. They can be fully understood only after definite types of experiment and discipline have brought the neophyte to a place where "reversed effort" can operate, where the aspirant has learned to use the mysterious energy embodied in "letting go." At last the ever-present, intrusive ego has stepped aside and it is then—to use an example from the practice of archery—that "bow, arrow and archer become one." At this point of psychophysical unity the archer does not shoot but "it" does it for him.

All this may seem, at first encounter, a long way from the usual idea of the religious life or a religious philosophy in operation. But although Zen has been called "the religion of no religion," its most noted modern followers assert unequivocally that it is a religion. It has, to be sure, dispensed with most of the accepted fundamentals common to other world faiths or theologies. Zen does not go along with the Judaic-Christian belief in a personal Savior or a God—outside the universe—who has created the cosmos and man. To the Zen view, the universe is one indissoluble substance, one total whole, of which man is but a part.

Ruth Fuller Sasaki, an American-born Zenist, head of a famous teaching center in Kyoto, and author of *Zen, a Religion,* has expressed this attitude in the most direct and simple terms:

> Only THIS—capital THIS—*is*. Anything and everything that appears to us as an individual entity, or phenomenon, whether it be a planet or an atom, a mouse or a man, is but a temporary manifestation of THIS in form; every activity that takes place, whether it be birth or death, loving or eating breakfast, is but a temporary manifestation of THIS in activity. Each one of us is but a cell, as it were, in the body of the Great Self, a cell that comes into being, performs its functions, and passes away, transformed into another manifestation. Though we have temporary individuality, that temporary limited individuality is not either a true self or our true self. Our true self is the Great Self; our true body is the Body of Reality.

The discovery of this "Reality" is the Zen goal.

There are in Zen no sacred gospels like the Hindu *shruti* or the Christian Bible that demand implicit credence from all followers. Zen makes use of certain Buddhist scriptures in its training centers and monasteries, but because of the emphasis laid on "finding out for oneself," it also delights in stories of repudiation, or even sharp scorn, of these same *sutras.* One of the most famous of Zen paintings shows a noted Patriarch tearing a religious manuscript into shreds and tossing it to the winds. This iconoclastic viewpoint is summed up in four classic Zen lines, a notably brief statement setting forth the nonformal and nonauthoritarian nature of Zen instruction:

> A special transmission outside the scriptures;
> No dependence on words;
> Direct pointing to the soul of man;
> Seeing into one's own nature.

Zen is fiercely Buddhist in its uncompromising emphasis on self-reliance. There is an old Zen saying, "Cleanse your mouth of the word Buddha," which is to say, no sanctimonious prating, no reliance on spiritual "authorities" supposedly unquestionable, not even the great Buddha himself. Zen would go even further in its drive to make this particular point: "If you meet a Buddha, kill him! If you meet Daruma [the Japanese name for the First Patriarch] or any other great Master, kill him!"

Westerners who find this shockingly violent are referred to the New Testament in which Christ, aiming at the same kind of extreme dedication on the part of his followers, states unequivocally, "If any man come to me, and hate not his father, and mother, and wife, and children, and brethren, and sisters, yea, and his own life also, he cannot be my disciple." (St. Luke 14:26)

Zen, which has had the advantage for centuries of a coexisting art of sharp and subtle commentary, delights in artists who poke fun at religious cant, or illustrate, with brush and special ink (*sumi*), Zen's uncompromising stand against mistaking *things* for *ideas,* or either of them for "reality." An eighteenth-century Zen painter, Fugai Mototaka, once sketched a very comical picture of a monk with his skirts pulled up warming his posterior at a fire made by the burning of a Buddha image. The picture illustrated a famous eighth-century anecdote in which a Zen monk on a very cold day set fire to a Buddha image to warm himself. When rebuked by another monk, who found this sacrilegious, the first monk replied that he was burning the image to "get the *sarira*"—an indestructible substance found only in the ashes of cremated saints. He went on to remark that since he had found no sarira in the ashes it was obviously not a saint he was burning, and as the day was bitterly cold they might just as well burn the other two images and keep warm.

Such extremism may be exemplary, but it is not, needless to say, in general practice among Zen followers. There are many beautiful, and certainly venerated, statues and paintings of Buddhas and bodhisattvas in Zen temples and monasteries, which are, as a matter of fact, repositories of many of Japan's most noted national treasures. These images, however, are not regarded as objects of worship but only as reminders that the attainment of *bodhi* (intuitive wisdom) lies within the grasp of any earnest seeker, just as the historic Buddha himself declared two thousand five hundred years ago. The traditional sculptured and painted Buddha pose of meditative serenity is also practiced daily by Zen monks and laymen alike, since the correct use, or posture, of the body is deemed essential to true contemplation and thereby to the attainment of self-realization. A description of this classic practice, *zazen,* and the meditative pose necessary for successful attainment, as quoted in Heinrich Dumoulin's *A History of Zen Buddhism,* reads as follows:

If you wish to attain enlightenment, begin at once to practice *zazen.* For this meditation a quiet chamber is necessary, while food and drink must be taken in moderation. Free yourself from all attachments, and bring to rest the ten thousand things. Think of neither good nor evil and judge not right or wrong. Maintain the flow of mind, of will, and of consciousness; bring to an end all desires, all concepts and judgments. Do not think about how to become a Buddha.

In terms of procedure, first put down a thick pillow and on top of this a second (round) one. One may choose either a full or half cross-legged position. In the full position one places the right foot on the left thigh and the left foot on the right thigh. In the half position only the left foot is placed upon the right thigh. Robe and belt should be worn loosely, but in order. The right hand rests on the left foot, while the back of the left hand rests in the palm of the right. The two thumbs are placed in juxtaposition.

The body must be maintained upright, without inclining to the left or to the right, forward or backward. Ears and shoulders, nose and navel must be kept in alignment respectively. The tongue is to be kept against the palate, lips and teeth are kept firmly closed, while the eyes are to be kept always open.

Now that the bodily position is in order, regulate your breathing. If a wish arises, take note of it and then dismiss it. In practicing thus persistently you will forget all attachments and concentration will come of itself. That is the art of *zazen.*

Zen asserts that in its very non-use of formal creeds, dogma, or mystic ritual lies its true spirituality. "The way is near, but men seek it afar." This saying from the Chinese summarizes one of Zen's often reiterated views. Another frequently quoted line is Lao-tzu's "Everyday life is the Tao"—a statement taken in Zen to mean that daily existence is not only the way to enlightenment but is in truth enlightenment itself. "What is the way to Wisdom?" inquires a disciple in one of Zen's provocative question-and-answer dialogues known as *mondo.* "When hungry eat; when weary sleep." The master who made this reply was not being flippant. It was merely his way, the abbreviated, oblique Zen way of expressing a humanistic emphasis on life in the here and now; that "gateless gate" that leads to understanding of the nature of the Real.

According to the Zen view, in "the moment," the simple moment—raking a garden path, typing a letter, watching a water bird, peeling a carrot, riding a subway—lies all the mystery and the meaning of the *you* and the *that*, or the eternal Is-ness of life itself. Grasp the moment before it flies; use it to enter the great Emptiness, that Void from which all the ten thousand things—leaves, rakes, typewriters, letters, birds, carrots, subways and one's own seemingly separate self—have sprung, and to which they still, and forever, belong.

Zen literature is replete with songs and verses celebrating the wonder of everyday observations and feelings. Some of these characteristically brief, pared-down verses are explicit, others indirect:

How marvelous, how miraculous,
I draw water,
I gather fuel.

The water-fowl
Lays its beak in its breast
And sleeps as it floats.

An old pine tree preaches wisdom
And a wild bird is crying truth.

The Zen "awakening" is not supposed to bring withdrawal from the world. It should rather, Zen claims, encourage participation, though never involvement of the tense egocentric variety that tends to produce the conflicts and breakdowns so common in modern life. The Buddhist idea that to be born a human being is a great privilege and one not to be neglected or carelessly accepted has full Zen endorsement. The Zen-man is not seeking something superhuman. He does not set out to become an anchorite or a saint or to create a supermundane state of Buddhahood. He simply wants to know how to become *totally* what he potentially is, "as the tree grows, the fish swims, the bird flies, the cloud forms." He wants to recover, uncover, discover his "true self." To use a modern Western slang expression, a true Zenist has indeed decided to "join the human race."

This emphasis on the importance of humanness accounts for a great part of the interest taken in Zen by Western psychoanalysts, who also seek to help their patients release wrongly repressed or diverted individual energies. At a seminar on Psychoanalysis and Zen Buddhism held a few years ago in Cuernavaca, Mexico, Dr. Suzuki in stressing the teaching of the "everyday mind as the Tao" had this to say: "By Tao Zen of course means the unconscious, which works all the time in our consciousness."

He then, however, went on to elaborate on the necessary development from a "purely instinctive unconscious" (common to children and animals) to a "trained unconscious." By this latter term he implied the kind of awareness proper to a really mature human being in which the unconscious experiences gone through since infancy are included as constituting a part of the whole being. He spoke of the proper use and understanding of the unconscious as "the fountainhead of all creative possibility," and without denying the importance of the mind, he uttered some warnings against the modern tendency to disconnect the brain from the larger field of man's total humanness. Elsewhere Dr. Suzuki has said, "The function of human consciousness, as I see it, is to dive deeper and deeper into its source, the unconscious. And the unconscious has its strata of variable depths; biological, psychological and metaphysical. One thread runs through them, and Zen discipline consists in taking hold of it in its entirety."

Zen tradition claims that methods for teaching "direct seeing into the heart of man" or "into one's own nature," the particular Zen way of liberation, were brought to China from India in A.D. 520 by a legendary missionary monk, the First Patriarch, generally known as Bodhidharma (though in Japan also as Daruma). Bushy-browed and eyelidless, fierce-looking yet with a rough kind of humor, this iconoclastic monk has been for centuries a favorite subject with Zen artists. There exists, however, scholarly disagreement about his authenticity as a Patriarch. Some disputants claim to see in Japanese Zen's emphasis on Bodhidharma's mission, title and importance merely a subtle way of discounting Chinese influence in Zen's development. As with most religious disputes, there can be little reliable evidence one way or the other. Certainly by the time Bodhidharma arrived from India, there were already well-established Buddhist organizations in both northern and southern China and also practices that could be termed yogic or meditative. Nonetheless, Zen Buddhism did develop its own peculiar teaching style and practice; and although some of it is obviously attributable to the influence of Taoism and Confucianism, as we have already seen, there is no reason to doubt that a revolutionary missionary from original Buddhist sources could have given new form to a variety of approaches to enlightenment and set in motion a fresh and lively teaching tradition. In any event, Bodhidharma enjoys among most Zenists the title of First Patriarch, though according to another tradition he was the twenty-eighth in a long unbroken succession of Great Teachers, going back to the very days of the historic Buddha himself and to a specific incident which is worth recording here since its inner meaning relates significantly to Zen's unusual viewpoint and methodology and to certain subtle canons of the Japanese aesthetic.

The story tells how on one occasion during his long Indian ministry the original Buddha, Siddhartha Gautama, was seated before a large assembly of people who had gathered from far and wide to hear him preach "the Law." The Buddha, remaining silent, took up a flower he had been given and quietly held it in his hand. Everyone in the congregation was puzzled by his silence and his deliberate gesture with the flower except one disciple, Kashyapa, who, looking at the golden blossom in the Teacher's hand, softly smiled. In his special inward smile the Buddha read Kashyapa's understanding of "that which goes beyond the word" or "the doctrine of thought transmitted by thought." Kashyapa became, at the Buddha's behest, the first of those twenty-eight Great Patriarchs who—by one reckoning—culminated in the missionary monk of the fifth century A.D., Bodhidharma.

To this day the canon of judgment brought to bear on a performance of Japan's ancient No drama (a theater rooted in Zen concepts) is whether it does or does not possess "the true flower," which is to say, whether it does or does not express that which is indescribable, ineffable, but plainly "visible" to those with insight. Similar aesthetic subtleties, grown in the rich Zen soil, will be taken up further on, but since Zen, it must be remembered, teaches more through insight than through direct instruction, it seems valid at this point, in the true Zen spirit, to digress a little further and make a comparison between Zen's approach to something as simple—and remarkable—as a single flower and a rather typical Western attitude.

Basho, a great poet of the seventeenth century, who wrote in the stripped seventeen-syllable form of classic Japanese verse known as *haiku*, is the author of one of these famous brief poems which says only:

> *When I look carefully*
> *I see the* nazuna *blooming*
> *By the hedge!*

In the original Japanese the last word of this verse is *kana*, which the English version can indicate only by an exclamation mark. (Kana is a particle used in Japanese to signify a special emotional response. As employed in Basho's haiku, it signifies a feeling of wonder.) Dr. Suzuki has pointed out that Basho, a true Buddhist practicing "harmlessness," did not *pick* the little flower he saw with such pleasure, blooming under a hedge. He did, however, "look carefully"—for not only is the nazuna a small, insignificant weed, easily invisible to a passerby with slow or "unopened" eye, but also the instruction to "look carefully" to be "constantly aware" is fundamental to all Zen teaching.

Having presented Basho's—or Zen's—viewpoint, Dr. Suzuki then suggests that we take a look at the English poet Tennyson and his "Flower in the Crannied Wall"—a poem known for decades to all students of English literature on both sides of the Atlantic. It will easily be recalled that Tennyson first *plucked* the flower "root and all" out of its cranny—thus abruptly terminating its existence. Then, holding it in his hand, he gazed at it and ruminated:

> *Little flower—but if I could understand*
> *What you are, root and all, and all in all,*
> *I should know what God and man is.*

Here a Western poet approaches the Zen view and at the same time veers sharply away from it. The real wonder of the blossoming plant is seen by both poets, but in almost a spirit of scientific inquiry the Occidental poet detached the flower from its place and after thus fatally interrupting its life process mused on it philosophically.

It should not be deduced from this single example that all Western poets are guilty of a similar approach to the countless wonders of the natural world. Many Western poets, in both the past and present—though there seem to be more behind us than around us—have given expression to essential Zenlike concepts. Wordsworth, Hardy, our own New England Transcendentalists—Thoreau in particular—are full of Zen thoughts. To cite but one example, Emerson's:

> *Hast thou named all the birds without a gun;*
> *Loved the wood-rose, and left it on its stalk?*

There are many illuminating examples, too, of the way in which Zen principles have been interfused into Japanese culture—and all of them offer certain insight into the Zen spirit. Just as there is a direct connection between the Buddha's silent holding of the flower, Bodhidharma's silent sitting (for nine years, it is claimed) and the suggestive evocations of the No drama and Japanese poetry, so—in livelier vein—one can trace a legend of the origins of the tea plant in Bodhidharma's day to the subsequent arcane rites of ceremonial tea-drinking.

The legend relates how sometime during the nine years this dedicated Great Teacher spent in intense meditation, seated in a cave in northern China, his back to the opening, gazing intently at a blank wall, his eyelids began to give him trouble by drooping with weariness. At last, in exasperation, the sage simply pulled them out and threw them on the ground. From the spot where the offending eyelids fell there grew an unfamiliar plant whose aromatic leaves were used by eager neophytes to brew a drink designed to keep them awake while they too sought the liberation of satori. This invigorating beverage, grown from the Patriarch's eyelids, is said to have been the first tea, and for centuries both in China and later in Japan the proper drinking of tea has played its part in the Zen way.

The occasional overprecious charm and self-consciousness displayed today by some participants in this ancient and honorable cult may serve to blur its original intentions, but, nonetheless, these intentions remain both profound and simple. The tea ceremony might be said to be a kind of group meditation—though not on strictly religious subjects. Its formalized manners and customs were initially designed to put the participants into a different frame of mind from that demanded of them in their daily lives in "the world." Taking tea—which rose to its greatest height of popularity and influence, surprisingly enough, during the turbulent medieval period in Japan—is, and always has been, a quiet coming-together of normally busy people in a secluded garden house, small, unpretentious and specially designed for the purpose, with an interior of such studied emptiness that its classic name is "the abode of vacancy." Here with the simplest—though, by virtue of association, perhaps very valuable—utensils and furnishings, the guests, who enter on their knees by a low door, sit quietly on the floor drinking a special souplike pale green liquid that is whisked, not steeped like ordinary tea. Guests and hosts must observe, with meticulous precision, prescribed manners of handling everything they touch. They talk in quiet tones and never of current affairs. Perhaps they speak of the history of some old valued object—pot or cup—in the host's possession, or the season of the year expressed in the one hanging scroll (*kakemono*) and special arrangement of flowers displayed in an alcove. Silences too are part of the formal tea reremony, enabling those present to hear such small soothing sounds as the fire burning, the iron kettle singing on the hearth, a pine bough brushing the roof, water dripping from a bamboo pipe into a stone basin outside. It is all designed as an experience in tranquillity and detachment, an appreciation of the simple, the old, the unpretentious and rustic expressed by two subtle Japanese words, *wabi* and *sabi*.

If the invaluable Bodhidharma's discarded eyelids led by devious routes to such long-sustained subtleties as those of the tea ceremony, it was supposedly the first of this great iconoclast's encounters with the Chinese Emperor Wu that helped to set the pattern for Zen's somewhat unorthodox approach to religious instruction. In the tale of this precedent-shattering interview one catches a glimpse of the kind of sharp, pithy exchange which was to characterize all Zen teacher-pupil relations for centuries.

At the time of Bodhidharma's arrival in China, so legend says, the Emperor, in residence at Nanking, was already a devout Buddhist of the orthodox kind, who had made many magnificent contributions to the Buddhist cause in his kingdom. Hoping, perhaps, to impress his renowned visitor, he invited him to the palace for a private audience and there proceeded to describe his good deeds in some detail. He spoke of the temples he had built in the Buddha's name, the many sacred scriptures he had ordered copied, the special privileges he had granted Buddhist monks and nuns. At the end of his recital, he ventured to inquire what degree of "merit," in Bodhidharma's opinion, all this had earned him. ("Merit" is a conventional Buddhist word implying, on the simplest level, the notion of reward on earth now or in another life.) Without a moment's hesitation, Bodhidharma replied bluntly, "No merit whatsoever." The astonished Emperor next inquired which among all the holy teachings of Buddhism was the most important, or, in other words, what did the learned sage consider the First Principle of Buddhism. "Vast Emptiness," replied Bodhidharma. Chagrined, nettled, but still curious, the Emperor then inquired, "Who are you who thus reply to me?" Bodhidharma's answer was "I do not know," and with that he took himself off, crossed the wide Yang-tze River upright on a floating reed, bound for his distant cave to sit down for a nine-year stint of meditation.

This account of Bodhidharma's conversation with the Chinese Emperor is not meant to suggest that Zen's First Patriarch was an ill-mannered lout who indulged in willful mystification. There was serious intention behind each of his replies—perhaps somewhat dramatically truncated during many centuries of word-of-mouth recounting. Most importantly, the story illustrates Zen's antipathy to lengthy verbalism. Also, in denying the possibility of merit for worldly deeds, Bodhidharma was not only forcibly rejecting the "doctrine of works"; he was also suggesting—without directly saying so—

that overattention to forms and rituals, intensive perusal of scholarly scriptures, would never bring "liberation." The real pursuit should lie in the direction of disciplined meditation leading to the goal of self-knowledge.

As for the answer that "Vast Emptiness" was Buddhism's First Principle, he appears here to be simply stressing the doctrine of the nondualistic eternal Void from which all life emerges and which, in Zen terms, must be personally experienced in order to grasp life's true meaning and significance. This idea of emptiness is a receptive rather than a negative concept in Zen. A part of Zen training in its early stages stresses "Empty the mind." Sometimes the aspirant is advised to "take as thought the thought of No-thought." Or again, it may be suggested that he not seek so hard after the truth but simply begin by "ceasing to cherish opinions." This latter point is illustrated in an anecdote about an old Tea Master who was asked by a learned professor to explain Zen to him. The Tea Master invited his intellectual acquaintance to tea, and as he served it, he deliberately kept on pouring from the pot until the tea ran over and the discomfited guest exclaimed aloud, "Sir, my cup is too full." "Just so," said the old Master, putting down the pot at once. "But how can I give you my tea unless you first empty your overfull cup?"

As for Bodhidharma's last reply to the Emperor—here one must tread carefully in the tricky field of explanation of which Zen is notoriously wary. Might it be said that he was simply employing an obliquity to avoid mouthing a lot of high-sounding words to the effect that in the vast Oneness of the universe there was truly no separate self or ego—a basic Zen concept as it is also a classic Buddhist concept? Or did he mean to indicate by his terse "I do not know" that "who" he was was essentially not an idea conveyable in ordinary conversation? One is warned, however, that his remark was a "plain fact stated in plain language." Yet it is perhaps worth noting that solving the meaning of Bodhidharma's third reply to the Chinese Emperor is one of the so-called koans—special conundrums—which play such a part in Zen training.

Bodhidharma's particular style—challenging the Emperor's curiosity rather than satisfying it—has remained Zen's style. It seems either to violently exasperate Western people or to mysteriously attract them. Whatever the reaction to its methods, Zen goes its ancient Bodhidharma way, a way that essentially reflects the attitude of the historic Indian Buddha, who may have handled his teaching with more *politesse*—as proper to a man born a prince—but who was equally uncompromising about getting involved in a long drawn-out discussion on subjects that could not, by their very nature, ever lend themselves to solution in words. When questioned about life's "meaning," about "the reality of the Self," about the "origins of the universe" or "the nature of Nirvana" (release), the Buddha maintained a "noble silence." This is also Zen's way. Such questions are considered essentially irrelevant to the problem of attaining spiritual freedom. Something more is involved in reaching the state of liberation than an exercise of the forebrain or one's wits. Intellectual curiosity, so Zen would say, is all very well in itself but it bears no promise of final release from the pressures and problems created by the restless, ever unsatisfied human ego. The most brilliant verbalism, no matter how seemingly irrefutable, cannot answer the fundamental human questions—Who? What? Why?—any more than ideas about water can quench a thirst or words about food satisfy the pangs of hunger. Reason, it is all too plain, can be used to refute itself, and one theory simply leads to another, on and on without end. A final "answer," real "peace of mind," cannot be reached by way of argument or any so-called facts.

Zen would not, however, substitute blind faith for intellection. It has other methods—time-tested and allegedly reliable—to force a student beyond the dualistic and dialectic pattern of ordinary thought processes. Zen's use of seemingly nonsensical replies to big questions is not haphazard, perverse or meaningless; it arises out of a long and honorable training tradition. Such non-sequitur answers, for example, to the question "What is the Buddha Mind?"—"The dirt-scraper in the courtyard" or "Three pounds of flax" (there are literally dozens of similar replies)—have a definite intention. Apparently such ridiculous irrelevancies are intended to focus attention on the truth that explanations "in words," or phrases explaining "meaning," are properties of thought and language, not of actuality. Zen claims that by effectively weakening the familiar involvement in a series of distinctions, discriminations and differences it can bring about a grasp of Reality; Reality being a condition transcending all opposites since it is by its very nature a "totality." The Zen acolyte is not being trained in analysis, rebuttal, or any other form of oratory or intellectual exchange. Instead he is being pushed relentlessly toward a personal *experience*, toward an illuminating *realization* of the unity of all life, the Is-ness, or Such-ness, of existence itself.

There are two chief schools of Zen teaching extant in Japan today—the Rinzai School, known as the "sudden" school and the Soto or "gradual" school. It is the former which has attracted more Western attention, not alone because of the extensive efforts of Dr. Suzuki, himself a Rinzai exponent, but also because of Rinzai's unorthodox methods, its use of the koan, that Lewis Carroll kind of riddle on which a Zen aspirant is asked to concentrate as a step toward the breakthrough into the enlightenment (satori) he is seeking. The Soto, or "gradual," school aims at the same ends as the Rinzai but proceeds somewhat differently. Soto stresses "quiet sitting," the practice of "observing one's mind in tranquility." It avoids the shock methods of Rinzai, the cries and thwacks with a stick to focus the beginner's attention. Both schools are concerned with gaining liberation from tension and conflict, with achieving peace in life, though not in any passive sense, rather with an increased—yet thoroughly relaxed—dynamism.

Heinrich Dumoulin, the Jesuit scholar who has lived and studied in Japan since 1935, says of these two main streams of Zen which were so successfully transplanted to Japan:

> "In the Rinzai sect we find the dynamic character of the daring *koan* experiment and of lightninglike enlightenment, while the Soto School is characterized by a preference for silent sitting in *zazen* and the quiet deeds of everyday life. . . . It appears [in Japan] . . . that adherence to one sect or the other is determined largely by the spiritual bent of the monks, who are inherently suited to one tradition or the other and pursue enlightenment in a way appropriate to their character. Thus one can find in the temples of the Soto sect men of brilliant wit and dynamic character who devote themselves to the *koan* exercises, while on the other hand certain Rinzai monks of subdued character can scarcely be distinguished from Soto disciples."

In relation to the word "sudden" as applied to Rinzai Zen's enlightenment, the notion of an abrupt breakthrough should not be taken to mean that without long and intense periods of concentrated and directed effort this result can come about. "Inwardness" must be unremittingly cultivated and practiced and the consciousness prepared by certain techniques—like the koan—carefully devised to throw the mind off its familiar track, out of its familiar habits of classifying, dividing, comparing this with that. An old Zen saying—one of the vivid images in which Zen abounds—makes its point about the difficulty of attaining true satori: To solve the riddle of existence requires from a man the kind of effort involved "in a mosquito trying to bite a bar of iron."

Yet the riddle can be solved, says Zen. Humanity's direct intuitional faculties, too often ignored or misunderstood, must be brought into meaningful play. Intuitive wisdom, inherent in all men, *can* be awakened and used. Zen case histories, both ancient and modern, appear to testify to the fact that the satori experience does, indeed, bring about a sort of "Copernican transformation," to borrow an apt phrase, in which the seeker is freed of the conviction that he is the master of the universe; he transcends, at first momentarily, but, with practice, permanently, the perpetual bifurcation of experience into subject and object, good and bad, mine and yours, and so on. In time he apprehends the truth—in Zen terms—that God, man and the universe are One, an indissoluble totality which only man's misdirected mind has split into seeming fragments. Once he has reached this place of profound understanding, there follows automatic release from the crippling restrictions of egocentrism and, with it, freedom from selfishness and greed. Here is the true source of compassion and love, for the awakened man can and will help his brother not because he is his "keeper" but because he has discovered that he *is* his brother.

This Zen teaching of the interdependence and oneness of all life is known in the Zen vocabulary as the *jiji muge hokkai*. It is, says Ruth Sasaki, the "realization that everything in the universe is constantly and continuously, freely and harmoniously interpenetrating, interconverting itself with every other thing. It is the realization of the universe as the expression of the eternal self-creating play of the Absolute. Thus experienced, the universe is seen to be one in time and one in space, or, rather, to be timeless and spaceless."

Although, as already noted, in the Zen view, human beings possess a temporary individuality, this temporary limited individuality is not a "true" self or any man's "real" self. To discover the true self, to get rid of the limiting and excessively dominant ego, and to learn to live in the Now, all schools of Zen employ techniques of individual and group meditation. In the Soto School the main emphasis falls on what is described as "sitting with a single mind" or "sitting just to sit." It should not be implied that this is the same thing as sitting in an ordinary, lethargic repose. The Zen sitter must remain "aware"; must, indeed, learn to cultivate the "mirrorlike awareness" that can alone lead him in due course to his goal: "becoming concentrated *but not in thought*."

Until a Soto Zen pupil has tried sitting "with a single mind," it may seem nothing at all, but once he has begun to practice, he soon discovers that he is the victim of constant compulsions rising from uncontrolled nervous and mental energy; the prey of formless apprehensions, of the seeming necessity to think *about* things all the time and to keep in restless movement. Before long it becomes clear that much of his ordinary daily activity, which has seemed so necessary and even useful, is actually a form of escape mechanism unconsciously devised to avoid facing basic problems and basic questions. Disciplined "sitting"—as taught today by Zen-oriented psychologists like Dr. Kondo of Tokyo—prevents the sitter from following habitual avenues of escape. In time—after inevitable periods of frustration and even perhaps increased restlessness—the sitter's scattered psychic energy is mysteriously re-collected into a more compact and directed unity. This new charge of psychic energy brings with it an unexpected feeling of completeness and fullness. The sitter, his mind no longer "separate" from the rest of his being and arrogantly trying to run the whole show, begins to feel in serene harmony with life, and, for the first time, *fully alive.* He is now in touch with what Zen would call "Such-ness" or "the Is-ness of the Is"—a state-of-being suggested by two brief Zen poems:

> *Sitting quietly, doing nothing,*
> *Spring comes and the grass grows by itself.*

> *In the landscape of spring . . .*
> *The flowering branches grow naturally*
> *Some long, some short.*

Neither poem is meant to suggest a mere passive acceptance but rather a dynamic realization of the great unified harmony that underlies all the phenomena of existence.

The original founder of the Soto School was Dogen, a Japanese scholar and mystic, who brought back from China in 1227 the Chinese Ch'an method of "sitting." Dogen, who was a philosophic genius as well as a teacher of what might be called yoga procedures—practices related to posture and breathing—wrote penetratingly on the troublesome subject of time. Since time in Dogen's teaching was located "here in this very body," it was by way of the body, through the right kind of meditation, that one could experience a rewarding and illuminating timelessness. "Live in the moment" was Dogen's advice; for in actuality there is only the Present, the Past is gone forever, the Future may never arrive. He was also concerned with bringing his followers to an understanding of the relativity of time and movement:

"If we watch the shore while we are sailing in a boat, we feel that the shore is moving. But if we look nearer to the boat itself, we know then that it is the boat that moves."

THE ART OF ZEN

The art of Zen—rooted in certain subtleties of Buddhist thought, nourished by the aesthetic canons of Southern Sung China (see text, page 143)—possesses rather special qualities. There is, first of all, little in the art of Zen (Ch'an in Chinese) that suggests "religion" in the accepted sense of the word, although many of its greatest painters were also Zen monks and Zen followers. Certain characteristics are easily discernible once the eye has been prepared to see them. Such general attributes as simplicity, seeming artlessness, inwardness, emptiness, suggestibility, deliberate incompleteness, are given expression by way of more specific techniques, which include economy of brush stroke (the so-called "thrifty brush"); the use of a "one-corner style" with empty space treated as something more meaningful than merely an interval between objects; a free-swinging "flung ink" style. Zen art of the first rank tells us that the artist has grasped life from within rather than from without. Any seemingly insignificant thing—a bird on a bough, a blossoming branch, a weed heavy with snow—can express life's totality and even, without preaching, make an evocative suggestion. "It takes only one blade of grass to show the wind's direction." It would be a mistake to infer that the often apparently careless, swift use of the special ink (sumi) that Zen painters preferred in their work indicates absence of discipline. Zen artists, like many of the mystic painters of old China, gave themselves over to an almost will-less intuition in the actual act of painting—almost as if the brush moved of itself—but this freedom came only after long and arduous training.

The few paintings included here which do not represent the work of avowed Zenists as such were chosen because they suggest something of what might be termed the "Zen mood," and indicate the profound influence of the Zen philosophy and the "Zen eye" on Chinese and Japanese art in general.

A monumental painting by one of the greatest of all Japanese artists, the 15th-century painter-monk Sesshu. The painting tells a story—generally accepted as apocryphal—about the monk Hui-k'o who came for instruction to the Indian missionary teacher Bodhidharma (known in Japan as Daruma). It was Bodhidharma who had brought to China in the 6th century A.D. that unconventional, dynamic, religious philosophy, founded on Buddha's original teachings, which was to become Zen. Legend says that Bodhidharma, after a notable dialogue with the Chinese Emperor (see text, page 153), left the haunts of men and took up solitary residence in a cave where he meditated for nine years. In Sesshu's painting the aspirant monk (destined in due course to become the Zen Master Hui-k'o, in Japanese, Eko), having failed to interest Bodhidharma in verbal expressions of his earnest desire to attain enlightenment, has gone so far as to cut off one arm and present it to the Great Teacher as proof of his invincible will to find the path to enlightenment. The fierce challenging eye of Bodhidharma is echoed in the "eyes" of the cave's rocky wall and the anxious, agonized eye of the would-be disciple. The whole composition is permeated with the explosive vitality and disciplined containment of the Zen "way."

92

Over and over again, with consummate
subtlety, Chinese and Japanese artists have
painted the scene of friends—sages or
scholars—seated together in a lonely, wild
or rustic setting, conversing, listening to
music or sharing their unspoken thoughts,
hearing what was called the "stringless
lute"—meaningful silence—as in (92) *Two
Sages Under a Spreading Plum Tree,* Ma
Yuan, late 12th–early 13th centuries. Of
the two seated figures in this famous painting in the Boston Museum of Fine Arts,
James Cahill has written: "like a pair of
parentheses enclosing nothing, but expressing a perfect accord between the two." The

93

94

suggestion of man inspired and revitalized
by nature is another constant theme, as in
(93) *Man on a Terrace Viewing the Moon,*
attributed to Ma Lin, early 13th century,
Sung, but probably 14th century, anonymous, and (94) *Nobleman on a Stag Viewing Autumn Foliage,* Ma Lin.

Gifted Chinese and Japanese painters of
the past seemed never to tire of the theme
of man in contemplative mood alone with
nature. Sometimes the figure is shown in a
rustic hut or lonely pavilion built for meditation, sometimes standing on a terrace
gazing at a moon or seated beside a waterfall "forever different yet forever the same."
Again, at ease in an open boat a man gazes
quietly into the water or into the depths of
a space which is at once both "within and
without." (95) *Man Alone in an Open
Boat,* attributed to Ma Yuan, late 12th–
early 13th centuries, but probably an
anonymous later artist. (96) *Chou Muo-
shu Admiring the Lotus Flowers,* by Kano
Masanobu, 1434–1530 A.D.

96

95

97

98

In ink-monochrome landscape painting the aim was not accurate representation but poetic suggestion, the creation of an inward mood and of a special kind of aware silence which was to reflect itself also in the brief evocative Japanese haiku:

> In the dark forest
> A berry drops;
> The sound of water.

Poetry and painting were often linked together with poems painted directly on the scroll itself as in (97) *Landscape* by Sesshu, 1420–1506, done in the Zen "flung ink" or *haboku* style. The first lines of Arthur Waley's translation read:

> The dying remnants of the mountain mist lie across the hillside.
> Nature seems to present us with a ready-made poem.

Magically simple landscapes in wash, often veiled in mist, suggest abstraction and immensity and serve to refresh the viewer by momentarily lifting him away from the turbulence of daily life, as in (98) *Landscape* by Soami (d. 1525).

99

1478–1523 A.D.). (99) *Mountain Landscape in Moonlight with Man on a Bridge:* unsigned but attributed to either Kano Motonobu or Soami. Again there comes to mind one of those brief, evocative, seventeen-syllable Japanese poems:

> *I walk over it alone,*
> *In the cold moonlight;*
> *The sound of the bridge.*

100

The idea of man as the conqueror and master of nature is not a typically Far Eastern idea. Chinese and Japanese painters were prone to depict man "at one" with the mysterious forces of the universe. Landscape was not used as a mere backdrop for a portrait of a man's head and shoulders as in Western Renaissance art, for instance. Instead, the viewer has often to strain his eyes to see the tiny human figures going their indomitable way through a vast terrain of towering peaks and cliffs, lonely, misty valleys and rushing rivers. (100) *Spring Landscape* by Keishoki (active

The so-called "one-corner style"—or the convention of leaving the important central space unoccupied, perhaps with only a bird in flight or a frail branch to break the emptiness —released the imagination and served to quiet and still the mind. (101) *Swallows and Willow Tree,* Sung dynasty, by Mao I, 1165 A.D. Many deliberately brief and stripped poems strove for a similar effect:

> *The sea darkens,*
> *The voices of the wild ducks*
> *Are faintly white.*

(102) While the "storm dragon"— mistily suggested—occupies the central space in this painting, a simple little country man steps forth briskly, even jauntily, over a rickety bridge above a roaring torrent, his small self a related part of a great visible and invisible "totality." By Kano Tannyu (1602–1674).

101

102

103

104

The idea of the meaningfulness of empty space, that fruitful void or *shunyata* of the Buddhists, was carried over into the designs of Japanese interiors, the architecture of tea rooms, the planning of gardens. (103) Traditional interiors, as in this typical guest room, are never cluttered. The prescribed alcove or *tokonoma* will contain only a single hanging scroll—painting, calligraphy, a poem—and a single flower arrangement. (104) Entrance to a private tea room where the classic tea ceremony takes place. (105) The famous 15th-century Zen garden of Ryoanji depends for its charm merely on a walled rectangle of finely raked white sand and fifteen carefully placed dark rocks of different sizes and shapes: a type of abstraction in art to which the West was to come 500 years later.

105

106

107

Chinese and Japanese painters who had subjected themselves to specific spiritual and aesthetic disciplines were able to suggest, in themes drawn from nature, meanings that far exceeded the boundaries of mere representation. (106) *The Six Persimmons,* Mu Ch'i (Mokkei), 13th century A.D. An inspired example of the so-called "spontaneous style," a masterpiece of skilled brushwork in varied tones of blue-black ink, this famous Zen painting conveys a calm, compelling mystery, a vital reality or "truth" which goes well beyond a merely artful arrangement of six fruits in empty space. (107) The eternally green bamboo's combination of yieldingness and stubborn strength, the living "emptiness" of the hollow stalk, can convey messages to those who, through sympathetic participation, know how to read the subtle code. Sengai, Zen priest and painter (1750–1837). (108) Drooping plants, by their delicate nonresistance, easily shed snowy burdens. Artist unknown.

108

109

Han-shan (in Japanese, Kanzan) and Shih-te (in Japanese, Jittoku) were two favorite human subjects of *sumiye* (ink painting) by Zen artists. Inseparable friends and good-humored nonconformists who found life, for the most part, a great joke, the former was a poet-recluse of the Chinese T'ang dynasty, the latter a "nameless" orphan of unknown parentage. Noted for their unconventional dress and behavior, they give eloquent expression to Zen's subtle messages about the folly of self-aggrandizement, over-organization of time and energy, earnestness devoid of humor. The blank unwritten scroll in Kanzan's hands, the broom for "sweeping clean" always held by Jittoku, also have their special Zen significance. In (109), a painting by the 16th-century Kaihoku Yusho, the two happy iconoclasts seem as related to the "invisible rhythm of the universe" as the deer in (110): a celebrated early 17th-century work by Nonomura Sotatsu.

110

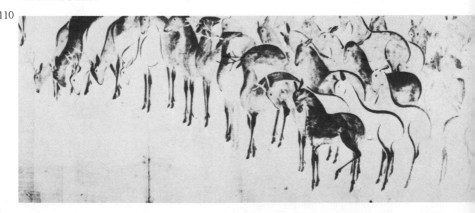

111

112

With unparalleled economy of brushwork,
painters revealed the varying characteristics of birds. (111) *Heron and King-
fisher,* attributed to Shokei, Muromachi
period after 1500. (112) *An Old Shrike
on a Leafless Tree,* attributed to Mu Ch'i
(Mokkei), late 13th century, evokes autumn's indrawn mood and reminds one of
a famous haiku by the poet Basho:

> *On a bare bough*
> *An old crow—*
> *This autumn eve.*

113

Their special way of "entering into the spirit" of whatever subject they were painting made it possible for the gifted artists of China and Japan to capture (114) the very tigerishness of the tiger (here said to be scowling at the rain), Mu Ch'i (Mokkei), late 13th century, and the monkey-ishness of monkeys (113), Morikage, 17th century. Many famous monkey pictures were painted in the centuries before Morikage by Mu Ch'i, Sesshu, Sosan and others, but the Morikage seems to illustrate rather aptly (although it was not necessarily the artist's intention) certain Zen teachings about "the moon in the water." The moon remains the same, no matter what waters reflect it or what eyes respond to it. Neither moon nor water plans the "happening" of reflection; both are in that state of receptive "no-mind-ness" which Zenists strive to attain.

114

Two paintings which, although done in different painting styles, illustrate a similarly daring use of space. (115) *The Zen Priest Choka, Seated High in a Tree* (also identified as *The Priest Lin-chi Seated in a Bird's Nest*), Nonomura Sotatsu, 1576–1643 A.D. Of this illustration of a Chinese anecdote, painted by a gifted Japanese Zen artist in an extreme assymetrical style, Sherman Lee has remarked: "Of few paintings can it be more truly said that one's praises are for what is not there." (116) *Heron in a Tree,* Kano Tsunenobu, 1636–1713 A.D. Although not

115

116

a practitioner of pure Zen styles, Tsunenobu, like his uncle Kano Tannyu who trained him (see plate 102), made use of themes and subjects from earlier Chinese and Japanese periods. Birds and trees as subject matter have appealed to many generations of Japanese artists. They often appear to reflect the mood of the classic poem:

An old pine tree preaches wisdom,
And a wild bird is crying out Truth.

Bodhidharma, Zen's first Patriarch, floating on a reed leaf on a wide expanse of water
—whatever his destination (and there are several versions)—provided many Zen
artists of China and Japan with a superb opportunity to express Zen's supreme faith
in life as embodied in the calm figure giving himself up to the unknown and unpredictable while yet remaining his own master. (117) *Bodhidharma Crossing the
Yangtze on a Reed,* China, Yuan dynasty, 1280–1368. (118) *An Early Zen Patriarch
Tearing Up a Scroll of Scripture,* a great painter's treatment of a famed episode in
Zen's annals, expressing Zen's viewpoint that direct experience, rather than canonical
dogma, is the way to enlightenment. Liang Kai, early 13th century.

117

118

119

(119) and (120) Two Zen masters in "composed states of mind," one resting on a tiger who appears to share the master's mood of quiet absorption. Both attributed to Shi-k'o (in Japanese, Sekkaku), 10th century. Two particularly fine examples of the effectiveness of free-sweeping brush strokes in the hand of a master. The physical poses, the presence in one picture of a subdued tiger, indicate that this "meditation" is in reality an intense looking into the very nature of things, a comprehension of life's "suchness" or the "Is-ness of the Is."

120

121   122

(121) A famous Zen painting of Hotei (in Chinese, Pu-tai) the Chinese-Japanese god of good fortune, here seen studying, with supreme detachment, two fighting cocks. The artist, Miyamoto Musashi (1584?–1645 A.D.), was a famed swordsman as well as a student of Zen. Daisetz Suzuki asks: "Was he, the artist, in the role of Hotei observing the fighting techniques of embattled birds (from which he might presumably learn something practical) or was he philosophically contemplating the Zen teaching about the void in which there is no killing, no killer, no killed." (122) A notable 15th-century portrait (part of a triptych painted by Soga Jasoku) of an actual historical 9th-century Zen Master, Tokusan, here shown waiting—with brilliantly expressed concentration and energy—to use his stick, if necessary, on a backward neophyte. Of this painting the French scholar and art critic René Grousset has said: "One of the profoundest portraits of a thinker produced by the art of all time, and worthy of the Descartes by Frans Hals."

123

124

The circle—symbolic of fulfillment—is often left by
Zen artists suggestively half-finished, not unlike the
appearance of the sun itself in this 19th-century painting (123) of *Sun and Waves* by Hashimoto Gaho
(1835–1908). Calligraphy is considered an art form
in both China and Japan. Zen artists played as freely
with formal script as Western abstract painters were
later to play with objects. Sengai's painting (124)
reads: "When your desires are few, your mind is
naturally tranquil."

Similarly, he said, we get the notion that our mind is constant and the universe moving around us. Actually nothing could be less fixed or constant or "there" than our minds; a truth we shall soon discover, asserted Dogen, when we pass through the difficulties—and the final rewards—of getting our random thoughts under firm control.

The Rinzai, or koan-method, School of Zen was brought to Japan from China somewhat earlier than the Soto, having been introduced by the famous Japanese Master Eisai (1141–1215)—said to be also responsible for introducing the tea cult to his homeland. Although Rinzai Zen, like Soto Zen, as already indicated, uses both individual and group meditation (zazen), Rinzai further emphasizes a formal personal interview (sanzen) between master and individual pupil during which the latter is asked to answer the koan on which he is working in such a manner that the roshi (teacher) knows he has grasped its essential point.

The word koan originated in a Chinese legal term, kung-an, referring to any case where decision had become a precedent for subsequent cases of a similar nature. (This idea of precedence is not without significance, even though it does seem to violate—in Zen's often paradoxical manner—the stress Zen lays on spontaneity.) Koans are used as a means of opening up the student's intuitive mind and as tests of the depth to which it has been opened. They have been described by Alan Watts as a kind of "spiritual dynamite," and although their irrational wording makes them unsolvable by use of the reasoning process, they do have a meaning within the context of a special type of Zen meditation known as kufu and are soluble in these terms.

Zen would freely admit that it is impossible to explain koans, for they have all been designed precisely to prevent "thinking about." They are intended to circumvent logic, analysis, all ratiocination; to create a true mental impasse, a state of sustained tension out of which there should eventually come, with proper instruction and perseverance, an illumination sudden as a flash of lightning. Here the student has reached the same level of intuitive understanding from which the master first spoke the koan to him. Since each koan has, in a sense, a "classic" answer, a student will finally bring to his master an answer that will approximate that of all the Zenists who have solved the same koan in the past. So close, so intimate and total, is the true relationship between instructor and pupil, however, that the easy parroting of one of these solutions would never for a moment deceive a master. "Awakening," in Zen terms, could hardly take place without reactions and responses that go far beyond merely correct phraseology. Similarly, ever since Buddha's wordless communication with Kashyapa over the golden flower, "intuitive transmission" has been a valid Buddhist method of ascertaining truth. Zen would hold that explanatory words too often merely hold us to the world of "multiplicity and relations," whereas Zen is in pursuit of an experience which cannot be stated in intellectual terms. Words are, finally, only noises standing for things, and enlightenment is much more than a collection of so many letters or symbols.

Koans, of which there are said to be some seventeen hundred in existence (though only a small number of these are used today), reveal very little to the uninitiated:

> What was your original face—the one you had before your parents gave birth to you?

> You can make the sound of two hands clapping. Now what is the sound of one hand?

> What is that which makes you answer when you are called?

The problem often presented to a Zen beginner is the famous koan known as "Joshu's Mu." Joshu, a Chinese Zen master who lived in the late eighth and early ninth centuries, was once asked by a young monk whether the Buddha nature was also in a dog. (According to Zen the Buddha nature is in all things.) In replying, Joshu said simply *"Mu,"* the equivalent of "No." He said the word, however, in a manner which indicated that he refused to answer the question. The implication here is that had he affirmed or denied, his reply would have been equally false, for this would have been to admit to discrimination, and the Absolute, "which is above all opposites and classes," cannot be expressed through either Yes or No, but can only be directly "experienced."

In *The Pilgrimage of Buddhism*, written some years before Zen became a commonplace topic in the West, its author, J. B. Pratt, tells how one of his Japanese students at Williams College, an enthusiastic Zen follower, worked on the Mu koan for several years and felt that he had gained not only a deepened understanding of life's meaning but new powers of self-control. Another of Pratt's Japanese students at Williams worked on "the sound of one hand" koan. He felt he had not satisfactorily solved "listening for the voice of one hand," but Pratt—who had become interested in the koan technique—did meet a young Japanese lieutenant, traveling in America, who had heard this "soundless sound" which has its origin in a personal realization of "the nature of the One, the Absolute." (The point behind this koan would seem to be that two hands make a sound *in relation to one another*. In the Absolute there are, however, no relations and no distinctions. The "sound of one hand" koan is therefore merely one of the many ways of bringing the pupil to Zen's goal, the essential final realization of life's oneness.)

Sometimes old Zen stories have a connotation reminiscent of the surrealists and even the dadaists who, after World War I, set out to bring about "a general and emphatic crisis in Western consciousness." This they attempted by a number of unusual devices. In painting they played the game of *trompe l'oeil;* on their canvases one frequently finds two or more objects presented as one. Dali's early painting of his old nurse—a familiar example —shows her spine as a crutch-propped aperture through which one gets a glimpse of sea and sand. In writing as well as painting the Dadaists delighted in unlikely juxtapositions of images and ideas: "the cave bear and the lout his companion, the *vol-au-vent* and the wind his valet, the cannibal and his brother the carnival, the Mississippi and its little dog" or the often-quoted "beautiful as the chance meeting on a dissecting table of a sewing machine and an umbrella."

At dadaist gatherings in Switzerland and France, speakers would sometimes sit in silence, or ring bells, or "make poetry" by poking holes through bits of paper. In Zen—where, to be sure, the motivations were of a somewhat different order—there are many stories like that of a Chinese Master who was asked to preach a sermon on Bodhidharma. "Ring the bell for assembly," he said. The bell was rung. The pupils gathered. The Master went up to the teaching platform and descended immediately without a word. When asked to describe the Buddha nature, another Master answered, "I know how to play the drum, dong-do-ko-dong"; and the great Joshu—he of the famous "Mu"—when asked "All things return to the One, but whither does the One return?" replied with some facts about the weight of a certain robe he had once possessed. Many lines from the famous group of French dadaist and surrealist revolutionaries—Éluard, Breton, Aragon, Tzara—have a curiously Zen ring. Among Éluard's *Proverbs* one reads:

A crab by any other name would not forget the sea.

Who hears but me hears all.

I came, I sat, I departed.

In Zen sayings one finds:

When Tom drinks, Dick gets tipsy.

Last night a wooden horse neighed and a stone man cut a caper.

A certain monk asked Hyakujo "What is truth?" Hyakujo said, "Here I sit on Daiyu Peak."

Yet one must take care not to press too far any comparison of dadaist or surrealist behavior with that of Zen, for their aims are widely divergent. This is particularly true when one compares Zen's goal of an active yet reflective serenity with surrealism's aggressive, often dogmatic pursuit of the irrational for its own sake. Zen's zany give-and-take strikes many Westerners as utterly, if inexplicably, comic and appealing, though the average response on a first encounter is apt to be the inquiry, sometimes with what would appear to be justifiable peevishness, "But why can't they just *say* what they mean?" To this question the only possible answer is "That is not the Zen way."

On the whole, the problems with which an aspiring Zenist is asked to struggle are not too bewildering if time is taken to absorb them quietly:

> *The cherry tree blooms each year*
> *in the Yoshino mountains.*
> *But split the tree and tell me*
> *where the flowers are.*

Or lines from another Japanese poem:

> *Now I know my true being has nothing to do*
> *with birth and death.*

Here a few hints might even be provided by a teacher: "Zen, it is asserted, has the aim of enabling you to see directly into your own nature. Very well, where is your true nature? Can you locate it? If you can locate it, you are then said to be free of birth and death. All right, you have become a corpse. Are you free of birth and death? Now do you know where you are? . . . Now your body has separated into its four basic elements. Where are *you* now?"

In attempting the solution of a Zen conundrum, the aspirant is advised to remember that he is "not to think about it, but just *to gaze at it closely.*" This type of attention immediately involves, in a physical way, parts of the body other than the brain. In fact, in practicing such an exercise the pupil becomes conscious of an active center of awareness in a section of the body just below the navel. Specific types of training emphasize the importance of this "field of the elixir of life," as the Chinese called it. Known in Japanese as *tanden,* this part of the physical organism is a central point of concentration in meditation exercises. (The Japanese have a little doll called a Daruma doll which is weighted in the abdomen; when knocked over, it bounces straight back. An American, visiting a Zen monastery, was once presented with two small legless dolls, one weighted, like Daruma, in the abdomen, the other weighted in the head. The latter when knocked over remained down; the other bounced back. Laughing heartily, the old abbot used the two dolls as illustration of the dangers of the Westerner's "top-heavy equipment.")

Zen might be said to offer something in the nature of a return to the simple and direct view of life possible to a child, because children, like "the enlightened," live wholly in the present. The awakened individual is said to experience a total, intense participation, free of self-consciousness and of all anxiety. He is spontaneous, fluid and adaptable, like the butterfly in another Zen poem, who "with every gust of wind lightly shifts his place on the willow."

In time, says Ruth Sasaki in *Zen, a Religion,* when Zen teachings have been thoroughly digested and assimilated, "there drops away the necessity to think about the philosophic or religious implications of our activities. Naturally and spontaneously we respond to the moment. Without thinking about anything we *naturally* act. This is the 'freedom' of Zen. This is also what is known as 'having nothing in mind and no mind in things.' This is the ultimate in the Zen way of life. It is only then we may say . . . 'The everyday mind is the Tao.' "

Long ago this same viewpoint was expressed in a favorite Zen saying: "Before you study Zen, mountains are mountains and rivers are rivers; while you are studying Zen, mountains are no longer mountains and rivers are no longer rivers; but once you have had enlightenment, mountains are once again mountains and rivers again rivers."

The universe is the same; only the perspective has altered.

The Zen concept of Emptiness, already touched on in Bodhidharma's rather cheeky bit of dialogue with the Chinese Emperor, is one of the most important points to grasp about Zen teaching. The theme is rehearsed daily in an ancient morning chant of Zen monks that carries a curious suggestion of certain contemporary scientific views: "Form is here emptiness, emptiness is form; form is none other than emptiness; emptiness is none other than form; what is form that is emptiness, what is emptiness that is form."

The Zen teaching that Emptiness, or the Void, is in no way "lacking" but is, indeed, equal to fullness when properly understood has played a significant part in the development of certain important canons of Far Eastern art. In old Chinese and Japanese painting, one sees space treated as a value in itself, not merely as something to be arbitrarily filled. In fact, many Westerners have found an opening into at least the outskirts of the Zen viewpoint by coming to understand and appreciate the intentions of certain Asian masters of the brush whose deceptively simple yet magic effects were produced not only by a rare skill in the manipulation of the tools of their trade, but were also an outgrowth of specific meditation on such concepts as the Oneness of all life, the significance of the Eternal Now, the relationship between Emptiness and the "ten thousand things"—of which man is only one, and by no means the arrogant master of all he surveys. Over and over again in these paintings one sees the human figure presented relatively small and frail, but never with any hint of sentimentality or pathos, as it goes its solitary, indomitable way in a vast landscape. A man may be shown viewing a moonrise; meditating beside some waterfall—"forever different yet forever the same"; playing a flute on a lonely mountaintop; standing with his *back* significantly presented to the spectator, his robes wildly blown by an autumn wind; laughing in glee—like those two joyful lunatic hermits Han-shan (Kanzan) and Shih-te (Jittoku)—at the sight of leaves falling, roosters fighting, birds nesting or any other ordinary, little-appreciated marvels of the Eternal Is-ness.

In these classic paintings each artist was motivated by his own personal awareness of that invisible rhythm which, in the ancient teachings of the Far East, moves through all life binding it together in a single harmonious totality. In the greatest days of Chinese and Japanese art, a young painter would be enjoined by his instructor: "Study and draw bamboo for ten years until you become a bamboo; forget all about copying bamboo, however, when you finally come to paint it."

The implication of such a suggestion was that when at last the artist took up his brush he should be free of all thought of himself in the act of wielding the brush, as well as any intention of exactly reproducing the bamboo. He should, instead, be capable of projecting onto the silk surface with a swift, assured immediacy the essential inner spirit of the plant. He should paint a forest "as it would appear to the trees themselves" and by overcoming man's basic anthropocentrism capture the very "tigerishness of the tiger." If he painted fruit, the artist was not to be concerned with creating a realism so intense that the viewer would be tempted to put out his hand to touch the flesh of the peach or plum; his concern should be rather to capture a moment in a process, one stage in an invisible chain of growth: seed, bud, flower, fruit. These almost unimaginably subtle aesthetic canons were natural outgrowths of the Zen Buddhist and related Taoist concepts, and their attainment was made possible only by the fact that artists practiced contemplation and understood the true meaning of subjectivity.

In the famous abstract gardens of Japan, one sees how their Zen-inspired creators, working only with stones of various sizes and shapes and surfaces of raked sand, expressed novel ideas about form and space to which Western abstractionist painters were to come many centuries later. (This is particularly well exemplified in the famous garden at Ryoanji.) As already indicated, the canons of the classic medieval No drama which have appealed so deeply to many Westerners (Yeats, Pound, Waley, Shaw, Claudel), and even a great part of the underlying ideology of the popular Kabuki theater, also find their sources in Zen; while in the composition of poetry, notably in the stripped, evocative haiku, one finds over and over again typical Zen attributes of simplicity and subtlety, love of nature and, very often, that earthy, almost rough humor in which, unlike all other religious philosophies, Zen abounds.

It is when we come to Zen's lively humor that the suggested resemblance between this Eastern philosophy and Western existentialism abruptly breaks down. Existentialism (unlike surrealism or dadaism), from Kierkegaard through Sartre, has little to do with spontaneous laughter. Zen—concerned as it is with life's many-sided Is-ness—finds it impossible to ignore the often wry comedy of human existence. Favorite Zen stories celebrate the ridiculous and paradoxical nature of daily living. Zen even enjoys deflating the achievement of enlightenment itself.

The late R. H. Blyth, an Englishman who spent most of his life in the Far East, a former professor at the Peers' School in Tokyo and the author of some illuminating (though occasionally exasperating) books on Zen, has written brilliantly about Zen's humor. He says that when he first read Dr. Suzuki on the subject of the koan he laughed at every one that was quoted, and the less he understood the more he was amused, for just as there is no way to explain a joke, so there is no way to explain a koan, yet they do affect many people, on first reading, as does the nonsense poetry of Edmund Lear or Lewis Carroll. Also in Zen, along with the immediacy of spontaneous laughter, comes a strong feeling that some inexplicable meaning lurks behind the seeming nonsense. Blyth says of Zen's deliberate use of humor: "Laughter is breaking through the intellectual barrier; at the moment of laughter something is understood. It needs no proof of itself. . . . When we laugh we are free of all the oppression of our personality, of that of others and even of God who is laughed away. One who laughs is master of his fate and captain of his soul."

Zen's countless amusing anecdotes appear to spring in part from its reluctance to be caught in any self-conscious high thinking or religious pomposity. In speaking of his first instruction in a Zen temple, Blyth remarks on how much struck he was with the almost total absence of solemn exhortation. He was, at the outset of his training, given only two seemingly insignificant rules of behavior, which were, however, to be observed very strictly. One rule was that whenever someone called out "Oi!" the person who heard must answer "Hai!" without a moment's hesitation and with real gusto. Shortly he found himself waiting for that frequent ringing "Oi!" and to find in it, and the swift response, a "kind of joke." As soon as this happened he "began to see a light, or 'get warm' as children say."

To judge from innumerable humorous Zen anecdotes, a kind of transcendental laughter often accompanies the sudden flash of satori. One story might stand as a prototype of many similar examples:

A monk came to a Master for help in working on one of the classic questions in Zen dialectic: "What is the meaning of Bodhidharma's coming from the West?" The Master to whom the question was put suggested that before proceeding with the problem the inquiring monk should make him a low salaam. As he was dutifully prostrating himself, the Master gave the disciple a good swift kick. The teacher's unexpected Marx Brothers response resolved in one stroke the murky irresolution in which the monk had been floundering for some time. At the impact of the Master's foot he "attained immediate enlightenment." Subsequently he said to everyone he met, "Since I received that kick from Ma Tsu, I haven't been able to stop laughing."

Even death is considered perfectly suitable as a subject for funny stories in Zen's opinion. Particularly is this true of any undue concern with worldly nonessentials in the face of the seeming "finality" of drawing one's last breath. There is particular enjoyment if the story deals with a supposedly enlightened monk's death, as in the account of the manner of dying employed by a certain Chinese Zenist of the tenth century. Zen annals relate that the usual posture in which masters died in the past was in the attitude of zazen (meditation), suggesting that some Zen followers in those days were so evolved they knew (perhaps could even choose) their moment of departure. A certain aspiring monk wished not to die in any of the accustomed poses. He looked carefully into the various ways of dying—sitting in meditation, taking seven deliberate steps and expiring with the seventh, lying down peacefully on one side like the Buddha at the time of his voluntary demise—and discovered that no Master had yet died upside down. "Never have we seen such a thing," his fellow monks all assured him, so he proceeded to die standing on his head. Curious crowds came from all directions to witness this phenomenon. Their awed astonishment was so overwhelming that no one dared take him down and cart him off for cremation. Finally his sister, a Zen nun, appeared on the scene. She cast just one swift look at him and remarked, "When you were alive, you took no notice of laws and customs, and even now that you're dead you are making a perfect nuisance of yourself." She then gave her brother a good stiff poke with her forefinger, and when his body toppled over, she ordered it off to the burial ground without further delay.

Much of the credit for the current dissemination of Zen thought in the West belongs—as already mentioned—to the elderly Japanese scholar, Dr. D. T. Suzuki, who through his many books, his seminars at Columbia, Harvard and elsewhere, and the effect of his extraordinary personality, has turned a number of able minds to the study of this particular branch of Buddhism. Among the noted psychologists who have given Zen explicit study are Erich Fromm, Hubert Benoit and the late Carl G. Jung and Karen

Horney. A number of successful writers, painters, dancers and musicians—Aldous Huxley, Jack Kerouac, J. D. Salinger, Kenneth Tynan, William Barrett, Gary Snyder, Allen Ginsberg, Mark Tobey, Morris Graves, Robert Rauschenberg, John Cage, Merce Cunningham, Martha Graham, to name only the ones that come most readily to mind—have admitted to Zen influence on their thinking and in their creative work. Zen has found itself of recent years linked with such scholarly names and titles as Martin Heidegger, B. L. Whorf, Werner Heisenberg (the physicist responsible for the revolutionary "principle of indeterminacy" which has laid such a sobering restriction on man's notion of a controllable universe cut to his own pattern), and the General Semanticists stemming from Korzybski. Of particular relevance is the recent appearance of two books, written by eminent Roman Catholic scholars—one a Jesuit, Heinrich Dumoulin, already mentioned in these pages, the other a Benedictine, the Very Reverend Dom Aelred Graham, prior of the Benedictine Community and head of the Governing Body of the school in Portsmouth, Rhode Island. These books, designed for the general public, appraise with admirable balance Zen's possible significance to modern Westerners interested in a re-evaluation of their own religious viewpoints and activities. The title of Dom Graham's book, *Zen Catholicism,* with the subtitle *A Suggestion,* is particularly relevant.

Because Zen has become in the United States identified in the public mind with the rise of the so-called beats and a new Bohemian cultism, it might be well to mention again that no matter how startling, even bizarre, some of Zen's methods and manners appear to be, nonetheless Zen considers itself a direct extension of the original serene yet challenging teachings of Siddhartha Gautama, the historic Indian Buddha. The much publicized and perhaps overmaligned beats have been accused of lifting from Zen—out of context, one might say—certain elements of spontaneous, unconventional, even designedly irresponsible behavior. These somewhat one-sided Zen borrowings have supposedly lent support to the beats' determination not to live their personal lives according to socially acceptable national patterns. Drawing psychological support from the famous happy "have-nothing" followers of Zen's past who would certainly have greeted the affluent society with a hoot of hearty laughter, a new wave of young iconoclasts is firmly on record as wanting none of togetherness, backyard barbecues, installment-plan buying, gadget-gathering, designed obsolescence of consumer goods and a whole list of other concomitants of the "good life."

If it is true that some of the beats have manipulated to their own purposes, and as an excuse for social irresponsibility, childlike, anti-intellectual, even irrational elements of which Zen makes deliberate use, it must be acknowledged in all fairness that Zen emphasizes these qualities with quite other ends in view. It should also be noted that daily work is a main precept of the Zen life and has been ever since an eighth-century abbot formulated the strict rule "A day without work—a day without eating." If Zen monks still go forth formally in Japan to beg alms or their daily food, it is only as a reminder of the original Buddhist practice of renunciation of all physical possessions.

In conclusion, one could not perhaps do better than quote again from Dr. Suzuki:

> The world in which we live is an old world, yet we have not exhausted its contents, not only in larger things but in smaller things too. But we can never reach the end of our researches as long as we limit ourselves to the fields of sense and intellect. This is the very nature of the human constitution. . . . Yet strangely enough as soon as we quit the realm known as objectivity and turn *inward* and go in this direction with resolution and persistency, we finally come to a gate known as "the gate of all wonders." We enter it and find ourselves in the field of Emptiness where our being is firmly rooted. [This is the] treasure house behind the consciousness where all sorts of potentialities have been kept in imprisonment.

Whether Zen will penetrate any deeper into the West in the years ahead is anybody's guess. Those who have been affected by it so far have apparently been led to a reappraisal of the two main historic influences on the Occidental mind: the Greek and the Hebraic-Christian. They have come to question whether there may perhaps be another "free-er" way of looking at existence; not as in Greek dualism, where the "intellect" is set apart so distinctly from the "senses" and where "reality" is solely resident in "thought." And not, either, as in the Judaic-Christian dualism of God-versus-creature, that essentially tribal paternalistic pattern with its attendant burden of primordial guilt and its "eternally nagging conscience."

Critics of Zen point out that its presence in the culture of Japan seemed to do little to stem the tide of recent all-out imperialistic war. They also assert that young people in Japan today appear to be moving inexorably toward the most superficial and disheartening aspects of Western culture. This may not, however, necessarily indicate that Zen is dead in the land of its greatest achievement. Zen's roots are deep and very old. It appears to be a sturdy plant, still capable of bearing seeds. As a part of Mahayana Buddhism, it also represents more than two thousand years of periodic movement, transplantation, and adaptability. It seems likely that it will take more than the unregenerate military mind (the same the world over) or the blue-jeaned motorcycle and jazz buffs of postwar Japan, or even its espousal by American beats to undermine Zen permanently. In the words of an ancient poem:

> *When one looks at it, one cannot see it;*
> *When one listens for it, one cannot hear it.*
> *However, when one uses it, it is inexhaustible.*

ACKNOWLEDGMENTS

I am indebted in varying degree to a number of institutions and individuals who have given me specific help and/or psychological support during the five years in which I have worked on *Three Ways of Asian Wisdom*. I am most particularly grateful to Professor Joseph Campbell of Sarah Lawrence College, Dr. Amiya Chakravarty, now of Smith College, Gerald Heard of Santa Monica, Elizabeth Jay Hollins of New York City, and Ruth Fuller Sasaki of Kyoto for carefully reading the manuscript in its early stages and offering me invaluable suggestions and warm encouragement. I am specially indebted in this respect to Dr. Chakravarty who, two years ago, took time from his heavy teaching schedule at Boston University to discuss with me at some length certain subtle and frequently misinterpreted aspects of Hinduism.

I am grateful to the Asia Society of New York City, on whose board of directors I have served since its founding in 1956—an association which has helped to widen and deepen my already vital interest in Asia; to John D. Rockefeller III, the Society's founder, who invited me to become an active board member and thus, indirectly, led to my daring, some time later, to assume the responsibility of writing the present book; to all the members of the Society's diligent, dedicated and always helpful staff, and specifically to four officers of the Society: the Honorable Kenneth Young, former ambassador to Thailand and the Society's present President, Paul Sherbert, executive director of the India Council, both of whom opened to me many new avenues of participation and interest in Asian subjects; Gordon Washburn of the Asia House Gallery who was unfailingly kind and generous in making the Gallery's photographic files available, and Lionel Landry, the present executive director of the Society, who went over the galleys line by line and wrote me a rewarding letter that I shall always cherish. I also owe special thanks to the Bollingen Foundation of New York City for the gift down the years of its entire list of publications, many of which have been of inestimable help to me, and to John D. Barrett, Jr., president, and Vaun Gilmor for many courtesies.

I can never properly thank Nirmal J. Singh of the Indian Consulate who cheerfully went to endless trouble to procure photographs from the Indian Archaeological Survey—to which I now want also to offer my most sincere thanks for their generosity, and to Grace Morley of the Indian National Museum in New Delhi for her assistance in these transactions.

Alexander B. Griswold of Bangkok, Thailand and Monkton, Maryland, put at my disposal a number of photographs of the so-called "Walking Buddhas" from the Breezewood Foundation in Maryland. For this I formally thank him, and also for presenting me, some years ago, with a then unpublished manuscript on *The Buddhas of Sukhodaya.* I am indebted to Dr. Stella Kramrisch of the Philadelphia Museum of Art for the loan of two rare photographs and for generously sharing her enormous erudition in the field of Indian art, and to Dr. Jane Gaston Mahler of Columbia University for finding time in the midst of many pressing demands to go over with me the section on Buddhist art and to suggest special iconographic points and source material. Douglas Overton of the Japan Society of New York City and Dr. Donald Keene of Columbia University also, on occasion, gave prompt and helpful assistance on specific questions.

The Cambodian Mission to the United Nations freely gave me access to its photographs of Angkor Wat, and the Indonesian Consulate, through Mrs. M. Washington of its staff, made available its photographic files on Borobudur. *Life* magazine—specifically through the generosity of Valerie Vondermühl and Maureen Mullen of the photographic department—made it possible for me to work on tentative layouts by providing photostats from the magazine's extensive files. *The New Yorker* ungrudgingly and promptly provided tear sheets from certain back issues.

A number of museums and their expert personnel should be mentioned for prompt response to requests for certain photographs and for an occasionally difficult identification: The Boston Museum of Fine Arts, the Cleveland Museum of Art, the Fogg Museum in Cambridge, Massachusetts, the Freer Gallery in Washington, D.C.; in New York the Metropolitan Museum of Art, the Museum of Natural History and the Riverside Museum, the Newark Museum in New Jersey, the Rijksmuseum, Amsterdam, and the Seattle Art Museum. Here, too, belong my thanks to the New York Public Library and, once again, in particular to Francis W. Parr of the Oriental Division and Naomi Street of the Art Division.

Mary Bradley Watkins and Patricia Young gave the manuscript careful reading and contributed some excellent suggestions; Gerstle Mack read galleys for "typos" with his famed eagle eye; two devoted and interested friends, Maud Oakes and Margot Loines Wilkie, have often in the last few years been called on to bolster the author's flagging will, as has my long-suffering husband, Stanley Young. At a particularly low point in my personal feelings about this book Dr. Paul Mus of Yale University and the Collège de France lifted my spirit immeasurably by a talk I heard him give at the Asia Society and by a letter he subsequently wrote me.

Lastly I am indebted to Max Schuster of Simon and Schuster who first suggested that I undertake the task of writing a book on Asian religious philosophies for general readers; to Henry Simon, the most interested and painstaking of editors, who so patiently helped me chart a course between mystification and over-simplification; to Robert Gottlieb who gracefully substituted as a pinch-hitting editor during Mr. Simon's enforced absence near the book's end, and, above all, to Edith Fowler whose consummate tact, unruffled calm and hours of patient creative work with me on illustrations, captions, the book's general design and endless last-minute details are quite beyond repayment.

As a footnote let me add that in thanking the various scholars and experts in the Asian field with whom I have consulted during the preparation of this book, I in no way wish to evade full responsibility for any and all errors of fact, judgment or interpretation which critics may discover in these pages.

GLOSSARY

ahimsa: Harmlessness in relation to all life; non-injury or non-violence in thought, action and speech; a basic tenet of Mahatma Gandhi's campaign for Indian freedom.

Amida: A Japanese name for the Buddha of the Pure Realm. See also *Amitabha.*

Amitabha: Another name for the Buddha of the Pure Realm or the Buddha of Boundless Light and Compassion.

anatman: Sanskrit term for the doctrine of nonego. See *anatta.*

anatta: Pali word for the Buddhist doctrine of nonego, the denial of a permanent unchanging "self."

anicca: Impermanence; in Buddhism a basic characteristic of all existence.

arahat or *arhat:* The ideal of Hinayana (Theravada) Buddhism; one who has freed himself from all ego cravings and thus attained enlightenment.

Arjuna: The hero of the Indian epic the *Mahabharata* for whom the god Krishna acts as charioteer and counselor.

Arya Samaj: Modern Hindu "reform" organization stressing a "return to the Vedas," early Hindu scriptures.

Aryan: Name given to themselves by the early invaders of India, from Arya, "noble."

asanas: Bodily postures used in Hindu and Buddhist meditation.

ashram: A hermitage where holy men live.

Ashoka: The third century B.C. Indian emperor who spread Buddhism throughout India and parts of southeast Asia.

atman: Sanskrit word for the soul or divine element in man. In Hinduism believed to be one with Brahman, the Supreme Principle of Life, therefore also Supreme Reality.

aum (also spelled *om*): Sacred syllable or mantra used in higher forms of invocation or meditation.

Avalokiteshvara: The Buddhist bodhisattva of compassion and love, known as Kuan-yin in China, Kwannon in Japan.

Avatara: the descent of a god into the world, a divine incarnation.

avidya: Ignorance.

Bardo: The after-death state which forms the theme of the Tibetan *Bardo Thödol* or *Book of the Dead.*

Beats (also known as beatniks): American social phenomenon, post-World War II.

Bhagavad-Gita: The discourse between Krishna and Arjuna that forms a part of the Indian epic the *Mahabharata.*

bhakti: Devotion, worship of a god through personal love.

[191]

Bhakti Yoga: The way to union with the Supreme Principle of life by way of selfless love.

bhikkhu: Pali word for monk, used in Hinayana Buddhism. (Sanskrit: *bhikshu*)

bhoga: Enjoyment of a blissful, supersensual kind, as a way to spiritual enlightenment.

bodhi: A term used in both Sanskrit and Pali meaning perfect wisdom or enlightenment.

bodhi tree: The tree under which the Buddha attained enlightenment. Sometimes referred to as the *bo* tree.

Bodhidharma: An Indian missionary monk who came to China in the 6th century A.D. Regarded as the founder of the Ch'an (Zen) School of Buddhism. (Known in Japan as Daruma.)

bodhisattva: In Mahayana Buddhism one who having attained enlightenment (*bodhi*) is on his way to Buddhahood but postpones his goal to keep a vow to help all life attain salvation.

Bon: Animistic, shamanistic religion of Tibet, preceding Buddhism and influencing it.

Borobudur: Great Buddhist temple compound built in Java in the 9th century A.D.

Brahma: God as creator; a *mythological* concept; member of the classic Hindu triad of gods: Brahma-Vishnu-Shiva.

Brahman: Supreme Principle of Being; a *metaphysical* term.

Brahmanas: A section of the Vedas.

Brahmin: Name used in the present text for the priestly caste of Hindus.

Brahmo Samaj: Reform movement in Hinduism founded in the early 19th century.

Buddha: An Awakened One. Refers usually to Siddhartha Gautama, the Indian prince who became an All-Enlightened Being, the historic founder of Buddhism.

buddhi: Wisdom in the sense of highly developed intuition, the principle through which pure consciousness is reflected.

buji: Japanese Zen term meaning "Nothing going on" or "Take no thought for the morrow."

bushido: The cult of the warrior class, the knights of medieval Japan.

chakra: A wheel; in yoga one of the psychic centers of the body.

Ch'an: Chinese name for Zen. (See also *dhyana.*)

cha-no-yu: Term for the Japanese tea ceremony. Literally, tea and water.

chit: Hindu term meaning pure consciousness. See *sat-chit-ananda.*

Dalai Lama: The periodically incarnated spiritual and temporal head of the country of Tibet, now in exile since the Chinese Communist invasion.

darsanas: The various schools or viewpoints of Hinduism; the literal meaning is "demonstration."

darshan: A silent transmission of spiritual experience to an audience or an individual.

Daruma: Japanese name for the First Zen Patriarch, Bodhidharma.

Dependent Origination: Theory of the chain of causation by which karma is carried on; teaching central to Hinayana Buddhism.

dhamma: Pali word for righteousness, duty, law. See *dharma.*

Dhammapada: A collection of Buddhist teachings; a part of the Pali canon of Hinayana (Theravada) Buddhism.

dharma: Sanskrit word (*dhamma* in Pali) used in both Hinduism and Buddhism, meaning variously, according to context, the way, the law, righteousness, reality. "The path which a man should follow in accordance with his nature and station in life."

dhyana: Sanskrit word for dynamic meditation or contemplation leading to enlightenment. (The words Ch'an and Zen are corruptions of dhyana.)

Diwali: Hindu festival of lights.

do: Japanese word meaning "a way of doing."

Dravidian: Name given to the pre-Aryan peoples of India.

dukkha: Buddhist word meaning suffering, pain, "dislocation."

Durga: Hindu goddess; one of the many forms of Shakti, the Divine Mother or Great Goddess of Hinduism.

Eightfold Path: Buddhism's formulation of the eight steps necessary for "awakening."

emptiness: See *sunyata.*

Eternal Now: Buddhist teaching about "living in the moment."

Existentialism: Modern Western philosophy emphasizing man's responsibility for his personal life through the choices he makes.

Fa Hsien: A Chinese pilgrim to India in the early 5th century A.D.

First Patriarch of Zen: See *Bodhidharma.*

Four Noble Truths: The Buddha's teaching that (1) existence involves inevitable suffering for all people; (2) this suffering springs from egocentrism; (3) egocentrism can be rooted out; (4) this rooting out can come by following the Eightfold Path.

Four Signs: In Buddhist legend also the Four Sights—an old man, a diseased man, a corpse and a holy man—that influenced Prince Siddhartha Gautama to leave his luxurious home and go forth on the search for enlightenment that led him to Buddhahood.

Gandhara: Sanskrit name for an Indian district, now part of Pakistan and Afghanistan, famous for early Buddha images in Greco-Roman style.

Ganesh (also *Ganesha*): Elephant-headed god of good luck, son of Shiva and Parvati.

Garuda: The bird associated with Vishnu.

Gautama: Family name of the historic Buddha; also spelled Gotama.

ghee: Clarified butter used in Hinduism for the anointing of sacred images.

Gita: Name often used in referring to the *Bhagavad Gita.*

gopis: Cowherd girls in the stories of Krishna's life as a cowherd; enthralled devotees of Krishna.

Gotama: See *Gautama.*

Great Demise: Term for the Buddha's death.

Great Departure: Buddhist term for Siddhartha's departure from his father's palace.

Great Renunciation: The silent and secret leave-taking from his family, including his wife and infant son, of Siddhartha Gautama, the Buddha-to-be.

guru: A spiritual guide; one who takes disciples for religious instruction.

haiku: Seventeen-syllable Japanese poem.

Hanuman: The monkey god who helped rescue Rama's wife, Sita, from the demon king of Ceylon in the Indian epic the *Ramayana.*

Harijans: Literally "Children of God," Gandhi's name for the untouchables of India.

Hatha Yoga: One of the four types of yoga; this discipline stresses control of physical processes.

Hinayana Buddhism: The "Lesser Vehicle of Buddhism" as compared to the "Larger Vehicle," Mahayana; refers to the scope and range of interpretation and permissiveness in relation to the Buddha's doctrine. See *Theravada Buddhism,* preferable term.

Hsuan-tsang (also spelled Hiuen Tsiang): Chinese scholar and monk (7th century A.D.) who visited India and Afghanistan, returning with many Sanskrit scriptures and Buddha images; wrote brilliant accounts of his travels.

Hui-k'o (Japanese Eka): famous early Zen Patriarch, pupil of Bodhidharma. (See plate 91.)

"Idiots": Famous Ch'an (Zen) characters; Han-shan and Shih-te (Chinese), Kanzan and Jittoku (Japanese).

Islam: Meaning "submission to the will of God"; a general term for the religion of the Muslim (Moslem) world.

Is-ness: Term used in Zen to emphasize the immediate state of being.

Jagannath: The image of Krishna that is worshiped in Puri, Orissa, India.

Jatakas: A collection of Indian folk stories about the Buddha's former lives.

jen: Chinese word meaning "human" in the very best sense.

ji: Japanese word of several meanings: technique or "tricks"; also things.

jiji muge hokkai: Doctrine of the Kegon Buddhist school of Japan, meaning the realm of harmonious relationship of all forms of life or things (ji), unimpeded interdiffusion, or the recognition of the complete non-duality of all manifestation.

Jittoku: One of the two "happy idiots" of Zen. (In Chinese, Shih-te.)

Jnana Yoga: Union with God through transcendent knowledge.

Joshu: Famed Zen master of the late 8th and 9th centuries.

"Joshu's Mu": Joshu's classic reply to a question that was put to him by a fellow monk; one of the famous koans of Zen. (The Chinese term is *wu.*)

Judo: A Japanese method of weaponless offense and defense built on principles of nonaggression.

juggernaut: English word derived from the annual Jagannath (Krishna) festival in Puri.

ju-jitsu: Another name for judo; ju means gentle, jitsu, art or practice.

Kali: One of the many names for India's Mother Goddess.

Kali Yuga: In Hinduism, one of the four ages of world time; a dark period of declining morality and rising calamity and distress.

kalpa: In Hinduism, an eon, a vast period of time that encompasses the creation and dissolution of a universe.

Kamma (Pali): See *Karma* (Sanskrit).

Kanzan: One of Zen's famous "happy idiots." (In Chinese, Han-shan.)

Karma: Literally "action"; the law of cause and effect, sometimes interpreted personally as punishment or reward for deeds performed in former lives.

Karma Yoga: The Yoga path that leads to release through selfless activity.

karuna: The Mahayana Buddhist term for compassion; a trait of bodhisattvas.

Kashyapa: First of the 28 great patriarchs of Mahayana Buddhism; the disciple who understood the Buddha's silent "flower sermon."

kendo: Japanese swordsmanship.

koan: Term used in Zen Buddhism describing a problem which cannot be solved by the intellect alone.

Krishna: One of the incarnations of the often-incarnated Hindu god Vishnu.

Kshatriya: The second of India's four major castes; rulers and aristocrats.

Kuan-yin: Chinese name for the bodhisattva known in Indian Buddhism as Avalokiteshvara; often presented in female form.

kufu: A Zen exercise.

kundalini: A term used in certain esoteric yoga practices for the "serpent" or "thermal" power that lies dormant at the base of the spine until awakened through yogic disciplines and exercises.

kung-an: Chinese legal term from which the word koan originated.

Kwannon: Japanese name for Kuan-yin, q.v.

lama: Tibetan term for a Buddhist monk or spiritual leader.

lingam (also written *linga*): The symbol of Shiva in the form of a phallus, indicating his divine creative function.

Mahabharata: One of the two great epics of India; contains the *Bhagavad-Gita.*

Mahatma: A personal incarnation of divinity; title given in Hinduism to universally acclaimed "great souls" like Mahatma Gandhi.

Mahayana: A Buddhist term meaning "Larger Vehicle" applied to the northern Buddhism of Tibet, Mongolia, China, Korea, Japan. It has many schools and forms.

Maitreya: The Buddha of the Future.

mandala: A diagrammatic picture used as an aid in meditation or ritual; sometimes a symbol of the universe, or a representation of a deed of merit.

mani walls: Name given to the walls in Himalayan Buddhist countries which have been painted with the words *Om Mani Padme Hum* (Hail to the Jewel in the Lotus).

Manjusri: The bodhisattva of Meditation whose image—as personification of Supreme Wisdom—is usually seen in Zen meditation halls.

mantra (or *mantram*): A Sanskrit term used in Hinduism signifying a sacred word, verse or syllable which embodies in sound some specific deity or supernatural power.

Mathura: Ancient Buddhist center near modern Agra where early Buddhist images were made.

maya: A word used in both Hinduism and Buddhism signifying the "illusion" of the world's appearance.

Maya, the Lady Maya: The name of the Buddha's mother.

merit: A Buddhist term used in connection with the performance of good deeds.

mettu: Pali word meaning loving-kindness; the basis of a meditation in the Theravada school of Buddhism and the subject of the *Metta Sutta.*

Middle Way: Buddhism's description of the path lying between all extremes as, for instance, asceticism and self-indulgence; advocated by the Buddha as the proper path for man to follow.

mindfulness: Buddhist term; "awareness."

Mithuna (or *Maithuna*): Tantric art; couples sculptured in close embrace.

moksha: Liberation from the bondage of finite existence.

mondo: Japanese word used in Zen; a rapid-fire question-and-answer technique employed to overcome conventional conceptual thought patterns.

Moslem (also spelled Muslim): Name given to followers of the prophet Mohammed, members of the Islamic faith; believers in the One God Allah.

mudra: A mystic or symbolic gesture of hand and fingers.

Muslim: See *Moslem.*

Naga: A snake deity.

Nandi: The sacred bull associated with Shiva.

Narayana: Another of Vishnu's titles.

Nataraja: Shiva in his dance, symbolizing the eternal cosmic processes of birth and death.

nazuna: The name of a Japanese flowering weed, used in a famous haiku.

neem: Medicinal Indian tree whose twigs are used for cleaning the teeth.

Nibbana: Pali word meaning Nirvana.

Nirvana: The attainment of final enlightenment; freedom from rebirth.

No drama: The ancient drama of Japan, rooted in Zen concepts.

nonego: See *anatta.*

om: The most sacred mantra of the Vedas. (See *aum.*)

Om Mani Padme Hum: See *Mani.*

Padmapani: A name for the bodhisattva Avalokiteshvara; "lotus carrier" or lotus-born.

Padmasana: Classic yoga pose.

Pali: The language of the Theravada (Hinayana) Buddhist canon, claimed to be the language used by the Buddha or similar to it.

Parinirvana: The final or perfect Nirvana, ending all earthly existences, implying no further rebirth.

Parvati: One of the wives of Shiva; an embodiment of the Divine Mother Goddess; a daughter of Himalaya.

pata (or *patta*): A plaque of metal or stone, carved with a god's figure.

Pitaka: Literally "basket"; the three Pitakas, or the Tripitaka, represent the main body of the Pali canon of Buddhism.

prajna: Wisdom; spiritual awakening.

puja: Worship of any god by way of an image.

Punjab: A section of northern India whose courts produced, in the 18th and early 19th centuries, delightful paintings of the Krishna saga and other folk themes.

Puranas: Ancient Hindu texts telling stories of gods, goddesses and mythological events; a part of the folklore of Hinduism embodying also social and religious instruction.

Puri: City in Orissa, scene of the Jagannath festival.

Radha: Chief *gopi* love of Krishna.

Raja Yoga: One of the four schools or disciplines of Hindu yoga teaching the highest self-realization.

Rama: A human incarnation of Vishnu; hero of the great Indian epic the *Ramayana.*

reincarnation: Belief in the living of more than one life.

ri: Japanese word; law, general principle, wholeness.

Rig Veda: One of the ancient authoritative scriptures of Hinduism.

Rinzai: One of the two main schools of Zen Buddhism in which training involves the use of the koan and mondo.

sabi: Japanese word meaning rustic unpretentiousness, as in the standards of taste applied to the tea ceremony.

sadhu: Indian holy man.

Sakti: See *Shakti.*

Sakyamuni: See *Shakyamuni.*

salagramas: Name given stones gathered from riverbeds; sacred to Vishnu.

samadhi: The supreme goal of yogic effort; superconsciousness.

samsara: The ceaseless round of becoming; the life of phenomena; opposite of Nirvana.

Sangha: The Buddhist monastic order.

sannyasin: A person who has renounced the world.

Sanskrit: The ancient language in which many of the religious texts of Hinduism and Buddhism have been written.

sanzen: A type of Zen training.

sarira: A special substance found in the cremated remains of saints.

sat-chit-ananda: Existence, consciousness, bliss, constituting the nature of Absolute Reality.

Sati: Name of one of Shiva's consorts.

sati: The decadent Hindu rite of immolation of a widow on her husband's funeral pyre.

sattipatthana: The name of a type of meditative Buddhism practiced in a Rangoon, Burma, monastery.

satyagraha: "Holding to the truth"; an ancient Indian tenet basic to Gandhi's teaching.

Sesha: Name for the great serpent who symbolizes Time, on whose coils Vishnu sleeps before periodic reincarnations.

sesshin: Period of intensive meditation practiced in Rinzai Zen.

Shakti: The feminine essence of the universe embodied in a consort of Shiva; *shakti,* energy, force.

Shakya: The name of the Buddha's "clan."

Shakyamuni: "The sage of the Shakya clan" —one of the Buddha's various titles.

Shih-te: The Chinese name of one of Zen's "happy idiots." (Jittoku in Japanese.)

Shinto: The indigenous religion of Japan.

Shiva: One of the three deities of the classic Hindu triad of deities.

Shiva-Shava: Shiva alive, Shiva as corpse. (See Plate 21.)

shruti (or *sruti*): Hindu term for the most ancient sacred scriptures, "that which was revealed."

Shudra: The fourth of the four major castes of Hinduism.

shunyata: The void, or emptiness; a basic concept in certain schools of Buddhism, Zen in particular.

sitting: A term used in Soto Zen in reference to meditative practice.

skandha: The five aggregates which, in Buddhist terms, make up an individual.

smrite: Hindu term for "that which was remembered." (See *shruti*.)

Soto: Zen sect which stresses quiet meditation and "sitting with awareness"; founded by Dogen who brought Chinese Zen teachings to his homeland, Japan, in 1127.

stupa: Originally a mound for relics, in particular the Buddha's; developed into elaborate architectural forms: chortens, dagobas, pagodas.

sutra: The Sanskrit word for Buddhist scriptures, meaning a discourse by the Buddha, or a disciple, accepted as authoritative teaching; literal meaning—"A thread on which jewels are hung."

sutta: The Pali word for sutra, or scriptures.

swami: A Hindu initiate of a religious order.

tanden: A Zen term for a center of "awareness" in the abdominal region; used in certain meditative practices and in judo instruction.

tanha: Sanskrit word for thirst or craving; in Buddhism, the cause of rebirth. (See also *trishna*.)

Tantra or *Tantras:* A body of esoteric Hindu religious literature said to have been revealed by the god Shiva for man's guidance in the present age, *i.e.* the Kali Yuga. These scriptures place emphasis on the worship of the female essence of the universe, the Divine Mother or Shakti. (See also Mayhayana Buddhism.)

Tao: Literally the Way or the Absolute; the teaching found in Chinese Taoism and in the often-translated *Tao Te Ching* attributed to the philosopher Lao Tzu; influential in forming the Zen viewpoint.

Tat Tvam Asi: Sanskrit formula expressing the fundamental identity of the individual soul and God: "That art thou."

Tea ceremony: The formal Japanese way of serving tea; related to Zen meditative practices.

Theravada Buddhism: The School of the Elders, another—and preferred—term for the Hinayana or southern school of Buddhism: Ceylon, Thailand, Burma. Thera means "elders."

Theosophy: Teachings developed by the Theosophical Society founded in New York in 1875 by H. P. Blavatsky and Colonel H. S. Olcott, dedicated to investigation of psychic phenomena, the comparative study of all world religions and development of man's "latent powers."

Tipitaka (Pali for *Tripitaka*): Literally the "Three Baskets"; the basis of the Pali canon of Theravada Buddhism.

Tripitaka: See above.

trishna: Pali word for thirst or craving. See *tanha*.

Unconscious: That part of the mind lying outside or below consciousness.

Upanishads: Sanskrit for "secret teachings"; the third section of the sacrosanct Vedas which form the basis of Hinduism's highest spiritual concepts.

urna: The small protuberance or "jewel" between the Buddha's eyes, representing the "third eye of intuitive wisdom."

ushnisha: The cranial protuberance on top of the Buddha's head; one of the marks of his supernatural anatomy.

vahana: The "vehicle" which carries a Hindu god; his mount, or the animal associated with a particular deity.

Vaisya: The third of the four major Hindu castes, engaged in commerce and agriculture.

varna: Original word for caste, meaning color.

Vedanta: Literally "end of the Vedas"; the main source of modern intellectual Hinduism; also the classical Hindu school of non-dualistic philosophy.

Vedas: The sacred scriptures of Hinduism, held to have been "born of the very breath of God"; primary scriptures of Hinduism.

vihara: Buddhist term for a dwelling place for monks.

Vishnu: One of the three great gods of Hinduism; a member of the classic triad: Vishnu-Shiva-Brahma or Vishnu-Shiva-Shakti.

wabi: A Japanese term meaning simplicity, unpretentiousness, implying "not being in the swim or trying to keep up with the Joneses"; a tea ceremony term.

wu wei: A Chinese Taoist term, literally "non-action"; implying deeds performed without thought of self, hence without karma.

yantra: A magic diagram.

yoga: Literally to unite (or be yoked with) God. There are various schools and methods of yoga discipline taught in Hinduism as a means of "liberation," or for attaining union with God.

yogi: One who practices yoga.

yuga: A division of world time. See *Kali Yuga.*

zazen: A type of Zen discipline.

Zen: One of the main schools of Japanese Buddhism, original Japanese pronunciation of the Chinese ideograph Ch'an, derived from Sanskrit *dhyana.*

BIBLIOGRAPHY

The following reading list does not comprise the author's bibliography in its entirety. On the whole, it stresses books of a more general nature, but includes also some books for those who wish to delve deeper. Asterisks indicate not only books most likely to appeal to beginners but also those which have proved most valuable to the author during the preparation of the present volume or have given most enduring pleasure in the past.

HINDUISM

*Behanan, Kovoor T., *Yoga, A Scientific Evaluation*. Institute of Human Relations, Yale University. New York, The Macmillan Company, 1937.

Bouquet, A. C., *Hinduism*. New York, Hutchinson's University Library, 1948.

*Chakravarty, Amiya (editor), *A Tagore Reader*. New York, The Macmillan Company, 1961.

Chatterjee, Satis Chandra, *The Fundamentals of Hinduism*. Calcutta, Das Gupta & Co., 1950.

*Chatterjee, Satis Chandra, and Dutta, D. M., *An Introduction to Indian Philosophy*. Calcutta, University of Calcutta, 1950.

Daniélou, Alain, *Hindu Polytheism*. New York, Bollingen Foundation, 1964.

———, *Yoga: The Method of Reintegration*. London, C. Johnson, 1949.

Dowson, John, *A Classical Dictionary of Hindu Mythology*. London, Routledge & Kegan Paul Ltd., 1950.

*Eliade, Mircea, *Yoga: Immortality and Freedom*. Bollingen Series. New York, Pantheon Books, Inc., 1958.

Farquhar, J. N., *An Outline of the Religious Literature of India*. London, Oxford University Press, 1920.

*Fischer, Louis, *Gandhi, His Life and Message for the World*. New York, Signet Key Book, 1954.

*Gandhi, M. K., *The Story of My Experiments with Truth*. Washington, D.C., Public Affairs Press, 1948.

*Hiriyanna, M., *The Essentials of Indian Philosophy*. London, George Allen & Unwin Ltd., 1949.

———, *Outlines of Indian Philosophy*. New York, The Macmillan Company, 1932.

*Hume, Robert Ernest, *The Thirteen Principal Upanishads*. London, Oxford University Press, 1934.

*Isherwood, Christopher, *Ramakrishna and His Disciples*. New York, Simon and Schuster, 1965.

——— (editor and contributor), *Vedanta for the Western World*. Hollywood and New York, The Marcel Rodd Company, 1946.

*Isherwood, Christopher, and Prabhavananda, Swami, Bhagavad Gita: The Song of God. London, Phoenix House, 1947.

*Morgan, Kenneth W. (editor), The Religion of the Hindus. New York, The Ronald Press Company, 1953.

Monier-Williams, M., Hinduism. Calcutta, Susil Gupta Ltd. First published 1877; still useful.

Nikhilananda, Swami, The Gospel of Sri Ramakrishna (originally recorded in Bengali by M., a disciple of the Master). New York, Ramakrishna-Vivekananda Center, 1942.

———, The Upanishads (a new translation). New York, published by Bonanza Books, a division of Crown Publishers, Inc., by arrangement with Harper & Brothers, 1949.

*Radhakrishnan, Sarvepalli, The Bhagavad Gita. New York, Harper & Brothers, 1948.

*———, The Hindu View of Life. New York, The Macmillan Company, 1931.

Rajagopalachari, C., Mahabharata (a retelling of the Indian epic). New Delhi, The Hindustan Times, 1950.

*Rawlinson, H. G., India, A Short Cultural History. New York, Frederick A. Praeger, Inc., 1952.

*Renou, Louis, Hinduism. New York, George Braziller, Inc., 1961.

Sarma, D. S., The Prince of Ayodha (a retelling of the Ramayana). Madras, Shri Ramakrishna Math, 1946.

———, The Renaissance of Hinduism, India, Benares Hindu University, 1944.

*Sheean, Vincent, Lead Kindly Light: Gandhi and the Way to Peace. New York, Random House, Inc., 1949.

Tennyson, Hallam, India's Walking Saint: The Story of Vinoba Bhave. New York, Doubleday & Company, Inc., 1955.

*Thomas, P., Epics, Myths and Legends of India. Bombay, D. B. Taraporevala Sons & Co., Ltd., no date.

*———, Hindu Religion, Customs and Manners. Bombay, D. B. Taraporevala Sons & Co., Ltd., no date.

Wadsworth, Cleome Carroll, Bhagavad-Gita, A Psychological Recension. New York, Pageant Press, 1965.

*Wood, Ernest, Great Systems of Yoga. New York, Philosophical Library, Inc., 1954.

Woodroffe, Sir John, Shakti and Shakta (4th edition). Madras, Ganesh & Co., 1951.

BUDDHISM

Ali, Aamir, The Story of the Buddha. London, Oxford University Press, 1952.

Anesaki, M., History of Japanese Religion. London, Kegan Paul, Trench, Trubner & Co., 1930.

Arnold, Sir Edwin, The Light of Asia. (The Life and Teaching of Gautama, Prince of India and founder of Buddhism.) Long narrative poem first published in England in the 1890's. The Peter Pauper Press, 1946.

*Babbitt, Irving, The Dhammapada. New York, New Directions Paperbook, 1965. Also published by Oxford Press, 1936.

*Beal, Samuel, Buddhist Records of the Western World. London, Kegan Paul, Trench, Trubner & Co., (translated from the Chinese of Hiuen Tsiang, A.D. 629), undated.

Bode, Mabel Haynes, The Pali Literature of Burma. London, The Royal Asiatic Society, 1909.

*Burtt, E. A., The Teachings of the Compassionate Buddha. New York, Mentor Religious Classic, New American Library, 1955.

*Conze, Edward, *Buddhism: Its Essence and Development.* New York, Harper Torchbooks, 1959.

*——— (Editors: Conze, E., Horner, I. B., Snellgrove, D., Waley, A.), *Buddhist Texts Through the Ages.* Oxford, Bruno Cassirer, Ltd., 1954.

*Coomaraswamy, Ananda, *Buddha and the Gospel of Buddhism.* London, George G. Harrap & Company, 1916.

Dasgupta, S. B., *An Introduction to Tantric Buddhism.* Calcutta, University of Calcutta, 1950.

David-Neel, Alexandra, *Initiations and Initiates in Tibet.* London, Rider & Co., 1931.

———, *With Mystics and Magicians in Tibet.* New York, Penguin Books, 1931, and University Books, Inc., 1964.

*Evans-Wentz, W. Y., *The Tibetan Book of the Dead.* London, Oxford University Press, 1951.

———, *The Tibetan Book of the Great Liberation, or the Method of Realizing Nirvana Through Knowing the Mind.* London, Oxford University Press, 1954.

Goddard, Dwight (editor), *A Buddhist Bible.* New York, E. P. Dutton & Co., Inc., 1952.

*Grimm, George, *The Doctrine of the Buddha.* Berlin, Akademie-Verlag, 1958.

*Grousset, René, *In the Footsteps of the Buddha.* London, George Routledge & Sons, Ltd., 1932.

*Hesse, Hermann, *Siddhartha.* New York, New Directions, 1951.

*Holmes, Edmond, *The Creed of Buddha.* London, The Bodley Head, 1949.

Horner, I. B., *Women Under Primitive Buddhism.* London, George Routledge & Sons, Ltd., 1930.

*Humphreys, Christmas, *Buddhism.* England, Penguin Books, 1951.

*———, *A Popular Dictionary of Buddhism.* New York, Citadel Press, 1962.

Keith, A. B., *Buddhist Philosophy in India and Ceylon.* Oxford, The Clarendon Press, 1923.

McGovern, W. M., *Introduction to Mahayana Buddhism.* London, Kegan Paul, Trench, Trubner & Co., 1922.

*Morgan, Kenneth W. (editor), *The Path of Buddhism: Buddhism Interpreted by Buddhists.* New York, The Ronald Press Company, 1956.

Narada, Thera, *Buddhism in a Nutshell.* Colombo, Ceylon, The Ceylon Daily News, 1954.

——— (translator), *The Dhammapada.* Wisdom of the East Series. London, John Murray, 1954.

Norbu, Thubten Jigme (the brother of the Dalai Lama), *Tibet Is My Country.* New York, E. P. Dutton & Co., 1961.

Nyanaponika, Thera, *The Heart of Buddhist Meditation.* Colombo, Ceylon, The Word of the Buddha Publishing Committee, 1954.

*Pratt, J. B., *The Pilgrimage of Buddhism.* New York, The Macmillan Company, 1928.

Ray, Niharranjan, *An Introduction to the Study of Theravada Buddhism in Burma.* Calcutta, University of Calcutta, 1946.

Reischauer, A. K., *Studies in Japanese Buddhism.* New York, The Macmillan Co., 1917.

*Shattock, Rear Admiral E. H., *An Experiment in Mindfulness.* New York, E. P. Dutton & Co., Inc., 1960.

Subhadra, Bhikkhu, *The Message of Buddhism.* London, Kegan Paul, Trench, Trubner & Co., 1922.

Takakusu, Junjiro, *The Essentials of Buddhist Philosophy.* University of Hawaii, 1949.

Thomas, E. J., *Early Buddhist Scriptures.* London, Kegan Paul, Trench, Trubner & Co., 1935.

*———, *History of Buddhist Thought.* London, Routledge & Kegan Paul, Ltd., 1953.

————, *The Life of Buddha as Legend and History.* New York, Barnes & Noble, Inc., 1960.

Thomas, E. J., and Francis, H. T. (selected and edited by), *Jataka Tales.* England, Cambridge University Press, 1916.

Waddell, L. A., *The Buddhism of Tibet.* Cambridge, W. Heffer and Sons, 1934.

*Waley, Arthur, *The Real Tripitaka, and Other Pieces.* London, George Allen & Unwin Ltd., 1952.

*Wells, Kenneth E., *Thai Buddhism: Its Rites and Activities.* Bangkok, Post Publishing Co., Ltd., The Bangkok Times Press, 1939.

ZEN

*Benoit, Hubert, *The Supreme Doctrine: Psychological Studies in Zen Thought.* New York, Pantheon Books, Inc., 1955.

*Blofeld, John, *The Zen Teaching of Huang Po (on the Transmission of Mind).* New York, Grove Press, Inc., 1959.

Blyth, R. H., *Haiku* (in 4 volumes). Tokyo, Hokuseido Press, 1950.

————, *Oriental Humour.* Tokyo, Hokuseido Press, 1959.

*————, *Zen in English Literature and Oriental Classics.* Tokyo, Hokuseido Press, 1942.

*Chang, Chen-Chi, *The Practice of Zen.* New York, Harper & Brothers, 1959.

*Dumoulin, Heinrich, S. J., *A History of Zen Buddhism.* New York, Pantheon Books, 1963.

Fromm, Erich, Suzuki, D. T., and Martino, Richard de, *Zen Buddhism and Psychoanalysis.* New York, Harper & Brothers, 1960.

Gatenby, E. V., *The Cloud Men of Yamato,* London, John Murray, 1929.

*Graham, Dom Aelred, *Zen Catholicism.* New York, Harcourt, Brace & World, Inc., 1963.

*Herrigel, Eugen, *Zen in the Art of Archery.* New York, Pantheon Books, Inc., 1953.

*Humphreys, Christmas, *Zen Buddhism.* London, William Heineman, Ltd., 1949.

*Ikemoto, Takashi, and Stryk, Lucien, *Zen Poems, Prayers, Sermons, Anecdotes, Interviews.* New York, Anchor Books, Doubleday & Company, Inc., 1965.

*Kapleau, Philip, *The Three Pillars of Zen.* New York and Evanston, Harper & Row, 1966.

*Leggett, Trevor (compiler and translator), *A First Zen Reader.* Rutland, Vermont, and Tokyo, Charles E. Tuttle Co., Inc., 1960.

Masunaga, Reiho, *The Soto Approach to Zen.* Tokyo, Layman Buddhist Society Press, 1958.

Ogata, Sohaku, *Zen for the West.* London, Rider & Co., 1959.

*Reps, Paul, *Zen Flesh, Zen Bones, A Collection of Zen and Pre-Zen Writings.* Rutland, Vermont, and Tokyo, Charles E. Tuttle Co., Inc., 1958.

*Reps, Paul, and Senzaki, Nyogen (translators), *101 Zen Stories.* Philadelphia, David McKay Company, no date.

*Ross, Nancy Wilson (editor and contributor), *The World of Zen.* New York, Random House, 1960; Vintage Paperback, 1964.

*Sasaki, Ruth Fuller, *Zen, A Method for Religious Awakening.* Kyoto, The First Zen Institute of America in Japan, 1959.

*————, *Zen, a Religion.* New York, The First Zen Institute of America, 1958.

*Sasaki, Ruth Fuller, and Miura, Isshu, *The Zen Koan.* New York, Harcourt, Brace & World, Inc., 1965.

*Suzuki, Daisetz Teitaro, *Essays in Zen Buddhism.* (3 vols.). London, Luzac and Company, 1927–1933, 1934.

*————, *The Essence of Buddhism.* London, The Buddhist Society, 1947.

*———, *The Essentials of Zen Buddhism* (Selected from the writings of Daisetz T. Suzuki, edited and with an introduction by Bernard Phillips). New York, E. P. Dutton & Co., 1962.

*———, *An Introduction to Zen Buddhism*. New York, Philosophical Library, Inc., 1949.

———, *The Zen Doctrine of No-Mind*. London, Rider & Co., 1949.

*———, *Zen and Japanese Culture*. New York, Bollingen Foundation, Inc., Pantheon Books, Inc., 1959.

*Suzuki, Daisetz Teitaro, *Zen Buddhism* (Selected writings of Suzuki, edited and with an introduction by William Barrett). New York, Anchor Books, Doubleday & Company, Inc., 1956.

*Waley, Arthur, *The Way and Its Power*. Boston, Houghton Mifflin Company, 1935.

Watts, Alan W., *The Spirit of Zen*. Wisdom of the East Series. London, John Murray, 1935.

*———, *The Way of Zen*. New York, Pantheon Books, Inc., 1957.

*Welch, Douglas, *The Parting of the Way: Lao Tzu and the Taoist Movement*. London, Methuen & Co., Ltd., 1958.

GENERAL

Alpert, Richard, Leary, Timothy, and Metzner, Ralph, *The Psychedelic Experience. A Manual Based on the Tibetan Book of the Dead*. New Hyde Park, University Books, 1964.

*Basham, A. L., *The Wonder That Was India*. New York, Evergreen, Grove Press, Inc., 1954.

*Brown, W. Norman (editor), *India, Pakistan, Ceylon*. Ithaca, Cornell University Press, 1951.

*Campbell, Joseph, *The Hero with a Thousand Faces*. Bollingen Series. New York, Pantheon Books, Inc., 1949.

*———, *The Masks of God, Oriental Mythology*. New York, Viking Press, 1962.

*Coomaraswamy, Ananda, and The Sister Nivedita (Margaret E. Noble), *Myths and Legends of the Hindus and Buddhists*. London, George G. Harrap & Company, 1920.

*Coster, Geraldine, *Yoga and Western Psychology*. London, Oxford University Press, 1934.

Creel, H. G., *Chinese Thought from Confucius to Mao Tse-tung*. New York, Mentor Book, New American Library, latest paperback printing 1964.

Eliade, Mircea, *Mephistopheles and the Androgyne, Studies in Religious Myth and Symbol*. New York, Sheed and Ward, 1965.

*Eliot, Sir Charles, *Hinduism and Buddhism* (in 3 volumes). London, Routledge & Kegan Paul Ltd., 1954.

*Hall, H. Fielding, *The Soul of a People*. London, Macmillan & Co., Ltd., 1899. (About Burma).

*Hawkridge, Emma, *Indian Gods and Kings*. Boston, Houghton Mifflin Company, 1935.

*———, *The Wisdom Tree*. Boston, Houghton Mifflin Company, 1945.

Heard, Gerald, *The Five Ages of Man*. New York, Julian Press, Inc., 1963.

*———, *The Human Venture*. New York, Harper & Brothers, 1955.

*Huxley, Aldous, *The Perennial Philosophy*, New York, Harper & Brothers, 1945.

Gunther, John, *Inside Asia*. New York, Harper & Brothers, 1939.

*Jeans, Sir James, *The Mysterious Universe*. New York, The Macmillan Company, 1930.

*Jung, Carl G., and Wilhelm, Richard, *The Secret of the Golden Flower*. New York, Harcourt Brace & Company, 1938.

*Kaplan, Abraham, *The New World of Philosophy*. New York, Random House, 1961.

Krishnamurti, J., *Commentaries on Living.* (First, second and third series.) New York, Harper & Brothers, 1956, 1958, 1960.

*Lamb, Beatrice Pitney, *India, A World in Transition.* New York, Frederick A. Praeger, Inc., 1966.

*Landon, Kenneth P., *Southeast Asia, Crossroads of Religion.* Chicago, University of Chicago, 1947.

*Mi Mi Khaing, *Burmese Family.* Bloomington, Indiana University Press, 1962.

Neumann, Erich, *The Great Mother: An Analysis of the Archetype.* New York, Bollingen Series, Pantheon Books, Inc., 1955.

*Northrop, F. S. C., *The Meeting of East and West* (An Inquiry Concerning World Understanding). New York, The Macmillan Company, 1946.

*Pallis, Marco, *Peaks and Lamas.* New York, Alfred A. Knopf, Inc., Revised edition, 1949.

*Radhakrishnan, Sarvepalli, *East and West in Religion.* London, George Allen & Unwin Ltd., 1949.

*———, *Eastern Religions and Western Thought.* London, Oxford University Press, 1940.

———, *Indian Philosophy* (in 2 volumes). London, George Allen & Unwin Ltd., 1951.

Radhakrishnan, Sarvepalli, and Moore, Charles A., *A Source Book in Indian Philosophy.* Princeton, Princeton University Press, 1957.

*Ross, Floyd H., *The Meaning of Life in Hinduism and Buddhism.* Boston, The Beacon Press, 1953.

Sansom, Sir George, *Japan: A Short Cultural History.* New York, Appleton-Century-Crofts, 1962.

Sharma, Chandradhar, *Indian Philosophy: A Critical Survey.* New York, University Paperbacks, Barnes & Noble, Inc., 1962.

*Shway Yoe (Sir James Scott), *The Burman: His Life and Notions.* New York, W. W. Norton & Company, 1963.

Siu, R. G. H., *The Tao of Science: An Essay on Western Knowledge and Eastern Wisdom.* Boston, The Massachusetts Institute of Technology, 1957.

*Taylor, Edmond, *Richer by Asia.* Boston, Houghton Mifflin, 1947.

*Toynbee, Arnold, *Christianity Among the Religions of the World.* New York, Charles Scribner's Sons, 1957.

———, *A Study of History* (in 10 volumes). London, Oxford University Press, 1934–1954.

———, *The World and the West.* New York, Oxford University Press, 1953.

Vogel, J. Ph., *Indian Serpent Lore or the Nagas in Hindu Legend and Art.* London, Arthur Probsthain, 1926.

*Watts, Alan W., *The Supreme Identity.* New York, Pantheon Books, 1950.

*Zimmer, Heinrich (edited by Joseph Campbell), *Philosophies of India.* Bollingen Series. New York, Pantheon Books, Inc., 1951.

ARTS

Some books related to the arts of Hinduism, Buddhism, Zen: painting, sculpture, literature, dance, drama and music.

*Anesaki, Masaharu, *A History of Buddhist Art.* Boston, Houghton Mifflin Co., 1915.

*Archer, W. G., *The Loves of Krishna in Indian Painting and Poetry.* New York, Grove Press, Inc., no date.

*Arthaud, Jacques, and Groslier, Bernard, *The Arts and Civilizations of Angkor.* New York, Frederick A. Praeger, Inc., 1957.

*Binyon, Laurence, *The Flight of the Dragon.* Wisdom of the East Series. London, John Murray, 1922.

*———, *Painting in the Far East.* (3rd revised edition). New York, Dover.

*————, *The Spirit of Man in Asian Art.* Cambridge, Harvard University Press, 1935.

*Bowers, Faubion, *Theatre in the East: Asian Dance and Drama.* New York, Thomas Nelson & Sons, 1956.

Bowie, Henry P., *On the Laws of Japanese Painting.* New York, Dover Publications. No date.

*Bowie, Theodore (editor), *The Arts of Thailand.* Bloomington, Indiana, Indiana University Press, 1960.

Briggs, Lawrence Palmer, *The Ancient Khmer Empire.* Philadelphia, American Philosophical Society, 1951.

Brown, Percy, *Indian Architecture.* (Buddhist and Hindu), Bombay, D. B. Taraporevala Sons & Co., Ltd., 1942.

*Bynner, Witter, *The Way of Life According to Laotzu* (An American Version of the *Tao Te Ching*). New York, The John Day Company, 1944.

*Cahill, James, *The Art of Southern Sung China.* New York, The Asia Society, Inc., 1962.

*————, *Chinese Painting.* New York, Skira, distributed by The World Publishing Company, 1960.

*Chiang Yee, *The Chinese Eye, An Interpretation of Chinese Painting.* London, Methuen & Co., Ltd., 1935.

*Chow, Fong, *Chinese Buddhist Sculpture.* New York, The Metropolitan Museum of Art Bulletin, May, 1965.

*Collis, Maurice, *The Land of the Great Image.* New York, Alfred A. Knopf, Inc., 1943.

Coomaraswamy, Ananda, *History of Indian and Indonesian Art.* New York, E. Weyhe, 1927.

*————, *The Dance of Shiva.* New York, The Noonday Press, 1957.

————, *The Mirror of Gesture.* New York, E. Weyhe, 1936.

Daniélou, Alain, *Northern Indian Music* (in 2 volumes). London, C. Johnson, 1949–1954. Vol. 2, published by Halcyon Press, under the auspices of UNESCO.

De Kleen, Tyra, *Mudras, the Ritual Hand-Poses of the Buddha Priest and the Shiva Priests of Bali.* New York, E. P. Dutton & Co., 1924.

*De Zoete, Beryl, *The Other Mind: A Study of Dance and Life in South India.* New York, Theatre Arts Books, 1960.

Drexler, Arthur, *The Architecture of Japan.* New York, Museum of Modern Art, 1955.

*Duthuit, Georges, *Chinese Mysticism and Modern Painting.* London, A. Zwemmer, 1933.

Edmunds, Will H., *Pointers and Clues to the Subjects of Chinese and Japanese Art.* London, Sampson Low, Marston & Co., Ltd., 1934.

Fenollosa, Ernest E., *Epochs of Chinese and Japanese Art* (2 vols.). London, Heinemann, Ltd., 1912. Revised edition, 1921.

Foucher, Alfred, *The Beginnings of Buddhist Art.* London, Humphrey Milford, 1917.

*Frederic, Louis, *The Art of India: Temples and Sculpture.* New York, Harry N. Abrams, Inc., no date.

*Gargi, Ballwant, *Theatre in India.* New York, Theatre Arts Books, 1962.

Getty, Alice, *The Gods of Northern Buddhism.* Oxford, The Clarendon Press, 1914.

Goetz, Hermann, *Five Thousand Years of Indian Art.* New York, McGraw-Hill Book Company, Inc., 1959.

*Gordon, Antoinette K., *The Iconography of Tibetan Lamaism.* Revised edition. Rutland, Vermont, and Tokyo, Japan, Charles E. Tuttle Co., Inc., 1959.

*————, *Tibetan Religious Art.* New York, Columbia University Press, 1952.

*Gray, Basil, and Vincent, J. B., *Buddhist Cave Paintings at Tun Huang.* London, Faber and Faber, 1959.

*Griswold, Alexander B., *Dated Buddha Images of Northern Siam.* Ascona, Artibus Asiae, 1957.

*———— (with Kim, Chewon and Pott, Peter H.), *Burma, Korea, Tibet*. (Art of the World.) London, Methuen & Co., Ltd., 1964.

Gropius, Walter, and others, *Katsura, Tradition and Creation in Japanese Architecture*. New Haven, Yale University Press, 1960.

*Grousset, René, *The Civilizations of the East* (Vol. 2, India). New York, Alfred A. Knopf, Inc., 1931–1934.

*————, *The Civilizations of the East* (Vol. 3, China). New York, Alfred A. Knopf, Inc., 1935.

*————, *The Civilizations of the East* (Vol. 4, Japan). New York, Alfred A. Knopf, Inc., 1934.

*Harada, Jiro, *Japanese Gardens*. Boston, Charles T. Branford Company, 1956.

————, *The Gardens of Japan*. London, The Studio Ltd., 1928.

*Henderson, Harold G., *An Introduction to Haiku*. New York, Anchor Books, Doubleday & Company, Inc., 1958.

Horiguchi, S., *Tradition of Japanese Garden*. Tokyo, Kokusai Bunka Shinkokai, 1962.

Ishimoto, Tatsuo, *The Art of the Japanese Garden*. New York, Crown Publishers, Inc., 1958.

*Keene, Donald, *Japanese Literature: An Introduction for Western Readers*. New York, Evergreen Paperback, Grove Press, Inc., 1955.

*Kramrisch, Stella, *The Art of India: Traditions of Indian Sculpture and Architecture*. New York, Phaidon Publishers, Inc., 1965.

*————, *The Art of Nepal*. New York, The Asia Society, Inc., 1964.

————, *The Hindu Temple* (in 2 volumes). Calcutta, University of Calcutta, 1946.

*Kuck, Loraine E., *The Art of Japanese Gardens*. New York, The John Day Co., 1940.

*————, *One Hundred Kyoto Gardens*. London, K. Paul, Trench, Trubner & Co., Ltd., 1937.

*Lee, Sherman E., *A History of Far Eastern Art*. New York, Harry N. Abrams, Inc., 1965.

————, *Ancient Sculpture from India*. Cleveland, The Cleveland Museum of Art, 1964.

*————, *Tea Taste in Japanese Art*. New York, The Asia Society, Inc., 1963.

Levi, Sylvain, and Monod-Bruhl, *Indian Temples*. London, Oxford University Press, 1952.

*Lippe, Aschwin, *Buddha and the Holy Multitude*. New York, The Metropolitan Museum of Art Bulletin, May 1965.

Marshall, Sir John, *The Buddhist Art of Gandhara*. England, Cambridge University Press, 1960.

*Minamoto, Hoshu, *An Illustrated History of Japanese Art*. Kyoto, K. Hoshino, 1935.

Munsterberg, Hugo, *The Arts of Japan*. Rutland, Vermont, and Tokyo, Japan, Charles E. Tuttle Co., Inc., 1957.

Okakura, Kakuzo, *The Book of Tea*, Rutland, Vermont, and Tokyo, Japan, Charles E. Tuttle Company, 1956.

Popley, H. A., *The Music of India*. Calcutta, Y.M.C.A. Publishing House, 1950.

Rao, T. A. G., *Elements of Hindu Iconography* (4 volumes). Madras, The Law Printing House, 1914–1916.

*Rexroth, Kenneth, *One Hundred Poems from the Chinese* and *One Hundred Poems from the Japanese*. (2 vols.) New York, New Directions Books, 1959.

Rowland, Benjamin, Jr., *Ancient Art from Afghanistan*. New York, The Asia Society, Inc., 1966.

————, *Gandhara Sculpture from Pakistan Museums*. New York, The Asia Society, Inc., 1963.

*————, *The Art and Architecture of India*. London and Baltimore, Maryland, Penguin Books, 1953.

*———, *The Evolution of the Buddha Image*. New York, The Asia Society, Inc., 1962.

*Sadler, A. L., *Cha-no-yu. The Japanese Tea Ceremony*. London, Kegan Paul, Trench, Trubner & Co., Ltd., 1930.

Sastri, H. Krishna, *South Indian Images of Gods and Goddesses*. Madras Government Press, 1916.

*Saunders, E. Dale, *Mudra. A Study of Symbolic Gestures in Japanese Buddhist Sculpture*. Bollingen Series. New York, Pantheon Books, Inc., 1960.

*Seckel, Dietrich, *The Art of Buddhism*. (Art of the World Series.) New York, Crown Publishers, Inc., 1964.

*Sickman, Laurence, and Soper, Alexander, *The Art and Architecture of China* (Pelican History of Art). Baltimore, Penguin Books, 1956.

Siren, Osvald, *The Chinese on the Art of Painting* (Translations and Comments). Peiping, Henri Vetch, 1936.

*Soper, A. C., *The Evolution of Buddhist Architecture in Japan*. Princeton, Princeton University Press, 1942.

*Soper, Alexander, and Paine, Robert Treat, *The Art and Architecture of Japan*. The Pelican History of Art Series. London, Penguin Books, 1960.

Suzuki, Beatrice Lane, *Nogaku, Japanese No Plays*. Wisdom of the East Series.

London, John Murray, first edition 1932.

Sze, Mai-mai, *The Tao of Painting*. New York, Bollingen Series, Pantheon Books, 1956.

Vincent, Irene Congher, *The Sacred Oasis (Caves of the Thousand Buddhas, Tun Huang)*. Chicago, Chicago University Press, 1953.

Waley, Arthur, *The No Plays of Japan*. New York, Evergreen Paperback, Grove Press, 1957.

Warner, Langdon, *The Enduring Art of Japan*. New York, Grove Press, no date (formerly published by Harvard University Press, 1952).

Winstedt, Sir Richard (editor), *Indian Art*. Essays by Rawlinson, Codrington, Wilkinson, Irwin. London, Faber and Faber Ltd., 1947.

Yashiro, Yukio (editor), *Art Treasures of Japan* (in 2 volumes). Tokyo, Kokusai Bunka Shinkokai, 1960.

*Zimmer, Heinrich (edited by Joseph Campbell), *Myths and Symbols in Indian Art and Civilization*. New York, Bollingen Foundation, Inc., Pantheon Books, Inc., 1946.

*Zimmer, Heinrich (edited by Joseph Campbell), *The Art of Indian Asia* (in 2 volumes). Bollingen Series. New York, Pantheon Books, Inc., 1955.

LIST OF PLATES

24 Durga slaying an Asura. Rajput painting; Punjab Hills, Basholi. The Detroit Institute of Arts. Photo: Ralph Burckhardt, courtesy Asia Society.
25 Kali stirring Shiva to life. Kangra. Photo: Courtesy Dr. Stella Kramrisch.
26 The Churning of the Milk Ocean. Angkor Wat, Cambodia. Photo: Eliot Elisofon, *Life* magazine (c) Time Inc.
27 The Descent of the Ganges (or Arjuna's Penance). Mahabalipuram. Photo: Archaeological Survey of India.
28 Detail from the Descent of the Ganges. Photo: Archaeological Survey of India.
29 Detail from the Descent of the Ganges. Photo: Archaeological Survey of India.
30 Krishna subduing the Naga Demon, Kaliya. Rajput painting; Punjab Hills. Metropolitan Museum of Art. Photo: Asia Society.
31 Krishna dancing on Serpent. Private collection, Gwalior State, India. Photo: Courtesy Dr. Stella Kramrisch.
32 Krishna subjugates the Serpent. Nepal. Photo: Asia Society.
33 Krishna and Radha embracing. Anonymous loan. Photo: Asia Society.
34 Sculptured lovers. Khajuraho. Photo: Gunvor Moitessier, courtesy Bollingen Foundation.
35 Krishna playing his flute. Rajput painting; Central India, Malwa(?). Anonymous loan. Photo: Asia Society.
36 Radha and Krishna in the rain. Rajasthan, Bundi. Collection George P. Bickford. Cleveland, Ohio. Photo: Asia Society.
37 Radha and Krishna watching a maid churning butter; Radha watching Krishna milking. (Picture in two parts.) Rajput. Seattle Art Museum.
38 Churning of the Milk Ocean. Busholi School, Pahari District. Seattle Art Museum.
39 Shiva and Parvati as Himalayan dwellers. Rajput painting; Punjab Hills. Albright Art Gallery, Buffalo. Photo: Asia Society.
40 The Hour of Cowdust. Rajput. Boston Museum of Fine Arts.
41 Two Sages in a landscape. Garhwal.

Collection William G. Archer, London. Photo: Asia Society.

BUDDHISM

42 The Preaching Buddha. Sarnath. Photo: Archaeological Survey of India.
43 North Gate, Sanchi.
44 Great Stupa, Sanchi.
45 Buddha's departure from home. Amaravati. Madras Museum. Photo: Archaeological Survey of India.
46 Worship of a Buddhist stupa. Bharhut. Freer Gallery of Art–Smithsonian Institution, Washington, D.C.
47 Setting the Wheel of the Law in motion, Buddha's first sermon. Nagarjunakonda. Photo: Press Information Bureau, Government of India.
48 Stucco head of the Buddha. Gandhara. Photo: Press Information Bureau, Government of India.
49 Seated Buddha. Gandhara. Photo: Press Information Bureau, Government of India.
50 Buddha as Ascetic. Lahore Museum. Photo: Archaeological Survey of India.
51 Dream of Queen Maya. Bharhut. Photo: Archaeological Survey of India.
52 Birth of Buddha. Gandhara. Calcutta Museum. Photo: Archaeological Survey of India.
53 Birth of Buddha. Nepal. Photo: Asia Society.
54 Buddha with Lotus Halo. Mathura. Photo: Press Information Bureau, Government of India.
55 Seated Buddha. Amaravati. Brooklyn Museum, Brooklyn, New York.
56 Standing Buddha. Sarnath. Nelson Gallery–Atkins Museum, Kansas City. Photo: Asia Society.
57 Buddha seated "European style." Ellora. Photo: Archaeological Survey of India.
58 Ashoka pillar. Champaran district of Bihar. Photo: Press Information Bureau, Government of India.
59 Standing Buddha. Ceylonese. Rijksmuseum, Amsterdam.
60 Buddha seated in meditation. Polonnaruwa, Ceylon. Photo: Archaeological Survey of Ceylon.

ZEN

INDEX

[213]

ABOUT THE AUTHOR

NANCY WILSON ROSS made her first trip to Japan, China, Korea and India in 1939. Since then she has traveled extensively in Asia and has written much on Asian subjects. Her last book, *The World of Zen,* was an outstanding success in America, England and France. *The Return of Lady Brace,* her most recent novel, had a Buddhist monk as a principal character. Her other novels, *The Left Hand Is the Dreamer, I, My Ancestor* and *Time's Corner,* are also known to a wide public here and abroad. In 1964 Miss Ross lectured on Zen Buddhism at the Jungian Institute in Zurich. She has served on the board of the Asia Society of New York City since its founding in 1956 and is on the governing board of the India Council. In private life she is Mrs. Stanley Young.